Roger Green is a writer and conservationist. He presented the Australian Conservation Foundation's case for preserving South West Tasmania to politicians and bureaucrats in Canberra in 1982 and 1983. After the Liberal-National Government of Malcolm Fraser decided not to save the Franklin River, Roger worked on the conservation movement's plans for electing a new Federal Government in 1983.

Roger's involvement in wilderness conservation began with the Colo Committee in Sydney in the mid-1970s. Later he convened the Pittwater Branch of the Tasmanian Wilderness Society.

Roger has worked as a freelance journalist for many newspapers and has also written for radio and television. He is currently writing about politics in Canberra.

Geoffrey Lea is a photographer who lives in Hobart. In 1976 he was drawn to Tasmania by accounts of Olegas Truchanas' journeys on the western rivers. He Liloed down the Gordon River and travelled much of the South West. In 1979 he returned to Tasmania and worked briefly for the Hydro-Electric Commission on investigations at the Gordon-below-Franklin dam site. Soon after, he joined the Tasmanian Wilderness Society and began working full time to protect the area.

Dedication

To the thousands of people around the world who have kept the Franklin River flowing free.

BATTLE FOR THE FRANKLIN

*Conversations with the combatants
in the struggle for South West Tasmania*

Interviews by Roger Green
Photographs by Geoffrey Lea

Fontana/Australian Conservation Foundation

Map page 7 by Anna Warren
Photograph page 8 by Melva Truchanas
Photograph page 275 by Russell Bastock
Photograph page 301 by Ross Scott

First published jointly by Fontana Books (the paperback division of
William Collins Pty Ltd), Sydney, and the Australian Conservation
Foundation, Melbourne, 1981.

The views expressed in this book are not necessarily those of the
Australian Conservation Foundation.

National Library of Australia
Cataloguing-in-Publication data:

   Battle for the Franklin.

    ISBN 0 00 636715 1.

    1. Conservationists — Tasmania — Interviews.
    2. Conservation of natural resources —
    Tasmania. I. Green, Roger. II. Lea,
    Geoffrey. III. Australian Conservation
    Foundation.

   333.78′2′0922

Typeset by Post Typesetters
Printed by Dominion Press-Hedges & Bell,
Maryborough, Victoria.

Contents

A Government Changes

The National Stage

Wild Rivers Saved

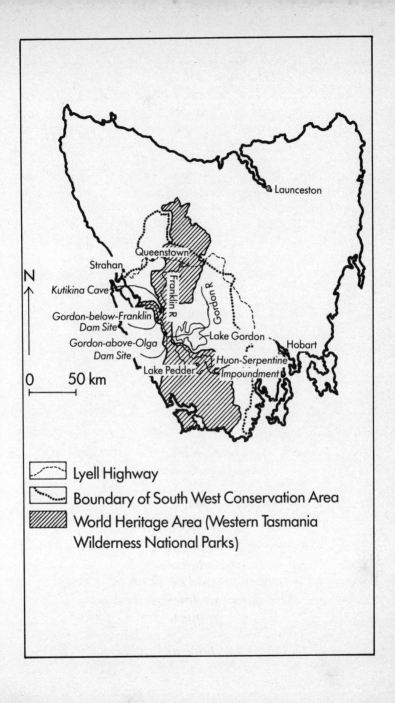

N

Launceston

Queenstown
Strahan
Kutikina Cave
*Gordon-below-Franklin
Dam Site*
*Gordon-above-Olga
Dam Site*
Lake Pedder

Franklin R

Gordon R

Lake Gordon

Hobart

*Huon-Serpentine
Impoundment*

0   50 km

------ Lyell Highway

········· Boundary of South West Conservation Area

▨▨▨ World Heritage Area (Western Tasmania
Wilderness National Parks)

Olegas Truchanas with his daughter, Rima, at Lake Pedder, 1970
Melva Truchanas

Introduction

At the beginning of 1972 the Serpentine River snaked across a highland valley in South West Tasmania and flowed into a placid lake lying between ranges of jagged mountains. The lake was Lake Pedder. A breeze blowing across its surface would stir a sea of diamonds, or as clouds covered the sun the sharp reflections of mountains would disappear into the lake's dark waters.

Paddling children run from the water up the wide white moon of sand. The rapidly-changing atmosphere brings cries from families and the clicking of cameras from photographers like Olegas Truchanas trying to record the swirling mists on the lake.

That was the last summer of Lake Pedder. No photograph could capture the beauty or the magic of that singular place, the excitement of those whose eyes beheld the scene, who whiffed the reaction between the weather and the lake, who heard the wind play the bent trees on the sandhills and the rain patter on the water. Lake Pedder disappeared under steadily rising water in the middle of 1972. A dam down the Serpentine River impounded water that rose to cover the river's banks, the swamps on either side, the lake, the beach and the dunes. A layer of the water at the top of the impoundment would later make hydro-electricity.

In 1972 Australia was changing. The people elected a reforming Labor Government whose first act was to pull troops out of the Vietnam War. There was hope for a prouder, independent Australia that cared for its people, its culture and its landscape.

In Tasmania little had changed. Doubts about the way things were done met a concrete-solid Establishment: for more than forty years the State's Hydro-Electric Commission had directed

9

Tasmanian development. The colony built on mining, logging and agriculture in the nineteenth century discovered, in the twentieth, that cheap electricity generated from fallen water could attract the industries that smelted the ores and pulped the wood. From the 1920s that single idea, propagated by the Hydro-Electric Commission, mesmerized the governors of Tasmania. In the 1960s its pursuit stirred environmental protest, but that opposition could not save Lake Pedder. Ten years after Pedder, in 1982, with the largest conservation battle in Australian history reaching its peak and with power demand below predicted levels, the Tasmanian Hydro-Electric Commission began work on another dam on the lower Gordon River, a dam that would flood the Franklin.

The Gordon, the mightiest river in Tasmania, was dammed once in association with the flooding of Lake Pedder. Downstream the river surged through slots in mountain ranges before winding a course between steep banks covered with rainforest. From the north entered the Franklin, the last major river in Tasmania surrounded by wild country and flowing free from its source to the sea. The Franklin and lower Gordon Rivers were at the heart of the Wild Rivers National Park, later inscribed on the World Heritage List. Below the junction of these rivers the Hydro-Electric Commission picked a site for the Gordon-below-Franklin dam, the last great dam site in Tasmania.

Late in 1982 conservationists from Tasmania and the mainland began arriving in the fishing village of Strahan on the windswept West Coast of the island. From Strahan a four-hour boat trip took protestors across Macquarie Harbour and up the Gordon River to their camp near the dam site. In mid-December conservationists started a blockade of dam work. The conservative government of Malcolm Fraser in Canberra, which had earlier said it would not intervene in the dam dispute, in January approved an offer of $500 million to Tasmania to leave the Gordon River and build a power station elsewhere.

The offer from Canberra was closely followed by a Federal election campaign and while the blockade continued the

Tasmanian dam was a major election issue. Bob Hawke, leading the Labor Party, promised to stop the dam, using legislation if necessary. The Labor Party won the election and attempted to negotiate a settlement with Tasmania. However the Tasmanian Premier, Robin Gray, continued to refuse Federal offers so the Federal Government passed legislation which was subsequently tested in the High Court. On 1 July 1983 the Chief Justice announced that work on the dam must stop. After five years' campaigning for the Franklin and more than fifteen years' battling hydro-electric development in the wilderness of South West Tasmania this was the Australian conservation movement's greatest victory.

Still, in Tasmania little has changed. Within weeks of the decision stopping work on the Gordon-below-Franklin dam, the Tasmanian Parliament approved the construction of seven more dams in the highlands and river gorges of South West Tasmania.

What makes the Hydro-Electric Commission want to keep doing it?

Building dams can be fun. Then, after a few times, it becomes a habit.

In Tasmania it must have been a terrific challenge to trek the wilderness in search of the perfect dam site. Once the place was found trails would be blazed, an access route built across rugged country and then a dam would be designed and built by the highly-skilled and ambitious young engineer keen to leave a mark on the world. Such activity would be even more satisfying for one convinced of the necessity of the project, convinced of the economic and moral good of the work being done. The joys of engineering could capture many a young graduate.

Some are hooked for life. In 1947 Russell Ashton graduated in civil engineering from the University of Sydney and began working with the Hydro-Electric Commission of Tasmania. The next year he was on the banks of the Franklin River in the wild South West, investigating its hydro-electric potential. Since 1977 Russell Ashton has been the Commissioner of the Hydro-Electric Commission. For more than 35 years he has been planning to build a dam on the Franklin River: no wonder he has been so keen to finish the job. He is still keen. For many

11

in the Hydro-Electric Commission the 1983 High Court decision stopping the dam is just a temporary setback. When the government changes in Canberra they believe work will resume on their Gordon-below-Franklin project. What is three or six years after thirty-five?

Why didn't the 1983 decision shatter the HEC world view and bring their world tumbling after? The Hydro-Electric Commission, like many other large institutions, has developed the resilience and survival instincts of a living organism. It has a life and destiny quite independent of the government that is nominally running Tasmania. This corporality, more than anything, sustains the Commission's enthusiasm for projects where the economics are unsound, the energy is unnecessary and the environmental effects are disastrous.

The HEC is more resilient than other institutions. No other authority operating 'under' a popularly-elected government could have survived so much public criticism, so many charges of impropriety and so many embarrassments without major structural changes. The Hydro-Electric Commission has been secretive, party-political during election campaigns, hostile to public review and unresponsive to changing needs. It has refused to carry out government policy, indeed lobbied for the removal of its Minister and the State Premier; but still it survives unchanged. There have not even been significant shifts of personnel.

The Hydro-Electric Commission sees itself above politics, it has a mission. The only reason that the Commission has survived so long is because a belief in the destiny of dams has infected more than the employees and their relatives; many Tasmanian people have succumbed to the condition, variously known as Hydro-philia or Dam-mania. How could Australia's natural or archaeological heritage be allowed to subvert such a reality?

The HEC is a dinosaur in its death throes, ransacking its own tiny island, cutting off its own life-support system. The Tasmanian dam builder is now an endangered species: its habitat is being destroyed as the State's dammable rivers and streams are progressively choked with rocks and concrete. With many of the surviving wild rivers now in reserves under Federal protection the species must migrate, mutate or face extinction.

Why do conservationists oppose the Hydro-Electric Commission's dam building? Why fight for years against the powerful forces of the State to save a trackless wilderness?

A love of beauty. Rows of glacier-gouged mountains fade into a misty distance. Water drips onto a quivering fern frond. An azure kingfisher flits along riverbank lighting on the fine, scaly branch of a huon pine. Nearby rapids crash on worn rocks.

The wild mountains, rivers and forests of the wilderness excite our senses so that even paintings and photographs of the landscape can stimulate our imagination wherever we happen to view them. The sheer physical beauty of wilderness unaffected by roads, buildings, agriculture or introduced species inspires those who work for its preservation.

But the beauty is more than skin deep. The experience and understanding of a natural area begins a relationship that adds more pleasure and intellectual satisfaction to that derived from the raw visual beauty.

A trip through the South West of Tasmania is an adventure where the challenges presented by rocks, water and the profusion of plants are, usually, surmounted and remembered for life. Nature is coloured by contrasting experiences: rough and smooth, wet and dry, sharp and blunt, enclosed and panoramic.

Wilderness travel is usually physically difficult, not only because the visitor has to be self-sufficient but also because it is only the least hospitable country that survives as wilderness — land that has failed to attract economic interest because it is too dry, too steep, too cold, barren or remote. Crossing such terrain can produce the same euphoria as performing before a large audience or winning a conservation battle.

Another kind of joy comes from knowledge of nature. Wilderness offers the chance to study complete ecosystems that have been minimally affected by humans. There is beauty in the detailed picture of an ecological niche, the food webs of a forest, patterns of growth and decay and the cycles of inorganic compounds and elements. Scientific understanding produces simple images of the fundamental particles and pathways that constitute the complexity and variety of a natural world. These theories have their own shape and beauty. The explanation of the nature of wilderness can please as much as the naive experience itself.

The wilderness also presents an object, outside of human direction, that may be interpreted in different ways. As in a great work of art observers can find many meanings in wild life — the different views of the scientist, artist, bushwalker and Aborigine and also different feelings about the meaning of life on earth. Whether it be melancholy, sublime or ridiculous there is no limit to the exegesis of nature. Limits come when the landscape is modified by human engineering. There are not many different responses you can have to a 100-metre-high dam wall; just awe, brute, head-cracking awe.

In nature we may find beauty in the most blasted heath, sheer cliff or desert. And just as in art, scarcity and the death of the Artist increase the objects' value so does the value of wilderness increase. No new Picassos or new wildernesses will be created.

There is more to natural beauty than its physical qualities and their interpretation. As with paintings the object itself has qualities that cannot be reproduced. A forgery perfect in every detail is not as valuable as the original. So a room equipped with machines that could recreate the sights and sounds, even smells, of a wilderness would be no substitute for the original. The experience would lack physical substance and does not have a history. It would be like sex without the flesh, without the other's personality and without the history of the relationship, however short. And while that is common it is a symptom of our video-alienation from life.

The sensual experience of wilderness is not essential for it to provide pleasure or inspire advocacy. The simple knowledge that a wilderness exists can provide enjoyment. An audio-visual presentation of the lost Lake Pedder, though extremely beautiful is also profoundly sad, tinged as it is with the knowledge that that wonderful place no longer exists. Knowledge of the existence of beauty, in nature, art and people, is a source of happiness whose loss compares to lost love.

The beauty of a wilderness exists today because of its history, natural and social. What we see now is a product of that history, and can teach us about it. In South West Tasmania can be found the story of the splitting of the ancient continent of Gondwanaland, the geological forces that shaped Tasmania and the glaciers that carved its mountains and valleys. Then those reaches were colonized by plants similar to those in the formerly-connected parts of New Zealand and South America and animals from what is now mainland Australia. Humans lived in caves by the rivers during the last Ice Age, about 20 000 years ago.

The preservation of South West Tasmania by our society adds another chapter to that history, showing a quality of Australian society in the late twentieth century. The scarcity of wilderness and the human domination of nature on this planet mean that Tasmania's wilderness survives only by our leave. In a way the existence of that wilderness beyond 1983 is one of our cultural artifacts.

Retaining wilderness is like collectively creating a work of art, a museum of nature full of the treasures of beauty and knowledge. The museum is not a heavy stone building filled with dusty boxes and glass cases but a light and open resort of the Muses, a place for the poetry and drama of nature. We value such a place, like Michelangelo's David, whether or not we see and touch it.

Through our understanding of and feelings for the complex beauty of wilderness we can develop a love of nature. An initial acquaintance with photographs may stir the curiosity enough for a strong attraction to begin. As in human relationships, perceived beauty can lead to love.

I grew up on the edge of a suburb surrounded by bush. My childhood playground nurtured an abiding fondness for Sydney's sandstone country. While the accident of my birthplace may make my particular affection seem arbitrary, my love for the scrawny trees and kookaburras over the back fence is easily generalized to Australia's surviving natural lands. And anyway all love is arbitrary.

Once a loving relationship begins there are no limits to the qualities that relationship may develop. The rapture of the soul in the presence of the other, the vicarious experience of the loved one's state, the care and concern for the other's well-being are all typical of the wilderness-lover.

This state need not be peculiar to rafters and bushwalkers. Anyone can appreciate the beauty of the wilderness, anyone can feel concern for life that is dependent on human actions as we are dependent on it. In any good relationship a sense of responsibility follows the satisfaction of the desire to experience beauty. Our emotions and moral sense dictate proper forms of conduct in dealing with nature as well as other people. Love is more than the pleasure of beautiful company, it involves more than the use of the loved object to serve the lover's interests. Even though the caring that is born of love may benefit both parties one does not care for that reason, conscious of the profit.

Our relationship with nature depends on the same qualities as our relationships with people — perception, affection, trust. When we love an untrammelled piece of wilderness we want it to live, for its own sake.

Tragedy may occur when the beauty of a forest or of a person is not noticed until too late. Without keen observers the value of a natural area will be overlooked and fail to become a social issue. There are many people who still do not see the beauty of wilderness and such blindness in our society threatens valuable natural places as much as callousness.

Though I emphasize the beauty of nature and natural processes I do not want to suggest that nature is just a decorative adjunct to human existence. We should not anticipate a change of taste that will lead to the destruction of wilderness. It has a use-value of other sorts. Like art it offers the chance for understanding of the world and of oneself: adventure and comradeship in the wild are amongst the best means of self-discovery.

Wilderness is materially important to our life in the city. Natural areas are the sources of valuable chemicals and genetic materials for use in medicine and industry, they offer reference areas for the study of urban and industrial pollution. And when we want to get away from that we can visit wilderness areas, supporting commerce in nearby towns. But the direct and indirect commercial uses of wilderness do not explain why conservationists fight for it. The love of its beauty does.

A few conservationists may espouse pantheistic or other religious beliefs; and the campaign for the Franklin may have seemed like a crusade complete with a spiritual leader, Bob Brown the Lionheart, but it was really just a band of secular people who wanted to protect the wilderness they love. Most would also care about the poor and weak in our society and have a keen sense of social and natural justice.

However, I do not believe that the plants and animals in wilderness areas have rights. Even the concept of human rights is hopelessly idealistic. My experience as an active conservationist has taught me the need to be a ruthless pragmatist. Only people with power have rights.

The South West Tasmanian struggle does show the power of ideas. The popular feeling that the wilderness should be saved prevailed, at least temporarily, over all the forces that could be mustered by the alliance of capital and state in Tasmania. These forces included all major industrialists, the Government and Opposition parties, the media and some unions. In spite of this confederacy a dam in the heart of the wilderness was stopped. Why was the Gordon-below-Franklin campaign successful?

Because thousands of people were convinced enough of the value of the World Heritage area in Tasmania to commit themselves to the fight. And because they managed to convince enough other people to make the political momentum of the campaign unstoppable.

Many were already motivated by memories of the Lake Pedder tragedy. Others who had been to the South West joined in. From that point the pleasure of fighting for good alongside one's peers, being part of a family as some have described it, spurred conservationists to greater efforts. Those efforts were directed so that the maximum publicity for the wilderness could be generated. Australia had to 'see' what was at stake. Even though this advertising has affected the wild quality of the Franklin, being rafted is better than being dammed.

The gradual escalation of the campaign from Tasmania to the national stage was assisted by the placing of ineffective obstacles in the conservationists' path by those who wanted to build the dam. Perhaps we owe thanks to our opponents: to the Tasmanian Legislative Council for its refusal to accept the 'compromise' Gordon-above-Olga scheme, to the Tasmanian

Labor Government for its outrageous 1981 referendum that did not offer a 'No Dams' option, to Malcolm Fraser for procrastinating just long enough to successfully raise the South West in the national consciousness and then offering Tasmania $500 million to prove the dam was a national issue after we'd been told it wasn't, to the Tasmanian Liberal Government for introducing just enough draconian measures to guarantee massive publicity for the Gordon River blockade but not enough to make any of the arrests stick and even to the Hydro-Electric Commission for refusing to appear modern and reasonable. Of course it would be better if all these people took a more benevolent approach to the wilderness.

The fact that they do not, perhaps indicates how few of the old beliefs have been changed. By exploiting traditional ideas and traditional paths of political procedure the movement to preserve the wilderness of South West Tasmania has accepted the legitimacy of those ideas and methods. There may have been some shift of ideas towards a greater appreciation of the value of wilderness but the political structures that produce dam-building proposals have not changed. In Tasmania the same old system goes on. There will be more dams, more power stations, nothing fundamental has changed. The same battles will be fought over and over again with the conservation victory being the exception. What can we do to change Tasmania?

At least, as Bob Brown says, the saving of the Franklin offers us hope. It shows that many people working together can achieve something.

This book is a first rough draft of history; it gathers together the accounts of those fresh from the clamour of battle for the South West Tasmanian wilderness, those who lived, if only in a limited sense of the term, to tell the tale, recorded by one of their number. Conservationists as well as politicians from both sides, and dam workers, tell their stories in their own words. The stories give an idea of the challenges, the risk of devoting oneself to a cause that, at the outset, seems to have little support, the tactics employed by both sides and the perceptions of those at the front.

These yarns throw up material that can be expanded, contradicted or criticized by those who follow. They contain clues to the values and ideals of the characters speaking and also hint more generally at the way the world works. The definitive history of the conservation struggle over the rugged and beautiful South West, a struggle that still goes on, will take years to write. This is just part of the story — the loss of Lake Pedder and the saving of the Franklin River — told by a few of the many thousands involved. There are other people with great tales to tell, other places that have been fought for and lost and others that may yet require protection. Much valuable wilderness remains outside the boundaries of the World Heritage area and is threatened by logging, mining and damming.

In the course of collecting the stories that make up this book I have noticed how people's manner changes as they move from being the struggling underdogs to winners. The nature of conversation changes from why something should be done to how we did it and how we'll do it again. Those who thought they had the power, change from being abrupt and dismissive and begin to justify their position and appeal for compassion. Such is the prerogative of the weak.

Many people working together have made the production of this book possible. I would like to thank all of them: those who told me their stories and the hundreds of others who could have, those who put me up and put up with me — Barbara Lane, Jill Hickie and Leonie Steindl in Hobart, Ross Scott and the Hooley family in Melbourne; my friends at the Environment Centre in Canberra and the Wilderness Society around Australia for their help and for the use of their facilities, Penny Figgis and Joan Staples at ACF in Canberra for their ideas and moral support during difficult times, Lincoln Siliakus for suggesting that I write a book, Monica McDonald from the Australian National University for getting my brain working after 12 months in ideological mothballs, Virginia Williamson for helping with transcribing, Geoff Lea for his photographs and his thoughts, others who offered photos, my parents for everything, and Haydn Washington, Milo Dunphy and Bill Dixon for getting me into the South West campaign in the first place.

Roger Green, Canberra, October 1983

Chronology

1955	Creation of Lake Pedder National Park.
1962	Formation of the South West Committee, a federation of groups concerned about the conservation of South West Tasmania.
1963	Commonwealth approval given for a road to the Gordon River.
1967	Formation of the Save Lake Pedder National Park Committee. Inquiry by the Tasmanian Legislative Council into the proposed flooding of Lake Pedder by the HEC.
1971	Formation of the Lake Pedder Action Committee.
1972 *March*	United Tasmania Group formed to contest Tasmanian elections. Dick Jones chairman.
April	Labor Party wins election. Eric Reece regains Premiership.
July	Lake Pedder disappears in hydro-electric impoundment.
December	Labor wins Federal election. Gough Whitlam Prime Minister, Moss Cass Minister for the Environment.
1973	Federal inquiry into the flooding of Lake Pedder.
October	Federal Parliamentary Labor Party decides to offer Tasmania finance for a

moratorium on the flooding. Gough Whitlam fails to make the offer to the Tasmanian Government.

Australian Conservation Foundation Council election. Geoff Mosley appointed Director.

1975 Conservation groups propose enlarged parks for South West Tasmania.

11 November Malcolm Fraser appointed Prime Minister.

1976
February First inflatable dinghy trip down Franklin River by Paul Smith and Bob Brown.

Tasmanian Wilderness Society formed. Kevin Kiernan founding Director.

Tasmanian Government establishes Advisory Committee on South West Tasmania (the Cartland Committee).

1977 Doug Lowe becomes Premier of Tasmania.

1978 Cartland Committee reports to Tasmanian Government.

1979 South West Conservation Area proclaimed within boundaries proposed by ACF to the Cartland Committee.

Bob Brown becomes Director of Tasmanian Wilderness Society.

October The HEC recommends Gordon-below-Franklin power development.

Evers Committee established to review Tasmania's future power development.

Legislative Council Select Committee reviews the HEC report.

1980 Norm Sanders elected to Tasmanian House of Assembly.

11 July Cabinet decides to build the Gordon-above-Olga dam instead of the Gordon-below-Franklin. The Franklin River is temporarily saved.

South West Conservation Area listed on the Register of the National Estate by the Australian Heritage Commission.

November House of Assembly passes Bill to proceed with Gordon-above-Olga dam.

December Legislative Council Select Committee recommends Gordon-below-Franklin dam. Council amends Olga legislation creating a Parliamentary deadlock.

1981
February Kevin Kiernan discovers archaeological significance of Kutikina Cave.

May Franklin-Lower Gordon Wild Rivers National Park proclaimed.

November The three Western Tasmanian Wilderness National Parks nominated for World Heritage listing.

11 November Doug Lowe defeated in Caucus, resigns Premiership. Harry Holgate becomes Tasmanian Premier.

December Referendum offering choice between two dams in South West Tasmania but lacking a No Dams option. 45% informal vote.

1982
May Tasmanian election won by Liberal Party. Robin Gray becomes Premier.

July Work begins on Gordon-below-Franklin project.

ALP national conference passes resolution opposing dams on Franklin and lower Gordon Rivers.

November Senate Select Committee report calls for moratorium on work on Gordon-below-Franklin dam.

4 December By-election in Federal seat of Flinders. 40% of voters write 'No Dams'.

8 December Federal Cabinet decides not to intervene in dam dispute.

14 December World Heritage Properties Protection Bill passes Senate. Four Liberal Senators vote against Government.

14 December Western Tasmania Wilderness National Parks inscribed on World Heritage List. Blockade begins on Gordon River.

24 December Norm Sanders resigns from Tasmanian House of Assembly. Later replaced by Bob Brown.

1983 Malcolm Fraser offers Tasmania $500 *January* million to build power scheme outside South West Tasmania. Offer rejected by Robin Gray.

March Labor Party wins Federal election. Bob Hawke becomes Prime Minister, promises to stop dam.

May Federal Parliament passes World Heritage Properties Conservation Act.

1 July High Court rules World Heritage Act valid. Gordon-below-Franklin work stops. Franklin River saved.

September Tasmanian Parliament passes legislation enabling the construction of two hydro-electric schemes in South West Conservation Area.

Abbreviations

AAP — Australian Associated Press

ACF — the Australian Conservation Foundation

ACTU — Australian Council of Trade Unions

ALP — the Australian Labor Party

ANZAAS — the Australian and New Zealand Association for the Advancement of Science

BP — before the present

CSIRO — Commonwealth Scientific and Industrial Research Organization

duckies — inflatable rubber craft used for floating down wild rivers

EIS — Environmental Impact Statement

G-Day — Green Day, 1 March 1983. The last major action of the blockade of HEC works

HEC, the Hydro — the Tasmanian Hydro-Electric Commission

IUCN — the International Union for the Conservation of Nature and Natural Resources; a non-government conservation organization

NVA — Non-Violent Action; a technique for peaceful protest

OTD — the Organization for Tasmanian Development; a pro-HEC lobby based on the West Coast of Tasmania

RMIT — the Royal Melbourne Institute of Technology

SWTAC — the South West Tasmania Action Committee

TCT — the Tasmanian Conservation Trust

TWS — the Tasmanian Wilderness Society, now known as The Wilderness Society

UNESCO — the United Nations Educational, Scientific and Cultural Organization

UTG — the United Tasmania Group

The Pedder Tragedy

*'God gave us the earth
to use and to care for.'*
ERIC REECE

Until the late 1960s Eric Reece's vision was the orthodoxy of Tasmanian development: building dams would provide cheap power, attract industry and make Tasmania wealthy. As Premier, Eric Reece championed the Middle Gordon scheme and that scheme's flooding of Lake Pedder.

When the intended flooding of Lake Pedder was discovered his vision was challenged. Ever since that time the adherence of the Tasmanian Establishment to Eric Reece's orthodoxy has been the wellspring of dissent by those who doubt the economic value of hydro-electricity and who wish to see the remaining South West wilderness preserved.

With Sir Allan Knight, the chief commissioner of the Hydro-Electric Commission of Tasmania from 1946 to 1977, Eric Reece directed Tasmania's development. Sir Allan Knight sustained and supported Eric Reece in his vision and was responsible for its implementation and the people's obedience to its principles.

Eric Reece was born on 6 July 1909 at Mathinna in the Fingal Valley, a coal-mining area. In 1917 his family moved to Queenstown on the Tasmanian West Coast. His father was a miner at Mount Lyell. Eric Reece worked at the Mount Lyell Company's smelters and then became the West Coast organizer for the Australian Workers' Union.

In 1946 Reece was elected to the State's House of Assembly. Within months he became the Minister for Housing. He was the Premier of Tasmania from 1958 to 1969 and 1972 to 1975. During the three year break in his holding of the office the Liberal, Angus Bethune, was Premier.

After the election of a Federal Labor Government in 1972 Eric Reece went to Canberra and told Gough Whitlam that he intended to go ahead with the scheme to flood Lake Pedder regardless of any inducements the Whitlam Government might offer. Later Federal Caucus decided to make an offer to Tasmania for a moratorium on the Middle Gordon development. However no offer was communicated to Eric Reece.

Eric Reece is a man of simple views and the will to power. He has been a good numbers man, amiable and persuasive. He lives in Glenorchy, a suburb of Hobart.

Hydro-electric development in South West Tasmania started back about 1960 when I made representations to the then Prime Minister, Sir Robert Menzies, to make money available to build a road to the South West in order to develop what is known as the Middle Gordon power scheme — that is, to Strathgordon. A grant of five million pounds was made available by the Commonwealth for that purpose.

The basis of the application was that it would make a contribution to national development. There were some forestry resources in the area that could be exploited, there were possible mineral resources in some areas of the South West that had not yet been examined and the power potential from there, from the waters that were available, would be available for power for industries. The rest of the application was confined to a description of the region with an average of about 100 inches of rainfall per year, the rainfall extending over about 270 days of the year and a regular supply of water was therefore available for utilization through power schemes. This was accepted by the then Federal Government as being a reasonable approach to development and they made the money available and that built the road to Strathgordon.

The State Government set out to develop what was known as the Middle Gordon. It was intended that the remainder of the water resources in those areas would also be harnessed for power development, and the Middle Gordon was the first section of that development. It was a large scheme from an engineering point of view in what was described as an appropriate site, and this meant damming the Serpentine River in order that that could supplement the waters from the Gordon River.

It was then that the controversy started over the Save Lake Pedder campaign. Lake Pedder was situated in the Serpentine area. It was about a mile square and had a sandy beach that was described as being unique and of great beauty. I agree that the beach was an uncommon occurrence. I think it was a recent geological occurrence and that there was a possibility that it would change as the centuries went by, but nevertheless that controversy continued in the community. Petitions were sent from all sorts of organizations throughout Australia. A great number were signed by schoolchildren and different classes in the schools and sent in bundles to the Premier's Office in Hobart. A petition was drawn up throughout the State of 7000 signatures and handed to me as a protest against Lake Pedder going out.

But the Lake Pedder development, although it did away with the lake itself, has created in its place a place of great beauty that is easily accessible. Before that, the only people who could really get into there were those who went in by light plane to the Lake Pedder beach or those who were able to walk there from the road. So for nearly 180 years there would not have been more than a couple of hundred people go in there in a year, it was just a bushwalkers' area and to some extent a mountain climbing area. It is a place that has been described by many in some lyrical terms but it is a place that hasn't been understood by a tremendous number of residents of Australia and not understood by a lot of Tasmanians. The greatest understanding they have got of it is their road journey into the development that took place for the Middle Gordon scheme.

What does the Middle Gordon scheme do? It doesn't take away anything of the character of the South West with the exception of the small lake that was there, and it gives access to a region that people didn't have reasonable access to before. But apart from that, it harnesses the energy that is available from the heavy rainfall flowing into the rivers. This is one of the things that makes Tasmania unique: it has the water resources to develop and these water resources were being developed in that particular scheme as a first stage.

We have got to keep developing. There have been times in my experience when the power need has doubled in a period of ten years here, so there is always growth. While there is an increase in population there will be an increase in consumption. Everybody that builds a house uses electricity, and the more houses that are built the more electricity is needed. The cheapest way to get it is by harnessing water. It seems to me to be absolutely criminal that there should be a non-use of the water resources that are now running out to sea. All I want to do is conserve them, use them, and then let them run into the sea. That is all the Hydro-Electric Commission was trying to do. They are carrying out their charter, under the Hydro-Electric Commission Act, to investigate these areas and to harness them for power needs. But they could not harness them without having the authority of Parliament, and nothing the Hydro-Electric Commission has ever done has been without parliamentary authority.

I have supported hydro-electric development from way back in the 1930s. The Labor Government came in in 1934 and the first thing that they did was to develop the Tarraleah power development. They started the power developments that have now taken place on the Derwent estuary. The whole of the Derwent river system has been harnessed from the commencement of that programme in 1934. Then they extended it to places like the Mersey-Forth area.

The Hydro-Electric Commission has been a very competent engineering organization. Some of their engineers are leading authorities and have been innovators and leading authorities on dam construction throughout the world. A man by the name of Thomas, who was their chief civil engineer at one stage, has written books on the construction of dams and the different methods used. They have been a public authority that has built up great expertise and have undertaken their task with great competency, and I don't think that anybody can say that they have left any region in a ragged state. They have cleared up after them and in many cases they have taken steps to improve the landscape after they have left.

I had a good relationship with the Hydro-Electric Commissioner. Sir Allan Knight was the Commissioner through all that period. He was a man that could be relied upon. There was complete openness and co-operation between us and at no time did he ever bring a proposition to me that was unreasonable. We got on particularly well together. He was one of the most competent sons that Tasmania has ever had, Sir Allan Knight, without doubt, and the organization built up mainly by him is one that has been very wrongfully condemned by critics in recent times.

After Lake Pedder was flooded and the Labor Party had won the 1972 Federal election, Eric Reece went to Canberra to meet the Prime Minister, Gough Whitlam. Proposals to reverse the flooding of Lake Pedder were current in Canberra.

I went up to Canberra, to Parliament House, and told him that we intended to go ahead with it. Mr Whitlam set up a committee of inquiry. I agreed to them making some inquiries but when the terms of reference were finally drawn up they were not those that I had agreed to. I protested about this very strongly to Mr Whitlam. Subsequently the committee came down here anyhow and after they had been down here making initial inquiries I met the committee one day and told them that I would not permit any government department to give evidence to the committee nor would I give evidence myself and I suggested that they talk to the Hydro-Electric Commission as to whether they wanted to give evidence.

After I had had this discussion I rang the Hydro-Electric Commissioner and told him what I had done. I did not try to coerce him in any way. I said I just want you to know that I have said I will not give evidence to the Commonwealth committee of inquiry, nor will I permit any department or departmental officer to give evidence. The committee went then and brought in their report without taking evidence from any Government source. There were all sorts of fantastic proposals for putting a concrete wall around and piping water past the Lake Pedder dam and all sorts of things. These of course to me were quite unreasonable propositions. There was a need for us to have power and this was the best resource we had. It was not an unreasonable proposition to build it. Most of the people now who go out there praise the area rather than condemn what we did.

I tried to instil some reason into the people who opposed the Middle Gordon scheme because I thought that they were being one-track-minded about it. To me, the conservation of the water and its use was extremely important, but they didn't give a damn about that. But I felt I had to be interested in it. Somebody had to hold the balance. My attitude was that that balance had to be held by the Parliament of the State and I asked the Parliament to do that and they did.

A simple example of the balance between conservation and development is in the Mersey-Forth. The hydro-electric operations go on alongside the wilderness and it is a most enjoyable and convenient place to go to because it has been roaded for power development and it is now there for enjoyment generally. People can see it at ease and enjoy it at ease.

I am a conservationist. The Gordon River Reserve has got my name on it. There were people who were talking about mining limestone in the Gordon River, this was way back — it might have been 1947 or 1948. I was Minister for Mines. There seemed to be a possibility that there would be some destruction there and I decided with the Scenery Preservation Board to put a reservation along the river. That has been there ever since.

The Gordon River was worth preserving, up to Butler Island. It is a beautiful river and it has beautiful scenery.

Butler Island is a short way down stream of the Gordon-below-Franklin dam site. I asked, why is the Gordon River worth preserving below Butler Island but not above it?

You have to look at whether there is room for both conservation and development. In all of the areas out there there is room for both. The mining on the Gordon River was quite a different proposition. That was going to scar it quite substantially.

God gave us the earth to use and to care for. I think that is a reasonable summation of why we are here. I believe in Christianity. I think that the Christian philosophy is a tremendous guide to humanity in general, the Christian principle. Whether you believe in God or not does not matter; it is the principle that counts.

There is plenty of room out there, in that area, for people to get lost in, be rescued from and in many instances to die in. People have been lost in there and have never been discovered. You have got to know those areas to know what the conservationists are asking for. They have taken away more than 20 per cent of Tasmania's surface just to be a wilderness and they are now claiming that there should not be any interference with it in any way. This to me is quite wrong. They do it because they want it personally to enjoy. There is a personal feeling in this as well as a group feeling.

I know bushwalkers who have not been against my ideas. I am not a city boy. I am a country bloke and I came from that region. I came out of the South West. I came from Queenstown. I lived there for many years. I was there when I was a boy. I know these regions. I have been all over the West Coast. I have walked it; I have ridden on motorbikes; I have travelled by train and road. I was in there before there was road access to places like Strahan from Queenstown.

Being Premier was a great responsibility. It is one of those things where you have to be fair to people, but having decided in a controversial situation that a certain course is the proper one to take then you set your determination towards achieving that objective and if you don't set your course and set your target you don't get anything done. I saw industries come here. I could see a lot more industries come here. Still there will be people who want to develop the resources of Tasmania.

The smelter at Bell Bay was put in in the first place by the Commonwealth Government. The Department of National Development during the last war wanted to smelt aluminium in Australia. Later, negotiations were carried out jointly between the Commonwealth and the State and eventually brought Comalco into existence. I always felt that the aluminium produced ought to have been fabricated in Tasmania too, but we could never achieve that. The companies concerned did not want to do it.

We wanted to get industries here because we felt there were sites and there was a labour resource available. The idea of chasing industry out has got to be questioned because somebody has got to be responsible for doing the dirty side. We can't all take the good things and not be involved in the basic things.

I was 66 when I retired. I was philosophical about it I

think. You always miss a thing that you go out of. But I adjusted all right. It took me about a year to say goodbye to people because I was given all sorts of functions around the State, about 100 of them altogether.

I would have liked to have been there when some issues were about because I don't think a lot of the trouble that has been caused in recent years would have taken place if there had been some resolution in the Government. I mean by that they would have said yes or no; but in the case of the Lower Gordon scheme they wouldn't say either. And they did this for two years after receiving a report that everybody could understand in a week.

I would have approved the scheme straight away. If they didn't want to, why didn't they knock it back straight away, instead of fooling around with it?

I don't think it would ever have got to the stage that it got to if I had been there, to be quite honest. It would have been decided before the end of 1979. A lot of the construction work would have been almost finished by now.

Mr Lowe is the man that sold Tasmania out. First of all he was not decisive and secondly the request for World Heritage listing went to the Prime Minister without him consulting Parliament or even telling the Tasmanian people he was doing it. You don't do those things. He was always talking about open government but when it came to that the Government wasn't open at all. Mr Lowe has been a calamity for Tasmania, a political calamity.

On 11 July 1980 the Lowe Government decided to save the Franklin but build a dam further up the Gordon, above the Olga River. This dam would still have flooded the spectacular Gordon Splits.

The Olga was one of the crudest compromises I've ever seen. Nobody wanted it. You might remember that the

Wilderness Society didn't — they acclaimed it in the first week and then said, no, we don't want it.

The Legislative Council was right in rejecting the Olga scheme. The Tasmanian people didn't want it. I went before the Legislative Council Select Committee that enquired into the matter and gave evidence. I used to meet the Councillors quite frequently, as I always do, and the subject came up almost inevitably.

There were some Labor people who agreed with my point of view but the majority of them didn't. I wrote a letter to them making a plea to them to make a decision that I favoured myself. In that letter I told them that if they went out of office they would go out for a longer period than they ever thought they would. Most of them replied to the letter. There were six people who said they supported my point of view.

Questions concerning Mr Lowe's leadership of the Labor Party were around for quite a while and different members of the Parliamentary Labor Party used to talk to me about it sometimes, tell me what their views were and what was going on and that sort of thing. I thought from these general rumours that there would be a challenge to Mr Lowe but it came a bit more quickly than I thought it would.

I didn't expect the reaction that came from Mr Lowe after he lost. When you are in politics and you are put there by a party, if anything comes along against you you take it on the chin and you fight your way back. For Mr Lowe, the prospects of fighting his way back in the Labor Party would be rather slim I would imagine. When you sign a pledge to support a party decision, you don't go back on your word. He should have resigned from Parliament if he was going to resign from the Party. That is my opinion.

The World Heritage listing should not have been asked for before there was some idea formed in the Tasmanian

Parliament about what could be done with the South West. The World Heritage listing, because of the attitude of the Commonwealth Government, has taken my ideas of using the water resources completely out of existence. They have just said: this doesn't matter, let the water run free too. There is room in the Franklin River area for both. I didn't want to see the dam stopped.

Now the decision has been made by the High Court everybody can sit down and assess the situation. Just what has Tasmania gained? Where has there been a win as far as the general public is concerned? Where do we go? Nobody has got any ideas about it. I have heard a lot about labour-intensive industries but all those who have talked about them haven't yet brought one here. It is as simple as that. You can talk and talk and have all sorts of high-faluting ideas but when it comes down to the practical grass roots of the situation, nothing happens. We tried to develop the things that we could develop.

Hydro-electricity was always the base on which we could make submissions to people who were likely to establish here. No matter what they were doing we would say, 'We can give you power at such-and-such a cost. It is a lower unit cost than it would be anywhere else.' In this it was a good talking point for our industrial development people. It was used always as being an advantage that people would have and when they did their sums, of course they included the cost of power in their calculations.

Apart from that we were always able to say that there was a reliable and competent workforce available, that people were adaptable and could be trained to undertake tasks that were a little different to what they had been doing in the past. These things were proven when they came to get them to do the job.

The best way to provide electricity at a reasonable cost, in my time, was to build dams because when you build a dam to conserve water, the water doesn't cost anything. The dam is the thing that costs the money. It is only the interest payments on the capital cost of construction that have to be paid and once you get this paid off the scheme is running at very low cost. It has got to. The water doesn't cost anything. It just flows into the dam and is used through the machines. If you use any other source of energy, any other source of fuel, oil or coal or nuclear power or anything of that description, they all cost more and will increase in cost as the years go by. But the water costs no more. It costs nothing. The water has always been there and always will be there.

'Pedder
was to be inundated.'
GEOFF MOSLEY

Geoff Mosley was working in the Australian Government's Department of National Development in 1964 and discovered that Tasmania had applied for money to build a road to the Gordon River. Ever since he has been involved in efforts to protect the wilderness of South West Tasmania.

He made a submission to the Tasmanian Legislative Council's Inquiry into Lake Pedder in 1967. The next year he joined the Australian Conservation Foundation as Assistant Director. In 1973 the Foundation's inaction on the Lake Pedder issue provoked a revolt by the membership. Geoff Mosley was made Director and has continued in that position.

On becoming Director he went to see Bob Hawke, then President of the ACTU, about the possibility of trade union bans on the Lake Pedder work. The ACTU referred the matter to the pro-dam Tasmanian Trades and Labour Council. They took no action.

Geoff Mosley studied Geography at Nottingham University, then worked in Canada and New Zealand before arriving in Australia in 1960. He gained his PhD at the Australian National University, for a study of national parks and Tasmanian recreation.

At the end of 1960 he made a long walk through the South West, visiting Lake Pedder. Over the next few years he visited many of the wild places in Tasmania and southeastern New South Wales. He helped to found the Canberra Bush Walking Club and became its first Honorary Life Member.

He was born on 14 September 1931 into a family of farming stock in Youlgrave, in the rugged Peak District of Derbyshire. In 1778 Daniel Defoe, who travelled through the northern Peak on horseback, described it as 'a houling wilderness'. Tastes in wilderness changed radically over the next 150 years.

When I was born into the area it was the subject of a conservation movement. The Peak District was a wild, moorland area. My interest in the natural environment came from those moorland areas and dales. I'm one of those people who love walking and climbing mountains.

The local branch of the Council for the Preservation

of Rural England were trying to make the Peak District into a national park from the thirties. I've got a book which is called *The Threat to the Peak* — it's full of photographs and so on, it's the sort of book that we would produce now — the date was about 1934. I grew up in that climate.

I appreciated the movement because it was going to prevent the area from becoming part of a city. Within 60 miles of the boundary of the national park there were twenty-five million people. If that national park had not been created, in 1950, those cities of Manchester, Sheffield, Derby, the Potteries, Leeds and so on would have all coalesced. There wouldn't be a rural area now.

In Tasmania you see a gradual development of conservation responding mainly to the idea of protecting the Tasmanian tourist resource and protecting the areas that Tasmanians loved and took an interest in; their fauna and their lakes and their trees. That developed in the latter part of the nineteenth century and manifested itself in the national parks. Tasmania was the first state to have a piece of legislation that set up a reserve system throughout the whole state and set up a central body to run it, the Scenery Preservation Board. That was in 1915.

You had parallel developments in Tasmania: on the one hand you had the appreciation and protection of the natural environment, the Scenery Preservation Board and, even earlier, painting — for instance paintings of Lake Pedder by Piguenit — photographs of the Gordon River and picture postcards of the West Coast and the rivers.

On the other hand you had the utilitarian stream of the HEC. You can draw a parallel between the Tasmanian clash of the utilitarian approach to conservation and the wilderness approach and the Pinchot and Muir streams of thought in USA in the early part of the century.

Gifford Pinchot, as President Theodore Roosevelt's forester, articulated the utilitarian view of natural resource management. His ideas still influence forestry administrators and other land-use planners. He was constantly in conflict with John Muir, transcendentalist and founder of the world's first wilderness society, the Sierra Club.

The HEC stream of thought began in a small way and became the conventional wisdom by the 1960s — Tasmanians had come to accept the HEC and the damming of rivers and so on. There hadn't been a great deal of conflict over the favourite places of the Tasmanian bushwalkers and the tourists. But clearly it was going to come on the Gordon River, and the Scenery Preservation Board was very much aware of that. Sir Allan Knight was a member of the Scenery Preservation Board; if you like he was a spook for the HEC, protecting the HEC's interests.

The South West issue came up first in 1963, with the road to the Gordon River. The Tasmanian Government applied for a grant to 'open up the South West'. In their application that went to the Department of National Development they asked for a grant that would enable them to build a road so they could explore for minerals in the area, tap the forests and, of course, most important of all, explore a dam site on the Gordon River. The site they had in mind was eventually the one where they built their dam.

It was a multi-purpose type of application, not stressing the hydro-electric interest, although everybody who saw the thing knew — there may have been a few stupid Commonwealth public servants who didn't. They got a grant of two and a half million pounds. There was no assessment of impact on the environment. As far as I know that wasn't even thought about.

They began to build the road about the end of '63. It was going well in '64, or badly, depending on your point of view. I first found out about the scheme when I went to Tasmania for the ANZAAS Conference in '65. There was still speculation as to whether it was going to affect Lake Pedder or not. The HEC was really keeping people in the dark at that stage.

After the ANZAAS Conference I took a week or so to do some walking with some friends. I was walking in the Frankland Range and Mount Anne and we went into an HEC hut on the Strathgordon Road. There we were shown plans that showed clearly that Pedder was to be inundated. Even then we weren't sure whether that was just one option. Now that we know what we know it's hard to realize how uncertain we were then. We didn't know what was going on.

At that conference in 1965 there was some discussion of the South West and its importance for conservation. The proposal for a South West National Park had already been around for a few years. Though the dam was looming up as a threat it hadn't materialized fully at that stage.

In general there was a great interest in the South West amongst bushwalkers. It was bushwalkers' terrain. That means the Hobart Walking Club, the Launceston Walking Club and the various people who came down from the mainland, from Sydney and Melbourne, every year to do summer trips.

There was a kind of ambivalence amongst Tasmanian bushwalkers towards the South West. They were split in their views between their feelings as citizens and their feelings as bushwalkers. They felt that there was probably something a bit selfish about wanting to keep this area as a playground for themselves. That sort of split personality, evident in the Hobart Walking Club then, has developed more widely in Tasmania since. However, there were a few brave souls who were able to resolve the matter quite clearly in favour of conservation. But there were an equally significant number who were undecided and even quite a number who came down on the side of development, because that was Progress.

That was an important point: even in the group of people who knew the area best and therefore you would expect to be in the forefront of the conservation movement, there was this ambivalence that was preventing them from developing an alternative future for the South West as a wilderness area, as a great national park. That idea was being fettered.

There was no such fettering of those people who were getting their living from planning to develop the hydro-electric power resources of the area. They didn't have any doubts. I would imagine there would be very few workers who have had any doubts. Of course we know a few of them — Bruce Davis, Olegas Truchanas and a few others. But in the HEC there wasn't the big doubt there was amongst Hobart Walking Club members.

That division came out into the open in 1967. You had the South West Committee concentrating on getting a good national park in the South West and they were aided by the Government wanting to appease those interests by creating a national park and then the few brave souls who did stand up for Pedder and be counted, who had been able to resolve the doubts in their minds.

The South West Committee still agonized over the proposed dam but they concentrated on their park proposal elsewhere. The Hobart Walking Club, which included a lot of South West Committee members, had been responsible for Lake Pedder being set aside as a national park in 1955. In 1967 the South West Committee weren't going to stab the others in the back but they wouldn't come out in a forthright way in opposition to the dam. Their complementary national park was declared in 1968.

Of the brave ones who took the view that we'd espoused, Peter Sims of Devonport was the leader. Peter, with little information, organized within weeks a petition of 8500 in a State that even now has a population of just over 400 000. That was a very remarkable achievement. Peter organized public meetings; he was up on the mainland organizing a major meeting in Melbourne; he came up to Canberra for the ACF annual general meeting. It was pretty much like the Pedder activities of '72 and the Gordon-Franklin campaign later. He was doing all that in '67.

There was a rallying of support for Peter in the Tasmanian community. So, while there was this ambivalence that I mentioned, there was already beginning to be a movement in the community towards a new kind of conservation, that is, conservation that stands up and defends areas.

The Australian Conservation Foundation was slow to defend Lake Pedder. However, dissatisfied members of the Foundation organized changes in the ACF Council in 1973 after Lake Pedder was under water.

Until 1970 the President of the Foundation had been Sir Garfield Barwick, a former Minister in the Menzies Liberal Government and then Chief Justice of the High Court of Australia. Prince Philip, the Duke of Edinburgh, succeeded Barwick as President.

Immediately after Lake Pedder the Foundation began work on the Gordon Power Scheme stage two. There was really no break. We knew that stage two was the Gordon-below-Franklin and we were working on that even before the stage one issue was over. In fact we inspected the Gordon-below-Franklin area from the air with Prince Philip and Sir Allan Knight — we flew over there together.

There were clashes between Sir Allan Knight and myself on some aspects of the impact of the scheme. Prince Philip was probably amazed that we should have this clash. As I recall it, Sir Allan Knight said something to Prince Philip and I contradicted it. Prince Philip said something like, 'Why on earth does Tasmania need so much hydro-electric power? What can it possibly do with it?'

We were trying to get the Tasmanian Government of the day to do the right thing by way of environmental impact assessment but, looking back on it now, one can see that it was not possible for Tasmania to resolve this issue in favour of the environment internally. The power of the Hydro-Electric Commission, or the power of that thrust in Tasmanian society, was so great, or at least the inertia was so tremendous, that the other stream that relates to protection of the environment was not strong enough to overcome it. In the end it had to be an outside force, it had to be the mainland appreciation of the South West, that finally saved the area.

I think Pedder was important in that it was the source of so many changes in our approach to conservation. It was the source of the Environment Protection (Impact of Proposals) Act. That Act was designed for a place like Pedder and it's just ironic that it was never used for it. The Task Force on the National Estate, and the Australian Heritage Commission Act, they were results of the Pedder conflict.

None of these had any impact on the South West. I don't think you could say that the fact that the area was on the Register of the National Estate made a great deal of difference. It was the World Heritage status plus the great development of public interest in the area. The fact that the Foundation persisted with the World Heritage nomination really paid off. We proposed South West Tasmania for the World Heritage List in 1974 and when the Cartland Committee carried out its investigation into the South West that was one of the main points in our submission. And that was in the final report of the Cartland Committee. We lobbied Doug Lowe about it and Doug Lowe vacillated but he knew about it and in the end he used it as a means of trying to stop the Upper House from building the Gordon-below-Franklin dam. And of course in the end the World Heritage listing was the basis for Federal intervention in the High Court case.

It just shows that if you plug away at these things, though at the time their true significance isn't quite evident, you never know how central they might become. It's a case for working on many different fronts.

All the different societies which were involved will have their own stories to tell, but what impressed me about the Foundation's approach was how everybody got on with the job, quietly without fuss, but with a lot of effect. It was as if they all knew what they had to do — members, Councillors, staff, everybody — and just did it. We are always asking ACF members to give, and they do for a wide variety of issues, but in 82–83, on top of everything else, they gave over $100 000 for the Franklin. Over 1000 ACF members were involved in the work at the General Election. It just shows that if the aim can be made clear cut and there is general agreement with it, everybody will put their shoulders to the wheel.

However the Tasmanians haven't been able to resolve their split and that is one of the big problems that we have in the future. They've responded positively to their environment but they are still exploiting it to get a livelihood, the HEC and Forestry Commission are trying to develop the State and provide employment.

The big disappointment of it all is that Tasmania is now a very hostile place for environmental conservation. Those Tasmanians who want to see a progressive examination of options must be feeling very frustrated.

On the national front the national role has been confirmed and it's respected and understood by many Australians. Wilderness conservation has come of age. We started out drawing lines on the map and saying, 'These are the areas that are still wilderness, we've got to keep them that way.' Now we have many people prepared to fight for the survival of wilderness.

But I think we're a lot further back than we in the movement think we are. We see victories like the Gordon-below-Franklin and that looms large but we haven't thoroughly insinuated ourselves into the fabric of Australian society, its laws and its forms of administration. If we had done so most of these brushfire-type issues that we get involved with wouldn't occur because proposals that destroy parts of the natural environment wouldn't be made. They would be sorted out by a bureaucratic system that would assess these things. You'd have a proper approach to planning our lands and resources.

Victories like this, while they're very welcome and spectacular, are not backed up by progress in legislation and government policy. Those things are much more conservative. To the extent that you can tell what the public wants, governments are well behind the public wish. Our politicians fail to realize what the public want and to provide leadership.

So where do you go from here? We've got to build on the recognition of the wilderness that we've gained and convert it into something a bit more solid and permanent. That's a difficult thing.

You may say that the most difficult thing in the world was to win the Gordon-below-Franklin — but at least it's a concrete target, you can marshal your forces around it, you know what to do. The other targets are a bit more hazy and more difficult because they require more diverse and diffuse effort. Working both on the political front and on the public education front is not easy.

What we don't do in Australia is think about our broad choices for the future in any coherent sort of way. Everything is dealt with on its own and in an ad hoc fashion. I'm talking about agricultural policy, forestry policy, population policy and so on. The economic matters are kept completely separate from these; it is mainly short-term thinking, nothing to do with the environment.

We need an approach which integrates both the environmental and development streams of policy. I am not saying that all conflict can be eliminated, or should be — debate over options is healthy — but we need an approach to development which is fundamentally to do with creating a good environment in all its aspects. If we had that, and you see the first tentative steps towards it in the World Conservation Strategy, wilderness conservation would not only be seen as having a rightful place in planning — a proper respect — it would have an adequate allocation of land.

*'Politicians have come to think
that anything goes.'*
DICK JONES

Dr Richard Jones is a professional environmentalist. Soon after joining the Botany Department of the University of Tasmania in 1970 he attended the meeting that formed the Lake Pedder Action Committee. He immediately became one of the group's leaders.

In March 1972 the sole Parliamentary representative of the Centre Party, Kevin Lyons, resigned, forcing an election. From the ashes of the Centre Party rose Australia's first Green Party, the United Tasmania Group. Dick Jones organized the UTG's election campaign with Milo Dunphy, the director of Sydney's Total Environment Centre.

The UTG won no seats. However Dick Jones' moral indignation about the political process that had led to the flooding of Lake Pedder fired him to battle on with the party for another five years. At the same time he established the Centre for Environmental Studies within the University of Tasmania. He continues as Director of the Centre.

In 1973 Dick Jones was at the centre of the 'coup' that changed the Australian Conservation Foundation from a conservative club to a lobby group more critical of governments. He was a vice-president of the Foundation from 1973 until 1981 and was made an Honorary Life Member in 1982.

Dick Jones was born at Sarina in Queensland in 1936. He did his PhD in plant ecology at the University of Melbourne and worked from 1967 till 1970 for the CSIRO at Deniliquin in New South Wales. He doesn't bushwalk because he has flat feet.

I was working in Deniliquin when I first heard of Lake Pedder. One day I got this letter in the mail saying, Cough up to save Lake Pedder. I had no idea what Lake Pedder was, it meant nothing to me whatsoever. I didn't cough up to save Lake Pedder. I never heard another thing about it.

I came to Hobart in 1970 to join the Botany Department of the University as the ecologist. Then one day in 1971 the Tasmanian Bushwalking Club — Brenda Hean and people like that — called a public meeting in Hobart

Town Hall. This followed the remarkable Easter of 1971 when 1000 people visited Lake Pedder. A colleague in the Botany Department thought I might be of assistance in trying to make the case and so it was suggested that I go. So I went along.

I have a very short fuse with regard to people being suppressed in public meetings. I was quickly aroused by some of the politicians there. The bushwalkers and other people who were interested in Lake Pedder were short on supporters so they quickly rallied me after the meeting. We agreed on the need for an action committee.

I offered the facilities of the Botany Department for meetings of those who wanted to participate in the continued efforts to save Lake Pedder. We had a meeting the next week and that's how the Lake Pedder Action Committee started.

A small number of people — less than twenty — attended. Within a few weeks the Lake Pedder Action Committee was Brenda Hean, Brian Proudlock and me. For any one group of days one of us would deal with the media. The Press couldn't stand it. They wanted a spokesman. They would give us publicity from time to time if they could show us in a bad light, if they could pretend that we were radicals. That gave more opportunities for the Premier to try to suppress us. I think they were always hoping that if they did that it would be the end of us, we wouldn't exist beyond the next week.

But we never went away. And that is something that politicians don't understand. They still talk about conservation being temporary, or say it's not being acceptable to the community or, in the economic downturn it will go away. But we are here to stay. People want a reasonable environment in which to live.

The real driving force behind the LPAC was Brenda Hean. She was an incredible lady. Brenda Hean was the Lady, part of Hobart society. An elderly lady, the wife of a dentist, she had appeared on the concert platform with the Symphony Orchestra, a pleasant lady who had access to society — but she was absolutely dedicated. Nothing could suppress Brenda — her good humour. She was a member of the Hobart Walking Club, she was in all sorts of organizations and wherever she went she just talked Lake Pedder. And she talked in terms of people's obligation to save Lake Pedder. She made people feel so uncomfortable in the most polite, pleasant manner that Brenda had about her. She was a nice person. People kept saying that it's all over, the decision's been made. What are you talking about? First of all they tolerated it — she'll get over it type of thing — then they got annoyed because they couldn't do their normal business because she always raised Lake Pedder, and they said, 'It's nothing to do with us.' But she said, 'Yes it is, because it's your conscience.'

They tried to keep her down but she was quite unsuppressible. She was the one who urged me on — I never got a chance to slack. She was always ringing me up with: Did I know this? Had I found that out? We had no information, we had never seen maps or diagrams of the thing.

People like Truchanas who worked for the Hydro were trying to indicate to us what the scheme was all about. Finally Brenda Hean prevailed on the editor of the *Mercury* — and she would have been the only person who could ever have done that — to actually publish, on the editorial page, the diagrams of the scheme. How we got hold of it I don't know.

We used to have meetings at Brenda Hean's house — we looked at the legal avenues. But we didn't know anything. In fact we were televised at Brenda's saying that we're going to investigate the legal situation. We really didn't know what we were talking about. One day somebody walked into my office and said, 'I can now tell you how to prove that this is illegal.'

We were willing instruments if someone had political advantage to gain by using us. Some of the younger people in the ALP could see opportunities to become Premier if Reece were toppled on the Lake Pedder issue and so they manoeuvred by back door means. The opportunity was there for other interests to provide us with information.

We just did what occurred to us. We tried to flush out people with information and then make that available through any sort of measure we could — public meetings, media. We spent our time recruiting people, persuading organizations, going to seminars, persuading those groups that supposedly have a conscience to take a public stand, attempting to do things that would attract the attention of television. We were exchanging letters with the Hydro, trying to get information in the Upper House — some incredible inconsistent figures were given in the Upper House. We were getting scientists involved, to increase their investigations of botany and zoology to determine whether there was anything unique there. We thought those were the types of things people might take notice of. We wrote to international scientific organizations to make statements.

The ACF was part of our problem. So we were becoming internally political in various conservation organizations.

It was not a very far step then to think about external political action based on the assumption that people would vote for something like this, on the basis of reasoned argument and information that had never been put forward, and also the fact that Tasmanian Parliaments were often evenly-balanced, with one person holding the balance of power. In 1972 that situation existed.

Here we were, the Lake Pedder Action Committee, the next thing we were the United Tasmania Group with three weeks to an election. We advertised on TV, we had an overflow at the Town Hall, we got support from the Australian Union of Students. Subsequently AUS used their facilities in Melbourne to print all our election material.

Milo Dunphy gave most rabble-rousing speeches. I asked Milo to be my co-director, so he came down from Sydney and we took up premises. There was a shop in Liverpool Street, the rent wasn't high so we said, 'Yes, we'll take it.' We had no idea where the money was coming from. That was the genesis of all the wilderness shops.

Designers dropped in from government departments and worked all night on newspapers. We were running around all over the place, not a minute to spare, telephones ringing. The atmosphere was fantastic. You felt that you were doing things. It was like a circus. Candidates were stomping around complaining that they hadn't got their stuff and we had to then get it out into letterboxes. We wrote a newspaper and distributed that.

We had a few candidates who had been dumped in one way or another, who had some sympathy with conservation, and thought that this might be their way back. And it darn nearly was. Candidates in Hobart went within a few hundred votes of election. It shocked people. A lot of disaffected ALP people wanted to give the Labor Party a shake-up. A lot of conservationists didn't vote for us — if they had it would have made a hell of a difference.

We were encouraged. It wasn't a hung Parliament. There was a swing to the Labor Party. The public flocked back to the Labor Party. The Liberals were decimated. People were sick of Bethune. Conservation didn't get a look in. Both parties said Lake Pedder wasn't an election issue and they left it to the Hydro to knock us off with their advertising.

They were saying to the public that if you vote for the

UTG we'll put your power prices up. They were scaring people. We put an ad in the paper saying that this was an outrage to the democratic processes, we called for a Royal Commission. There was not a sausage of response. Nobody took it up. That is where the public showed their lack of responsibility.

We moved on the Federal sphere. The Gordon road was being built by Federal money. We knew there must be something that could be done there.

Soon we were in a Federal election. It was an era of extraordinary politics where you couldn't draw the attention of the public to an issue like Lake Pedder before the overwhelming attention of the public diverted onto some extraordinary event. The public and the media did us over. The only things they would publish would be the conservation component of any statement we put out — to demonstrate the validity of their claims that the United Tasmania Group was a one-issue mob. They never publicized anything that we would say on economics or alternatives — they wouldn't have a bar of it. At one stage the *Examiner* made the mistake of publishing an editorial that said Dr Jones had produced more policies for Tasmania than all the other parties combined. That's the only recognition that we've ever had.

After the 1972 Federal election the Lake Pedder Action Committee, the UTG, whoever we were, focused on Canberra. We had to persuade these people to honour what we thought were promises, particularly Tom Uren's promise to hold an inquiry. We had a series of campaigns.

It was a great heady time in Canberra: all these new people in office, all their new assistants, finding them all in the corridors, trying to talk to them when all they were doing was settling down and starting to enjoy the first fruits of power. Leigh Holloway was invaluable. He went to Canberra, he was the main lobbyist, he would walk into anybody's office. He could get anywhere, he could persuade people.

We got into Ministers' offices. We learnt that you had to go to every politician, that Caucus was a large body and that a majority was required there. We were learning politics. We learnt then that everything had to be achieved piece by piece; there was a major campaign for each piece. So getting an inquiry established was only the first thing, you then had to get the inquiry to operate, when you had the inquiry operating you had to get a report, and once you got an interim report you had to then get a final report, and then you had to get action on the final report.

I don't think there are any parallels between the Franklin campaign and the Pedder campaign — it's just one continuum of experience and activity. That continuum can be traced in terms of several threads if you like — one thread would be the political sophistication of environmental activists, another would be the techniques for public arousal which you could trace through, and over and above all that you could trace through a thread of political and social responsibility abrogation.

To put it another way: I believe there is a fundamental breakdown in the operation of politics in Australian society and that Lake Pedder detected that in the early stages. The responsibility of politicians and the public has continued to break down — public decision-making and involvement in politics has only gone for worse — and that's a continuum.

It's particularly obvious in Tasmania. I would also involve the Kerr Affair — the dismissal of the Whitlam Government and the abandonment of precedent as a guiding principle. I would regard that as having a parallel in the Tasmanian situation. Here in Tasmania it involved earlier things like the lack of political representation of legitimate public views in Parliament — there was no way that views about Lake Pedder or views about resource development over energy could be expressed. There was a total lack of information to the public, secrecy. There was no way that any public representation in the forum of the people could be obtained.

When a number of citizens were contesting elections we had the Hydro-Electric Commission using its internal funds to influence the election in a most obvious and blatant way. That, too, is a breakdown of precedent — the involvement of semi-government organizations in the political process — and a complete winking of the political eye on all sides from all politicians, who felt that there was nothing wrong with that.

Those processes were showing breakdown in our traditional expectation of proper representation in Parliament. That led to the breakdown of a subsequent Parliament; where you had a Premier, Lowe, who was trying to do something about the HEC and found that it was not possible. The politicians reaped the harvest.

We have had politicians such as Norm Sanders petitioning the Governor to get rid of the Government. Politicians have come to think that anything goes. So when you look at conservation in Tasmania you have to look at this other business which is revealed about the Parliament.

I don't know what the cause is but I know that it's something to do with the Australian ethos of 'It's all right mate' and the cynicism in the Australian public about politics, about politicians — 'they're all crooks'. I don't know that everyone thinks our politicians are taking backhanders; Australian politics is supposed to be more free of that than other banana republics, but there is an enormous cynicism in the average Australian about politicians. Politics, particularly in Tasmania, is being conducted by a bunch of politicians for their purposes, not for the benefit of the electorate. They can conduct elections and compete for seats and ministries as a game between politicians.

Something has got to give on this because it has just reached absurd proportions. Instead of governing and looking at the problems that were raised by this issue, and seeing it as of great public moment, the politicians used the thing in order to compete for the top job. And the different parties were using the thing in order to get to the Government benches. They had no concern at all about the fundamental questions of the public good over this issue. The public, by being cynical in this way, have now got themselves into a situation where they don't know what is happening.

And so the abrogation of the responsibility of being a citizen is the other side of this equation. And you put those two together and we have total breakdown in our traditional system of government.

The public say, 'Don't bother us with facts, we've elected somebody to make those decisions and they should.' This was particularly prevalent in the referendum when I found there were a lot of people saying, 'We don't give a continental about the dam, we don't know about dams, we don't know about Olgas and Franklins and things like that — that's not for us. Now they've forced us to go to an election to make the decision for them and we're pissed off.'

Politicians hate idealists. They don't like people like me — intellectuals who seem to be working for ideals. One politician once asked: 'What does this fellow Jones want?' When he was told I didn't want anything he washed his hands of me. If I'd wanted something that was all right, they could understand me and do deals with me.

It's all very well for an academic to have a public conscience — academics have tenure, an assured job, and a good salary, and are in a position to query society. But it's not possible for many people in private industry to make public statements, or wear stickers on their car, or be candidates for election. They have been threatened with losing the company car, or company house, or even their job.

That leaves you with students, academics, housewives. Bushwalkers and mountain climbers would tend to use their organizations or the Conservation Trust. The Trust wanted to be respected and respectable. Having cups of tea with Ministers was regarded as social advancement.

There was a very big schism in the early 1970s between the Lake Pedder Action Committee and the traditional conservation movement. It was only people like Brenda Hean, who had a foot in all camps, that kept the peace at all. And she was regarded more and more by her colleagues in the Conservation Trust and the South West Committee as rocking the boat. Activists were regarded by other people who held the same beliefs as not doing the cause any good. We were bad news.

At a UTG annual conference in Launceston in the mid-seventies we discussed what the South West was. I said to Kevin Kiernan: 'Give me the largest possible area that you want in the South West.' Meanwhile the Conservation Trust were saying: 'Oh, you couldn't have all of that, we'll be reasonable and ask for a nice little area somewhere down in the south. We want to appear to be reasonable people and not ask for too much.'

So there was a big, bitter argument going on between the Lake Pedder Action Committee and some people in the Trust about what the tactics were. I said, 'I'm not going to argue about which bits should and shouldn't be included — I haven't been to any of these places — the natural thing to do is to talk about the wilderness which will encompass all your claims, all your interests.' Kevin produced a map and we passed a motion saying that this was the South West.

We passed it on then to the ACF and Geoff Mosley said:

'We need a lump up the top, and you haven't put this in.' So we put them in and that was the South West. When we finally got around to the days in the late 1970s when we had the Cartland Committee Inquiry they did exactly what I had argued. That boundary contained all the claims. Their report defined the South West.

You've got to be tactically unfettered. You have to be reasonable when it's necessary to be reasonable, you have to persist when it's necessary to persist. There are times when I wouldn't have persisted and other people, who seemed to be fanatical, dragged me along. Not that I objected. But I thought that it wouldn't work. But those people proved to be correct.

When ACF started I was a PhD student at Melbourne University. I was joined up by my supervisor. I just continued to be a member of the rather distant ACF. When the Lake Pedder issue came up we appealed to the ACF, whoever they were, to make supportive statements. Much to our surprise they didn't eventuate.

We were very chagrined. Why would our premier conservation body be so reluctant to take any public position? So we looked at who the people were. The ACF councillors were executives from ICI and top public servants from Victoria and university professors. So the ACF was run by people who were upper middle class, who had feet in other camps, who were very unlikely ever to have an activist view of conservation. They had always espoused the 'scientific' view of conservation, which in my book is a euphemism for doing nothing.

When we asked for help they said: 'Well, we've tried to enlist Prince Philip, who made it clear that he supported us, but of course he was constrained by his royal connections.' And he was getting advice from the ACF executive. It was only this fellow Milo Dunphy who was on the Council who was giving us inside information about the way that they were behaving and what was actually being said. Geoff Mosley was then an assistant in the system who was also putting different points of view but he was being suppressed — he was told he wasn't to say anything and was put further and further into positions that were less visible to the public.

We organized people. There were a lot of people upset about Lake Pedder in Victoria. So we had an enormous meeting — 150 people, whereas usually they hardly got a quorum.

Usually the councillors were able to change the Constitution at will because they were the only people that attended. They had it all set up and running for themselves. The club was becoming more comfortable, and with Prince Philip as the head it was becoming rather exclusive.

So we went to this annual general meeting and tried to put motions to say: 'This is what the membership want you to do about Lake Pedder. You haven't done it. We, the membership, have come to tell you that you're on the wrong track.'

Garfield Barwick ruled the putting of motions out of order — the Constitution didn't allow us to bring up other business. But he allowed us to talk ourselves out. And it was very acrimonious — some of the young people who came from Hobart were in tears of frustration and emotion at the terrible situation, and one councillor from Queensland was pouring scorn upon us as a rabble — unwashed and unclean. We got the distinct impression that our betters knew what was good for us.

We were totally rebuffed, it was totally undemocratic. The membership had overwhelming support for doing something about Lake Pedder. But the executive wouldn't move. It became clear that they were part of the anti-Pedder view.

We just said it wasn't good enough. The only thing we've got to do now is to change the Council, to the majority view. And so from that time on we organized.

Several of us had come to the same conclusion. Coming from Tasmania where we were very much involved in activism, we said: 'That's what has got to be done.' So we set about persuading people in other states that that had to be accepted and that we had to find candidates who could get up and would be elected and do the opposing.

Along came the Perth ANZAAS Conference so I went to that and lobbied round, made contacts there and talked to people and Geoff Mosley was doing the same thing — something had to be done. Others were doing the same in Victoria and new South Wales.

I was designated co-ordinator of this campaign. I wrote letters setting out what we wanted to achieve and the reasons and where the numbers were and produced lists of names and said these are the people we know who are to be supported.

We prevailed. In the 1973 Council elections we got five people elected in Tasmania, we tossed out all the people who were here as Councillors. In the other states we got a slim majority.

It was an awful blow. Prince Philip was mobilized to come and chair the meeting and it was felt that his presence was bound to overawe this rabble. So the Annual General Meeting was held — they looked at the legality of all sorts of things, they knew what was on by then — it seemed that legality was on our side. When the Council meeting was called the new Councillors were there to take their places. The old Councillors were very foolish in that they hadn't tied up this little end.

That meeting was tense in the extreme. Here we all were, sitting in the Academy of Science in Canberra, Prince Philip on the rostrum. And the first thing we had to do was sack the executive director, saying, 'You're terminated, right now.' That was a very hard thing to do. We could have lost all the membership. There were a few conservative people who were backing us, but they didn't like those sorts of actions.

The next thing was to appoint Mosley as Director, which we had arranged, then to appoint certain people as Vice-Presidents, which was arranged, and the executive was all arranged. Of course the residual people from the old guard found this totally abhorrent — you don't do that, you act as gentlemen. You don't have votes, you don't have opposition and argument, you simply do things because there is consensus.

Prince Philip was brought in to do that. He stood up there and made suggestions and we said no. Prince Philip carried on, so I get up and I say, 'I move ...' He totally ignored me, he went on — that was Prince Philip you know, Duke of Edinburgh — he was running the meeting on consensus, we don't want any motions.

I was moving that we conduct the elections seriatum. I forget whether we'd sacked jolly Thing — all of a sudden we called him in — Prince Philip had to wear this, he was there — and after all we are his subjects the same as the rest of them — much as he was uncomfortable we delivered the blow.

Everyone wanted to relax then. 'What have we done?' Blood on the hands. They'd really like to slink away. But that was only the first stage. We had to appoint Mosley, then we had to get on with all these other things. Of course this was going too far, this total re-organization.

Then a Councillor got up and walked out: 'I've resigned. You're a rabble. Disgusting.' Another left. Then they all walked out. They thought that was the end of us, we were destroyed and they would create another ACF.

I got up a second time and I said: 'I move that we call for nominations for vice-presidents and that we treat them seriatum.' None of this, we'll have the senior people as vice-presidents by discussion. Again he totally ignored me. Prince Philip.

The third time I got up and said: 'I demand that you call elections in the proper conduct of proceedings,' to Prince Philip. All my fiery jolly republicans were slipping down further and further in their chairs. Then he could see he had to, so he did. He just converted. I wasn't going to take any nonsense from Dukes of Edinburgh or anybody.

Then of course we go back and try to run the thing. We had to be democratic. Of course while we appointed ourselves vice-presidents, Prince Philip was the President, and that was very fortunate because none of us could be the boss. From then on, for the next several years, there was the left and the right tug amongst ourselves. It ended up with my having to leave because the right won. I resigned in 1981.

It was basically a power struggle, some of us wanted to reduce the salaries of the Director and have more people on the staff and run it a bit like the Lake Pedder Action Committee — that was totally open, nobody benefiting, no hierarchy.

People felt that the ACF, while it needed to be activist and more responsive, did get a lot of support from middle-class people. There was a role for using that, appealing to those people, building on that and not going too fast. If you just changed over to being a leftish organization then you would open the way for those people who left in a huff to form a new organization.

Our continued existence actually stopped that — the ACF was as strong as ever it was. So I sided with the right in that type of argument while the left were looking for me to be their spokesman. The lefties gradually got out.

I think the ACF has been much better since we took over. It has been able to go ahead to the point where in this last election they were able to form a coalition which took political action. That would never have been possible in the past. When we first took over ACF we were scared of the effects of not being neutral.

The people who are running ACF like to be respected, they like to be liked, they like to be in the corridors of power. A position in ACF is a sort of social having made it. People work very hard for those organizations but the satisfaction that they get, and everyone needs some satisfaction, is the social recognition that they get out of it. For people who otherwise wouldn't have any status in the community — Councillors of the ACF are like that — going to national meetings, making statements to the Press, is a social achievement.

In the Pedder days I got a lot of satisfaction because the action was important, the friendliness of the people, the humour that we could generate, the laughs that we had at opposition, the foolishness of their lack of any co-ordinated, sophisticated response to the things that we could do. It was hilarious. We had enormous fun. Even in the early days of ACF we had enormous laughs at the pompousness of people.

After a while it became very oppressive. The lack of success of the UTG finally got to me — it was my personality that had to keep it going. The bitterness of the wrangles we had on ACF — not so much on conservation issues but how to run the place, power within the business.

There were people who were accusing me of seeking power where I couldn't give a continental about power. I liked to be in the centre of things because I thought my ideas were good for the organization. I acted in a democratic way. I find that in a lot of cases democracy is the way to cut your throat. If you give people equal opportunity then there are those people who do want power, who will use that to consolidate them.

I'm tired now, I really am exhausted. I got burnt out over all those things at the same time as this Environmental Studies establishment was being created, out of nothing with no support and everyone expecting it to fall apart. And my organizing the coup in ACF, running the UTG, I really did get utterly exhausted. It was continuous, all the time, never giving up, no relaxation.

Bob Brown has given full time to the Wilderness Society. Peter Thompson, being a media-trained person, could see the value of promoting Bob as an image. Bob wouldn't have done it without Peter. Bob's gained in charisma, he's certainly met people's imaginations around the country, he has carried himself in the role magnificently. He is a phenomenon, whether he was made a phenomenon or not.

It's very hard to be entirely enthusiastic now. My interest is basically for the good of society. I don't know why that is the thing that I hold important. When we started the UTG my intellectual concern was for all the things that were wrong about this society. If we could save Lake Pedder along the way that was good.

To me Lake Pedder was one of the most beautiful places. Just seeing films now of Clive Sansom talking about it causes me an emotional response that I don't usually feel.

I was surprised at my reaction to Lake Pedder. Really was surprised at the impact that had on me as a physical place. The whole combination of flying in — the place was filled with cloud, the sun was shining brightly above — we circled a couple of times and then dived down through this cloud to this incredible beach. Then being on the ground looking at the swirling mists around me, the mountains and the water and the native vegetation. It seemed to be all there in one little place. Not only that but the moods were so ephemeral, they came and they went so that you could get enormously different experiences in the one place. You could go back to it again and again.

Brenda Hean found that her spiritual centre. She was an elder of the church and she tried to persuade the church to support her view from the moral position but they wouldn't. They were very conservative.

She was a very naive person in many respects — she just automatically expected the support of her other elders and the ministers. They represented the Christian view and the Christian view was one of appreciation of God's creations. Of course that's not true. In the end I think she transferred her allegiance from the church to Lake Pedder.

It's very sad. She was so disillusioned with her church — her centre was going to the Lake, she mounted part of the vigil there on her own. I think that she had come to the conclusion that if she gave her life for Lake Pedder that extreme sacrifice would move people. They'd suddenly say: 'This is not good enough, when such a nice person's life is lost for this.' In her mind I think she had made that decision. That's the only reason I can think that she could hop in an old Tiger Moth and set off from here to Canberra. She had made the mental adjustment and she was quite prepared to give her life in the cause.

But of course people's lives don't mean a thing. Brenda got in her plane and disappeared, and there was hardly a ripple. I'm glad she doesn't know.

In September 1972 Brenda Hean and her pilot, Max Price, took off from Hobart to take the fight for Lake Pedder to Canberra. They disappeared over Bass Strait. Conservationists around Australia grieved at their deaths.

'Gough said,
"Stay out of Tassie."'
MOSS CASS

Dr Moss Cass was Minister for the Environment in the Whitlam Government.

When Labor came into office at the end of 1972 Lake Pedder was already under water. In an effort to reverse that flooding Moss Cass set up an inquiry, the Burton Committee, which recommended a moratorium offer to Tasmania. Though the Caucus, the members of the Federal Parliamentary Labor Party, voted for it in October 1973, the Prime Minister, Gough Whitlam, never made an offer to Tasmania.

As Minister for Environment and Conservation, Moss Cass introduced a range of legislation on Australia's natural and built-up environment including the requirement for an environmental impact statement (EIS) to be prepared for major developments. In 1975 he became Minister for the Media.

Moss Cass was born at Corrigin in Western Australia in 1927. He studied medicine at the University of Sydney and has worked in medical research, children's hospitals and workers' health centres. He was Member for Maribyrnong in the House of Representatives from 1969 to 1983 and a member of the Left in Caucus.

In 1982 he was made an honorary life member of the Australian Conservation Foundation.

During the campaign for the 1972 election the people trying to save Lake Pedder had their little caravan outside Parliament House. And the Labor people all went over and said we support it and signed petitions and all that jazz. I wasn't in the midst of it all because I was only a backbencher but Tom Uren, who was then spokesman on environment, on behalf of the Party, promised that if we were elected we would see what could be done. We couldn't say we'd save anything, we said we'd see if it was possible. Now that has been a bit misunderstood actually. The dam was already finished, the locks had been shut and the lake was already flooded. Tom knew that.

So the promise was that we'd see if there was any way by which the whole process could be reversed. That was the election promise which he made with Whitlam's agreement.

When we got elected and I became the Minister, Tom immediately told me what had happened and said that I ought to do something about it. So I approached Gough and he said, 'Look, stay out of Tassie, don't go down to Tassie. A letter's been sent.'

So I sat around and didn't do much at all because contact had been made. There's a rule of protocol that Ministers can't approach the Ministers of another Government. There's got to be an approach to your own Head of Government, the Prime Minister, and the Prime Minister has got to get in touch with the Premier and then, if that's all accepted, you can contact your counterpart. Everything goes through Prime Ministers and Premiers.

So Gough having said that, I had to wait. It gradually dawned on everybody that nothing was happening, or nothing was going to happen. Worst of all I didn't have any power to do anything because there was no legislation backing the environment.

I eventually got so much pressure on me that I just went to Tasmania. I didn't bother asking Gough, I just went. I went late one afternoon and in the evening had a secret meeting with Reece in the State Parliament, I think in the Cabinet Room. I started talking to Reece and he told me all the terrible things that had happened to him — how people had abused him and his wife, thrown stones on his roof — all these dreadful environmentalists of course.

He had no objection to my going to have a look at the lake. He'd approved of the HEC people showing me around. It was clear that he was quite resolute in his mind that the whole thing was finished, the dam was now filling up and he wasn't going to do anything about changing that.

The lake had practically gone. Only the high sand

dunes were still above the rising water level. Some of the young environmentalists were camped there in tents, freezing and trying to put up a show of resistance. I was shown around by the Hydro people. What's there to say? We'd seen the dams and they were all terribly proud of the new bigger and better Lake Pedder. I didn't think much of it then, I just looked and had a swim in the lake — when we got there everybody dived in from the boats — that was the suggestion of the environmentalist people. It was terribly cold.

When I came back the proposition was not saving the lake but reversing what had happened and seeing if the lake might recover. I didn't quite know what to do. Peter Ellyard, my adviser, said, 'We've got to try and do something about it.'

I wanted to but Gough refused to have anything to do with it. He said, 'We're not interfering in the State's affairs. There's no head of power we can use to implement legislation or anything like that. Too bad. We can't do anything about it.' There was no legal action we could take.

It was still worrying me a lot and I kept trying to do something about it in discussion with my colleagues in the Cabinet Committee which dealt with urban affairs and the environment. I told them it was a real political problem in view of our pre-election promise. The complaint was there had never been an EIS — an EIS would have shown that the flooding was not sensible for all sorts of reasons, economic as well as other reasons.

Someone suggested doing a study on Lake Pedder as an example of how an EIS could demonstrate a possible alternative, such as not building the dam. That was agreed to. Of course we couldn't ask the HEC to do the study — they'd say, 'Go jump in the lake.' And they'd provide the lake. So Peter Ellyard proposed a fellow called Doug Hill (*now ACF's Deputy Director*), who'd been involved in an inquiry into a lake in New Zealand. His inquiry, and the data he presented to the New Zealand Government, persuaded them not to do it. Then he suggested a fellow called Burton from New England University who'd been involved in some way in environmental matters and hence we established what became known as the Burton Committee. (*Edward St. John Q.C. was also a member of the Committee.*)

They raced off and conducted their inquiry and by the time they'd finished they had found that the HEC information was very unreliable, to say the least, and particularly in their estimates of Tasmania's power needs. In the report Burton proposed a moratorium.

Armed with that, my Department prepared a Cabinet submission and I very carefully presented this as a discussion paper to the Caucus committee dealing with the environment. On the basis of their comments and understanding, the submission was fashioned into the document presented to Cabinet. So my Caucus backbench colleagues knew all about it.

The proposal was that we should offer money to the Tasmanians for a moratorium, during which they'd open the sluice gates and stop the building up of water, in fact let the new lake drain. And we would see whether or not the lake could be rehabilitated. The estimate of the cost was from practically nothing — $4 million or something like that to pay the workers to rehabilitate the area — to the other extreme of $70 or $80 million if in fact there was going to be a shortfall of electricity as claimed by the HEC.

That was put into Cabinet and debated there and I lost the debate. All the economic hardheads around the table — which included my good friend Bill Hayden — were more concerned with development in those days and I didn't get anywhere. My proposal was fairly easily defeated in Cabinet. Some said environmental issues are important and that we ought to do something about it, but it was defeated.

It then had to be reported back to Caucus that the Cabinet recommendation was that no action be taken. I gave the report and said, 'I regret to say Cabinet declined to endorse my recommendations.' I didn't say anything more.

There had to be some sort of motion or decision made by the Caucus so someone moved that Caucus endorse the Cabinet decision. Whereupon the chairman or the secretary of the Caucus Committee relating to the environment got up and moved, from the floor of the Caucus, as an amendment to the motion that Cabinet's decision be endorsed, all the proposals that had been contained in my Cabinet submission — in essence that there be a moratorium and that the necessary financial support be offered to the Tasmanian Government.

In 1975 Gough threw that at my head saying that I was a devious blighter, that I went behind Cabinet's back when I lost a fight and whinged to Caucus. The truth is I didn't have to whinge to Caucus, they knew all about it. My Cabinet submission was basically their proposal. In the debate, which was a long and spirited debate, the backbenchers won. The vote was to try and save the lake.

It was a good debate. Serious debates like that always are good. There was a disbelief about the Burton Committee's estimates of the cost by those who accepted the Treasury view that it was going to cost $70 million — they wouldn't believe the lower figure. But others fairly persuasively put the arguments in terms of how the community sees the environment as increasingly important. And we won.

Of course the news got out straight away, I mean that wasn't going to stay a secret. I was asked, 'Well, what do you do now?' and I said, 'It's up to the Prime Minister now, to get in touch with the Tasmanian Premier.' As soon as the Caucus made the decision the newspapers got onto Reece and asked him what he thought. He said, 'I'll wait till I hear from the Federal Government.'

They never heard from the Government. I thought that Gough had never told Reece at all but I subsequently learnt that he sent a letter simply saying Caucus passed the following resolution, and gave the text of the motion. Full stop. And Reece very cleverly said — and maybe they hatched it up between them — 'I will wait till I hear the Government's decision.' Now the Government's decision had to be conveyed by Whitlam. Whitlam never said anything about the Federal Government offering financial support. It was just a Caucus decision.

The Caucus technically is not the Government. The Government is the Prime Minister and the Ministers. So that was how the whole thing finished up. The offer was never conveyed Government to Government. I was rubbished and became known as the Minister for Lost Causes, but there was nothing I could do.

Most of us knew in our hearts that making the offer was probably a useless exercise but we would still have done it. I had no legislative power whatever. My department said to me, 'You can keep trying to fight this battle if you like, but the more you do the less chance you have got of getting any legislation up. And that's the "real" politics of the situation. All the other departments will be as shitty as hell.' At that stage the Environment Department people were trying to talk to the other departments to get agreement on the Cabinet submission for the EIS legislation, which was the only thing that would give us any power. Someone said there were going to be a lot of Lake Pedders. 'Do you want to kill yourself on the first?'

The environmentalists attacked me for a long time — they mistrusted me. Some gave the impression they thought I didn't say anything in Cabinet, that I didn't even try to save Lake Pedder. They failed to recognize what I was trying to do. I think the debate in fact helped educate the Australian community. It was useful.

When the inquiry report was presented and everybody saw what was in it they were happy. Why shouldn't they be happy? When nothing happened after that they abused the hell out of me for not saving the lake.

In the aftermath of the Lake Pedder debate I started to look into the role played by ACF, at the behest of the other environmentalists — they said that it was a waste of money, that money should be made available to other environmental groups that are really prepared to fight for these sorts of issues. They were getting about $150 000. In the lead-up to the '72 election McMahon offered them $150 000 a year for three or five years, as part of making it look as though the Liberal Party was all on the environmentalists' side. They gave it all to the ACF knowing that all the ACF people were terribly acceptable politically. There was no other money for any other environment group.

I had a meeting with the ACF, dinner down at their office. We finished up shouting at each other, I really lost my temper. I could feel that they were not wanting to stir on anything — in their view it wasn't their job to criticize government. There I was, asking them to criticize me. If they were only prepared to say nice things, the environment movement would never get anywhere.

After that dinner I decided that I was going to cut their money down to $50 000 and the $100 000 I was then going to offer the other environmentalist groups. I put that in my Cabinet bids and it wasn't objected to in Treasury so it wasn't even put up for discussion in Cabinet. It was accepted.

During a break in the Budget discussions I walked behind Whitlam and Crean, the Treasurer, saying that I wasn't causing them any troubles. I had noticed that they hadn't picked out anything. In fact they perceived that I was saving them money by just taking it off the ACF and giving it to other environmental groups. They both chortled and laughed. And said that's good.

A month or so later, before the Budget was presented, while Gough was overseas, I suddenly got a message from my department to say: We've just been informed by Treasury that all the money for environmentalists, $150 000, is all going to the ACF. I was flabbergasted because I had already told environmentalists that I was going to get some money for them. I'd made the commitment.

So I had to ring Gough in America. I said I had just received the information and what was that about. He said, 'Oh, yes, I'm not having you or anybody upsetting Barwick. He's the Patron of the Australian Conservation Foundation. We're not going to take their money from them, we're not going to reduce their grant.'

I said, 'Well, that's difficult because I've gone on record promising other environmentalists money.' He said, 'Too bad. If you can get any money out of Frank Crean that's your affair but that money is going to go to the ACF.'

I was on the spot. The word had got out, someone had leaked the message and I was interviewed and I had a very difficult time because the interviewer knew bloody well what the story was and I didn't know how to answer it. Fortunately my answer was so complex and confused, because I tried to rationalize and tried to defend my Prime Minister whilst at the same time not making me look a fool, that they didn't bother to broadcast it because it was so difficult to follow.

I rang up Crean and I recalled the little discussion we'd had. He said, 'Yeah, I remember that.' I said, 'Well, do you realize that Treasury has informed us, on Gough's instruction, that all that money is going to the ACF?' And he hadn't realized, he hadn't been told about that. He said, 'That's not fair.' And I told him the story of the phone call

I'd had with Gough. And Frank said, 'That's really not fair. I do remember that I do have some latitude and I'll give you the $100 000.'

So I finished up getting $250 000 instead of $150 000 without an argument. I was happy about that. (*In 1982–83 the Foundation's grant from the Commonwealth Government was $75,000.*)

By that stage I'd talked to a lot of the people, particularly in Tasmania, and I said, 'Look, you're stupid to sit on the sidelines whinging about what the ACF is doing or not doing. It's for all environmentalist groups, why don't you get in there and change it?' That's when they organized the coup.

That was terribly funny because Prince Philip came over and chaired the meeting of the ACF where it all happened. And I was invited to have lunch with them and I went over and said hello to him and he told me all that had happened. I knew damn well that it was going to happen. It was interesting to hear it from him. He didn't mind, he just took it that the young people had decided that they wanted a more vigorous ACF. He thought it was very good, the young people who had arranged things were well organized, they knew what they wanted and bang, bang, bang, it all went through. He was sorry at what had happened to Lake Pedder. He thought it was a mistake.

I had a tough time the whole time I was in that portfolio. We kept losing the battles but finally won the war. Ordinary people are beginning to realize that the environment means where they work and where they live.

The environment, in a sense is a class issue. The rich are well-enough off to look after themselves, even if it means going to greener pastures elsewhere. The poor finish up in polluted surroundings all the time. If you start showing them how that works in their factories, even if it is only noise pollution, then you can begin to get more understanding. I think that's what's happening.

Purists call me spineless, pragmatists call me hopelessly idealistic and not very worldly, and in reality that's what political progress is about. I could have easily gone down securing nothing at all. I could have been the solid, inflexible, uncompromising environment movement and got absolutely nowhere. It is a question of educating people.

I have the same fight even with my own colleagues in the Party. I'm a member of the Left. But if the Left's going to get anywhere it's got to get some of those funny, wishy-washy people in the centre to swing over to left before the Left's going to win any battles. The Left hasn't got the numbers otherwise.

The same applies to the environmental areas. It's no good being pure about the environment and never winning that large amorphous mass in the middle who are not sure, who are open to persuasion, but are always terribly nervous and will listen with a very open ear to all the soothsayers on the other side who would prophesy economic doom if we go ahead and save all these stupid old buildings, and parks that after all have just got trees or scrub in them. There could be minerals in the parks that you could mine, that would make you very rich. That's a very persuasive argument, particularly in times of economic recession, such as we've got now. A lot of the bitterness over the Franklin issue is on the question of unemployment.

The environmentalists have got to show where you find the jobs in saving the environment. That's the way you win the environmental argument. By showing that you can get more jobs, more secure jobs, by saving the trees, by growing the trees. That's the difficulty.

Discovering the Franklin

*'All over the bloody floor were stone tools
and I had just never noticed.'*
KEVIN KIERNAN

Kevin Kiernan will probably be remembered as the person who discovered fragments of an Ice-Age culture in Kutikina Cave on the banks of the Franklin River. The discovery only occurred because of Kevin's combined interests in caving, conservation and geomorphology.

Kevin Kiernan and some friends first saw Kutikina Cave in 1977. They named it Fraser Cave. However, Kevin did not recognize the cave's archaeological significance until his third trip there in February 1981.

Born in Hobart in 1952, Kevin was still at school when he joined the fight to save Lake Pedder. In 1971 he became secretary of the Lake Pedder Action Committee. He was with Olegas Truchanas when the photographer drowned in the Gordon River in 1972.

During the mid-seventies Kevin Kiernan was the mainstay of a number of Tasmanian conservation campaigns. He formed the South West Tasmania Action Committee in 1974. Two years later that group spawned the Tasmanian Wilderness Society. He was its first Director.

I can remember as a little kid I was taken to Hastings Caves. Later I brought acorns home from school and one of them sprouted and I can remember Mother planting it — it's all terribly symbolic — but while she was planting we started talking about time and what time was all about. Somehow a discussion of Hastings Caves came up and how long stalactites took to grow and she mentioned to me that there was this other cave up north that was as good as Hastings, really wonderful, but it had been blown up. I remember thinking at the time: 'What a stupid thing to do.' I don't think she pushed the fact that it was a stupid thing to do. She did not think it was very intelligent but my whole family was apolitical, they never got involved in anything. Maybe there are some origins there for two things — caves and conservation.

I took up caving with great enthusiasm in the late 60s and never really put it down again. For the first few years we got off on competitive trips like chasing Australian depth records. We got four. And then that got a bit tedious. The record when we started was 720 feet, then we got down to 800, then 850. I nearly drowned myself at 980 feet, trying to get to a thousand, once in a waterfall. That was a major epic — twenty-one hours of absolute abject misery in a cave, following a stream way down. This is back in the days of ladders and stuff, none of this whizz-bang, high-speed single-rope technology. Most of our lights went out and we were suffering from hypothermia — it was really quite amusing.

I got involved in wilderness-type caving in 1970, because of my involvement in wilderness issues. I'd had a letter-writing-to-the-*Mercury*-as-a-schoolboy career.

Wilderness conservation just seemed like a matter of decency to me. I've never really got off on a lot of the arguments that are advanced for conservation. I mean I can see the logic of things like gene pool preservation, I can see the logic of the economics, I can see the logic of recreation, the scientific opportunity and stuff but basically it's always seemed a matter of ethics and how you treat your fellow inhabitants of the planet and whether you've got the right to expect user rights over everything on the planet. I guess that was in my system quite early and it's never really got out. I've used these other arguments but I'm quite certain the basic motivation in me was never those arguments.

When I started on the Lake Pedder campaign I was at school. I went along to a meeting of the Lake Pedder Action Committee. After a couple of months I got involved in it, a couple of months after that I became secretary of it. I was pretty irate about Pedder. It just didn't seem the right thing to do.

I look back very fondly on the Lake Pedder Action Committee. It was a great group of people. There was a fairly realistic 'don't expect too much' streak but there wasn't much cynicism. I've got enormous respect for Dick Jones. Brenda Hean was head and shoulders, she was just great. She had a very strong Christian faith which carried her and guided her. In some ways I envied it.

We ran this meeting in 1971 at the Town Hall in Hobart and that radicalized us a fair bit. Milo Dunphy came down with this 'Ah, to hell with the Hydro' type image and started talking about revegetating the Gordon road. Everybody in that hall felt that, but no-one had ever had the guts to actually say it. Suddenly there's this bloody maniac standing up saying: 'We're going to revegetate the road.'

It was really inspiring. He described himself and said how some people had referred to him as a crazed left-wing extremist. The *Mercury* that night said: 'The HEC should be kicked out of the South West, according to a Sydney conservationist who has been described as a crazed left-wing extremist.'

Milo was important because he had abilities to deal with the media. He introduced us to just basic things like how to do press releases properly — he had a much punchier way of going about it. He was a much more media-oriented person where most of our work had been done writing submissions to select committees.

We were lost in the Tasmanian political scene. It's a very depressing place to be sometimes, Tasmania, as much as I love the place. It was nothing like as depressing as things got later, at the time we were still feeling quite spirited. I guess that's an indication of our naivete.

Look at some of our politicians and put it in the context of the current cave debate. They would have exterminated the Aborigines. The old squattocracy names continue on today in the Parliament; the whole thing is hereditary. They are passing down the ability to exterminate things Aboriginal, be they actual beings or their artifacts. I think the political scene is sick and the whole society of

Tasmania is grossly diseased and rotten at the core. Our only big hope is that there are some people around here that don't fit into that mould, that some of the shittiest people, the grabbiest sort of people, flee to the mainland to try and grab more, and then there's all these alterno-freaks who come down here to shove muesli into their veins and so on, and that changes the voting balance a bit. So we end up with the driftwood of Australian society down here — makes houmus, and eats muesli and milks goats — and it's improving Tasmania.

In 1972 there was the starting of some kind of nationhood for Australia, some kind of pride. Lake Pedder was very much part of it. It was recognizing the Australian landscape. It was at the forefront of this awareness of the value of the landscape in Australia. 1972 was that fantastic time prior to the election of the Whitlam Government. There was a terrific feeling of hope. Clearly we weren't going to get anywhere at the State Government level.

Howson was the Federal Liberal Minister for Environment, Aborigines and the Arts. He was useless. The LPAC in Victoria campaigned against Howson in the 1972 election and he lost.

What happened here in the 1972 State election was editorialized around Australia and it carried through into the 1972 Federal election. I suppose the defeat of Howson was the first obvious success from the greenies at Federal electoral things.

Shortly before that, Brenda Hean and Max Price were going up to Canberra to lobby politicians when their plane went missing. The circumstances of that were incredibly suspicious.

It was squashed very effectively afterwards when Eric Reece stood up in the House and claimed to have been threatened with bomb threats. He got massive publicity and it just killed the whole thing. All these nasty conservationists were threatening poor Eric. When the bomb threat was tracked down to three schoolgirls who had slipped in on their way home from school, it made page two of the *Mercury*, in very small letters.

The Federal Pedder inquiry recommended an offer. We were quite euphoric when the recommendation was finally accepted by the Caucus in October 1973.

I was down in the House that afternoon and Eric Reece stood up and indicated that he would want to know the details before he said anything. He couched that in a whole lot of stuff about how we don't really want to save Lake Pedder anyway. That was interpreted by a lot of the media here as meaning: Reece rejects. It was all pretty inflammatory sort of stuff — everybody in the media wanted to have a war. We were able to keep the Pedder issue alive a bit longer.

About 1972 Mineral Holdings made an application for mineral exploration rights at Precipitous Bluff. So while things were dying on the Pedder front we were pretty busy on other fronts.

We've never thrown up our hands on Pedder. The Federal Government had a defeatism which said that once it's under water we stop. I still believe it's feasible to drain the new lake. I still believe that that vegetation will recover; I still believe that the general quality of the place is intact enough to recover within a certain amount of time. I still believe it's a ludicrous economic proposition to have the dam there anyway.

I flew over it a few weeks ago — there's erosion around the shores but I think the Lake Pedder landform should be essentially intact. The sand-dune will be subdued. It will regenerate of its own accord over time. I'm quite sure within ten, twenty years you'd have quite a presentable thing there. Some of the endemic fauna's been stuffed by the introduction of exotic trout, though.

Pedder was never one issue. It started off with the lake but then became a set of nested issues that got onto things like who ran the State and where the State was going and hydro-industrialization policy. I see one of the reasons that the conservation movement has progressed so well in Tasmania has been that there always was this multi-faceted thing to the campaign, and there was never an Opposition. We became, in effect, the political opposition because of the implications of the issue that we were focused on. The Labor Party and the Liberal Party here tended to argue about who could do the same thing best.

Of the people who were involved at the core of Pedder I was the only one dumb enough to keep bashing on the main wilderness campaign. Dick Jones kept going through the UTG and the ACF, on broader issues.

By this stage I'd had a personal involvement in the Precipitous Bluff campaign. As a caver I wanted to do something that was interesting to me and would contribute to the campaign. So I organized an expedition to Precipitous Bluff to try and hunt up caves and perhaps get cave fauna and produce some of the sorts of arguments that we had used at Pedder. That was really successful — we had people from every state in Australia, a fair bit of publicity, and we collected a few new species.

By this time I was fired up by this notion that we were pursuing sites rather than regions. One of the things that I started to do was promoting the idea of looking more widely than issues — we'd had a Lake Pedder Committee, we'd had a Precipitous Bluff group, we had a Lower Gordon Committee set up by the Conservation Trust in about 1973 — but it was obvious that we needed to do something more broadly-based, so we set up this South-West Tasmania group — the South West Tasmania Action Committee — in 1974. At the same time there were similar groups set up in Sydney and Melbourne, so it was almost a national structure.

When we were pushing Pedder as a national issue to get the Federal Government involved we developed this letterhead which was plastered with addresses from all over Australia as to where our branches were — even if they were abour half a person and a dog — it looked good. So we adopted the same technique for the South West Action Committee.

The problem almost immediately with the South West Action Committee was that it was a bit too much confined to the South West. We had an issue come up in Freycinet, there were other people interested in the western central plateau or the Norfolk Range. So it was because of that that I suggested we have a wilderness society in 1976 at a meeting at Bob Brown's place. And that's where the Wilderness Society came from.

The main thing I spent my time on during those SWTAC days was trying to develop a larger park proposal.

The South West Committee, formed in 1962 and one of the oldest conservation groups in Australia, was also working on a park proposal.

It was a group mainly of bushwalkers some of whom the Pedder Committee found a problem. They were violently opposed to extending the South West campaign north of the Gordon River Road. My larger proposal was adopted by the UTG. It was the first formal proposal to include the Franklin in a national park.

That put the cat among the pigeons because it caused a huge split in the conservation movement. I feel now that it was in some ways the end of my really close, heart-in-it involvement because it was such a bitter and unpleasant time. We ended up with the Big Park and the Small Park people. And that got just so bloody vicious it was unreal. A Legislative Councillor once made a comment: 'Which group are we going to listen to: so-and-so's group with a thousand members,' that is, the members of the delegate bodies to the South West Committee, 'or this fellow Kiernan with his twenty rabble-rousers?'

It went on for some months and it was just horrible. I was really working my guts out on that thing. I knew there were going to be problems over it but it was the way the whole thing was done.

I don't think I contributed very effectively to negotiations between the sides because I tended to get frustrated with them and to go off the handle. I had friendships on both sides which were souring. And then a good mate — Paul Whitham — defected from the Small side, and that helped a lot. Eventually everyone adopted a Big Park, in one form or another.

Looking back, I suppose it was a bit of an ego-trip. You were forever in the papers. But I don't think anyone does anything for free. I think that anyone who gets involved in a voluntary conservation group still has to be being paid off in some way or other. So much of conservation seems negative. I had a big pay-off in trying to do something positive — in producing an alternative plan for a new park. It was a great feeling. I guess I think of it as my main contribution.

I used to get frustrated with meetings. People would come alone late and then expect you to go through the whole bloody ground again. And if you complained that they should have turned up on time they'd say: 'Ah, we're only volunteers.' And I used to get so pissed off with that sort of stuff. We had to be more professional.

The night before the Wilderness Society was officially supposed to form, I had a visit from three influential people. There had been some campaign-style difficulties about some of Geoff Holloway's tactics. I didn't feel there was too much problem with them, though. They came along to express concern that Geoff might have some role in the organization. I was really pissed off. We didn't always see completely eye-to-eye but we worked well together, and he worked, whereas some of the people who complained about him didn't. I listened fairly silently and said I'd think about it. By the time the morning had come I had decided I wasn't going to take on being Director of the Society because this was just so shitty.

So I went to the meeting in the Environment Centre here in Hobart, and when someone asked if I'd take on the job of Director, I said maybe I should not because I envisaged being away for some weeks. Some of the conservatives there were keen that I didn't and they jumped up and said: 'Isn't it wonderful, he's being so honest, what a shame we can't have him.' I left the meeting for while. Bob Brown was tending to be a bit of a middleman then. He and a couple of others came out and we had a talk and I said, 'O.K. I'll try it on.' So I took on the directorship for the first year but I suppose I was just getting soured by the interpersonal side of the whole movement at this stage. My attitude to groups never recovered and the loss of Pedder had affected me a great deal. It was my cathedral like the Franklin is Bob Brown's — only mine got desecrated.

The first I knew of Bob Brown was during the latter part of the Pedder campaign when there was an advertisement in the *Australian*. It had a date for the emu extinction, a date for the Aborigines, a date for thylacine extinction and another date for Lake Pedder and a big heading on the bottom: '400 000 Tasmanians making history'. It was signed RJB. I eventually found out it was this doctor guy.

Well, he came to a couple of the SWTAC meetings and we had reached the stage where we all got to know this guy called Bob Brown and he had this nice house so we started to meet there. I think on the second occasion we met there I suggested this TWS business. I stayed in a year as Director and I wasn't really enjoying myself, so I talked Norm Sanders into it.

Norm's attitude was that he didn't like organizations either. I thought he was good because he was good with the media. He's a bit abrasive but he wouldn't sell out. I was really fed up to the teeth with arseholes who would sell out all the time and would compromise on really basic things like being prepared to give away Hartz Mountains National Park to swap for Precipitous Bluff, this sort of thing. And so I was a very strong supporter of Norm's approach because he wasn't going to sell out. But on the other hand, he didn't want to go to meetings either and he used to laugh his head off about the raffles that were incessantly conducted. It was a raffle club basically for a long time. He stayed as Director for that year and never turned up; I was at the stage where I was just about to go back to University study and wasn't so much involved with it and they decided they'd better have a new Director and Bob Brown decided he'd take it on. It would have been nice if he could have taken it on before.

He had the ability to smooth things over. I suppose you are always fairly conscious of the things you don't see yourself as having — like diplomacy. I tended to be a bit too confrontationist; he's in the same trap as me now. You get addicted to that kind of situation because on one hand, well from my point of view it was exhausting and there were many times I would wish that there was assistance around and yet I never trusted the assistance enough to do the job. An egomaniac's trap I suppose. But then one day I steeled myself to hand over a particular task and it all went wrong. A patron resigned in anger and my original fears were compounded. I got worse.

The addiction is to running the group; I suppose some sort of power trip and also the feeling that you are doing

92

something worthwhile in society. I mean the thing that I've missed most since I drifted away was the feeling that I wasn't doing anything worthwhile in society any more.

By 1976 I was reaching the stage where the political stuff was burning out for me. I was not enjoying it any more. But by the same token once you're into a fight it sometimes is hard to pull out. I wanted to be doing something more positive for myself, so then I got into the geomorphology.

Since 1974 most of my hard caving had diminished and I was into wilderness-type caves. I had been doing trips since about 1974 to the Franklin River caves on a sort of Precipitous Bluff type of excuse — wanting to use my caving some way usefully, and it seemed that if I could go to the Franklin and find something useful there for the campaign that was doing both things. It was giving me recreational caving and it was doing something useful via my conscience without a lot of politicking involved.

The whole campaign to find caves on the Franklin was entirely politically motivated. The intention was to try and find something — we never knew what it was going to be, maybe a big whiz-bang cave or something — that would help the campaign. Whenever we came back from a trip we would splash out in the Press and we were always taking documentary film crews or even just a camera or two. There were a few half-hour TV segments produced on caving on the Franklin, back in the early days.

In 1977 we started naming caves after politicians which we'd previously done at Precipitous Bluff. We had one at Precipitous Bluff called Reece's Cave which was a huge hole with a howling gale coming out and absolutely nothing behind it. It was actually a tactic adopted previously on the mainland. So all these caves were named in 1977 after politicians. We found in that time probably in excess of 100 caves in the Franklin area, not all of them big by any means. It was a different scale of thinking to what we had been used to. They weren't actually caves that were 14 miles long and still going — deep caves. It was a totally different ball game and a totally different environment, different sport really because it was river related at the same time.

At first we tended to go up the rivers. On our first trips we had just an outboard motor power boat which we'd knock the propeller off at the first set of rapids, then walk up through the scrub and paddle a Lilo through the flat bits. It was pretty primitive.

The earliest trips I tried to have on the Franklin were overland. I was with Olegas in 1972 when he was killed and the intention of my going with him at that time was to get me to some limestone at the top end of the Lower Gordon, in the vicinity of the Splits. We weren't sure what we were going to get there but we thought it was worth having a look. Olegas was going down to get photographs because he could see the threat to the Splits. I had only met Olegas that previous Christmas at Lake Pedder and we got on fairly well and we both had the same ideas and so he said, 'Why don't you come down the Gordon River for the first few days and you can bash back up and I'll continue on down.' So that's how it went.

It was a disaster, we lasted about an hour. We were only on the first rapid when Olegas was killed.

The idea was that I travel by foot and be canoed over the puddles and then I was going to walk back up again. He was just going to show me various things that he thought were useful for me to know from the cave point of view. We crossed over on this flying fox, took the packs over and then we took Olegas' canoe down which was a bit awkward to get in the water. Then we launched the thing and paddled across a little pond. I hopped off and went to get the packs which we had brought down the track on the far side and had dumped. He was then going to haul his canoe in and pack his gear. So he shot through this other little rapid to come into a better landing point, it was only very small and there was a small embayment at the rocks. He was then going to trail his canoe around on the painter and just pull it up at this little embayment. As he trailed it round to bring it in to his pack, it swung sideways and filled up with water under a bit of a rapid. And as he tugged at it he lost his footing on this wet rock and slipped — straight in underneath this really nasty foamy bit. That was the last I ever saw of him.

There was just no way of saving him. I didn't know where he was because there was this big foamy bit of water and it went down under this big rock. It was aerated further on so that if you had been swept out you probably wouldn't have come to the surface, and there was another couple of small rapids. The first thing I did was I just sort of peered down, looking for him. The canoe came up and drifted off, but he clearly wasn't in it. I didn't know which piece of the river he was in so I did a couple of trips up and down the river looking for the most likely places, with a pole poking and probing in, in case he was caught somewhere and could grab onto the pole, in some air space, but I never picked up where he was. So I swam back across the river and went out for help.

Up in that vicinity of the Gordon Dam there was a spot where they could just doze some stuff across. So they dozed a bit of debris and held the water back for a few minutes. The water dropped and he was found caught under some logs right at the point he went in.

From 1974 on, most summers we spent two or three weeks looking for stuff on the lower Franklin with speleos from Sydney and a couple of locals. We found Fraser Cave in February 1977.

What we tended to do was just drift down the river looking at cliffs, looking for holes, and occasionally we'd go inland but we were lazy about going inland because there was all this scrub. But there was a low point in the cliff and I was ahead of everybody else and I rowed in and found this bloody great big cave mouth. Karen, my wife, was with us so I raced back and got her. She doesn't like caving, but I think she was impressed by this one. We didn't examine the cave deposits. We were cavers at the time, we weren't competent to interpret the sediments very much. We found all these stalactites up the back and thought, 'Oh isn't that nice?', named it after Malcolm and came away.

It was one of the more atmospheric caves I suppose that we found on the Franklin — very spacious and it had some nice little daylight holes and sunbeams coming in through the twittering water, little musical drips and all this other romantic stuff. We had found bones in Fraser Cave but because we were essentially looking at them from the eyes of cavers we just thought they were normal types of cave bones. But we did notice the deposit was fairly thick.

I started to wonder about this cave on the Franklin later. There is nothing like getting home in your armchair and thinking, 'You know, there was quite a lot of bone in that cave and there was no obvious place for it to fall down from and it couldn't have washed in there because it would have got smashed up.' I didn't know there was any archaeology in it by any means but I had it in the back of my mind. I was aware of a story of a human skeleton in a cave on the lower Jane — it had been told to me by a prospector — and I had a vague idea that I might be able to find it if I was lucky. Bob Brown said, 'Oh what a nice idea for a jolly', and Bob Burton said, 'Yes'. So the next thing, as TWS was wont to do, they grabbed a helicopter and said, 'Come, come, we'll go and find this. It will be wonderful publicity for the Franklin campaign if we can find a dead convict.'

So anyway in February 1981 we decided we were going to try to find this cave. And of course we failed miserably. We helicoptered in to the Jane — Goodwin's Creek's the place — and we thrashed around there for a while. Then we climbed Goodwin's Peak and we felt very nice about that and thought, 'My goodness, we were rugged pioneers coming up here; I bet no-one comes up here.' Then we leant against a tree on the summit that had axe blazes in it. We wandered back down to the creek and probably down a few kilometres and thrashed round — had a jolly nice time, went for a float and a walk through Humbaba Gorge and it was lovely. Then we went down and I showed Bob and Bob a cave on the Franklin.

I was keen to look at Fraser on the way past because I still had this thing about it. I'd seen it twice by then but on neither of those occasions had I done any appropriate University study. I couldn't read stratigraphy. We took an archaeologist with us in 1976 on the Lower Gordon and adjacent bit of the Franklin but he found nothing.

By 1980 I was starting to get into the geomorphology. I started to be able to read stratigraphy and understand it. Then in 1981 we went floating down.

Poor old Bob Burton was in for his second night in a row with a sodden sleeping bag and when we got to Fraser cave Bob Brown was being a good samaritan and helping him wring it out. I think Bob would really have liked to have come in but I didn't have any altruistic streak in me at all and I just thought, 'I'm going to go and look at this cave, I've been waiting too long.'

Now when I went into Fraser the first thing I found was exotic rock which couldn't have been washed there, and the second point, I probed in a little bit more and I found that some of the bone was burnt. By the time I had been in the cave a minute it was so obvious that we had walked over this massive midden. By the time I came away I was quite confident in my interpretation of the age of it as being a Pleistocene site. I found stone tools. The first thing I did was I went there with my pocket knife and I just probed in around some bones and I hit something hard and I scratched around it and it was exotic rock and that really set me going. Everything just went 'Twig'. I scratched around and I found some more stone tools and I scratched a bit more and I found this bone and I walked back up the top. All over the bloody floor were stone tools and I had never noticed! Incredible! I was pretty elated.

I went back to the river where Bob and Bob were still working. I said, 'Look at this, look at this.' I was probably incoherent when I first got back there because I was pretty excited about it. I guess they were pretty pissed off.

Then Bob Brown came in and started to find stone tools in parts of the cave that I hadn't looked at and so he was really getting off too and Bob Burton was there and we were all actually finding stuff. It was all really bloody exciting, we were absolutely elated. We were running around taking photographs of the stuff and of each other, produced a bit of a map and then we came home.

We pressed it out about a week later after I had contacted Rhys Jones. I wasn't an archaeologist but I had the stratigraphic skills and he had the archaeological skills so we got together and went for it.

The public impact of the archaeology hasn't been the fact that humans were there but *when* they were there. If you had to say, 'It's not an Ice Age site after all, but it's still an archaeological site,' people would have said, 'Oh, big deal.' It was the Ice Age connection that was so important. I picked an Ice Age date because you tend to get frost wedging of bedrock under cold climatic conditions. What you can get with the very cold conditions is masses and masses of angular rubble. Within Fraser Cave there was this massive amount of angular debris. I saw that on the 1981 trip and I thought that's it, that's the peak of the last glacial. I was fairly sure of that.

Because a creek had flowed across part of the floor and incised a little gully through the deposits I was looking at the side of this gully. So you've got the flow stone on top and you've got all these masses of rock rubble with stone tools and bones all the way through it and at the bottom of that, clays and gravels.

Kevin went back in March with Dr Rhys Jones, Senior Fellow in Prehistory at the Australian National University and the authority on Tasmanian Aboriginal archaeology, and Don Ranson, archaeologist with the Tasmanian National Parks and Wildlife Service.

By that stage we were having a little sweep and I guesstimated the deposit was about 19 000 years old. It eventually came out at 19 700. That trip, behind Fraser — Kutikina — I found Nothofagus Cave, a second Pleistocene site (its name is going to be changed).

We could find the stuff but when it came down to detailed techniques of excavation we were no good. We had to have an expert adviser like Rhys. His name has been significant because we felt we were working with somebody who'd be listened to. He has also been important because he's been the connection with ANU and there's been money there — most of our previous trips were just shoestring stuff — which has meant that at last we had enough money to at least have our food paid for if nothing else. And he's been terrific on publicity.

The Press has really pushed the idea that we made this wonderful accidental discovery out of the blue. But it was a conscious decision to go looking for stuff for the campaign. If it hadn't been for that campaign then probably we would have been playing silly buggers in grotty little holes in the ground somewhere else.

*'I like to think I'm carrying on
where Olegas left off.'*
PETER DOMBROVSKIS

Peter Dombrovskis was born in Germany of Latvian parents in 1945. His father disappeared during the war. He and his mother arrived in Sydney in 1950, moving to Hobart a few years later.

At 17 Peter met Olegas Truchanas and was introduced to serious photography and the outdoor life — canoeing, skiing, bushwalking. As Truchanas recorded Lake Pedder so Peter Dombrovskis has become the photographer of the Franklin. His striking landscapes, with extended exposures that make time seem frozen, have made the South West wilderness accessible to the world.

Peter's photograph of Rock Island Bend on the Franklin River was reproduced more than a million times in campaign advertising for the 1983 Federal election.

Before putting out his first calendar of Tasmanian scenes in 1972 Peter Dombrovskis studied science, art and architecture. In 1977 he began producing the Tasmanian Wilderness Calendar.

As well as publishing calendars he has produced two books: *The Quiet Land* in 1977 and *Wild Rivers*, with a text by Bob Brown, in 1983.

Peter Dombrovskis uses a large-format, Linhof Master Technika camera.

My mother introduced me to nature. Interest in the natural environment and the appreciation of nature largely stems from childhood experiences. I remember walking through the Cradle Mountain-Lake St Clair National Park when I was 12 or 13. From there I think Olegas Truchanas took over. And to some extent I suppose I became his disciple.

I happened to go on an adventure camp at Dover when I was 17 and Olegas was there. I went on a canoeing trip down the Huon River which was a completely new and exciting experience for me. Then the next year I built my own canoe to Olegas' design and became more and more involved in outdoor pursuits. Olegas introduced me to skiing. I'd always wanted to go skiing but I'd never had the opportunity. I've skied pretty consistently ever since except for the last couple of seasons.

His major bushwalking trips and canoeing journeys down the Gordon he did on his own. I did quite a lot of trips with him on the Huon and the Derwent. They were just for the sheer enjoyment of doing them, the physical exercise. There was nothing serious about them, though. We did make a photographic record of all the trips.

He put all of himself into anything he thought was worth doing. There weren't any half measures with Olegas. He was a perfectionist in everything, both in his enjoyments and in his more serious pursuits. I'd derive a lot from the intensity and the enthusiasm with which he tackled things. His enthusiasm was infectious. And there was a beauty about everything he did that appeled to me.

Making worthwhile photographs is a long-time exercise. You just can't do it quickly no matter how much effort you put into it, no matter how hard you try. You go away on a trip — two weeks — under ideal conditions you might come back with three or four really good photographs. Quite often I go away for two weeks and come back with nothing. Each year I do five trips, two weeks each.

Ideal photographic conditions are when things are happening atmospherically and you can work. If the weather isn't absolutely terrible you're working all the time. Moving around looking at everything.

It takes you a few days to get in the right frame of mind, to get in tune with, in rhythm with, the environment around you. Being receptive to what is around you takes time. To really start seeing what is around you and try to make sense of it. You start to feel and hopefully you start to hint at it in photographs.

What I'm trying to do I suppose is, through the photographs, convey how I feel about the land. To do that all sorts of things have got to be working for you.
When I went to Pedder I was more a bushwalking photographer, a record photographer. I wasn't really

aware of what I was looking at, I hadn't exposed myself to the land sufficiently. And I just wasn't mature enough to do anything worthwhile.

Olegas' photographs were absolutely crucial, vital. Those audio-visuals in the Hobart Town Hall were essential in creating a feeling in people's minds of what it was about, even for those who'd been there.

In any sort of campaign where you're trying to get people to feel for an area, to make some sort of decision about it, you've got to have both words and images. You need people who can talk about the area and about the issues involved, like Bob Brown, and you also need images to show people, to give people an idea of what those areas are like.

When I'm photographing I don't think about anything like that at all. The publishing side and the creative side are in two different boxes and I don't mix them at all. When I'm out photographing I don't take pictures which I think might sell or people might like. All those considerations are left behind in the city. I go out there to be renewed, to get in touch with the land, to get in touch with myself. When you go out there you don't get away from it all, you get back to it all. You come home to what's important, you come home to yourself.

What I'm showing is visual beauty, but wilderness is very much more than visual beauty. All the other feelings you have there you can talk about, but it really doesn't mean much until you actually go there and experience it. It's like trying to tell someone what love is, what faith is; it doesn't mean anything until you actually experience it yourself.

The calendar wasn't a wilderness calendar originally, it was more of a touristy thing that I wouldn't show around now. The first calendar had a cheap binding and a short print run. It sold because there was nothing else available. The calendar in its present format started in

1977. It needed to be bigger, to give more of an impression of what the place was like. Always in the back of my mind was turning it into what I wanted it to be instead of what I thought would sell and what the mass of people would want to buy. That became more of a possibility with each edition.

I use large-format rather than 35mm because I want to get as much information into that image as I can. Hand in hand with that goes trying to get the very best quality printing — fine screen printing with good colour balance.

A large-format camera imposes limitations — it's big, it's awkward, it's heavy, it's slow, it can't be used other than on a tripod. For that reason the images have a studied deliberateness about them. When you set the tripod up you compose everything very carefully, it's all composed on the ground glass.

It's difficult for me to photograph when I'm on the move. There's so much energy in simply lugging the pack that you can't appreciate what's around you, you're watching where you're going to put your next step so you don't trip up.

I find that recently I've been getting a little bit stale, going to the same places. I'd really like to travel, to see a landscape that's different, like Antarctica, or North America, Alaska, South America. You need a bit of excitement, a bit of change. On the other hand, the South West is so complex that the only limitation is your own imagination. If you spend enough time in small areas like Louisa Bay and you're in the right frame of mind you could produce enough good images to fill a whole book.

I think that what I am doing now is what I'm meant to be doing. I suppose I like to think I'm carrying on where Olegas left off, in my own way, finishing the work that he started.

'Bob wasn't all that excited
about the trip initially.'
PAUL SMITH

Paul Smith is a forester from Launceston. After Lake Pedder's flooding he knew the Franklin River would be on the HEC's list. In 1976 he interested a local doctor, Bob Brown, in making the first inflatable dinghy trip down the Franklin.

John Hawkins, John Dean and others canoed down the Franklin River in 1958. The only other recorded trip before 1976 was a makeshift raft voyage by Fred Koolhof and others in the summer of 1970–71.

Bob Brown often recalls his first Franklin trip as 'the best two weeks of my life'. Those weeks were a turning point, not only in Bob Brown's life but also in the struggle for Tasmania's future. Since that trip the Franklin has become so widely known and valued that its flooding to make electricity was no longer politically acceptable. Paul Smith realized the need for publicity.

At the beginning of 1977 he returned to the Franklin to make a film with Bob Brown, Peter Thompson, Ric Rolls and Sam Stark. *The Last Wild River* was the first of many 16mm films made on the Franklin.

Paul Smith was born in Hobart on 16 December 1941. He has worked for the Tasmanian Forestry Commission since 1966. Both within the Commission and outside he has promoted the idea and the value of wilderness.

I think I got an interest in the outdoors from my father, he was a keen trout fisherman. He used to go off fishing, nowhere wild, just places in the north-east and the Derwent River. In my early teens I can remember standing on the shores of Lake St Clair and it was virtually a blizzard. I was standing there shivering, waiting for my father to catch fish. It seems a strange occupation to me now. It's a wonder it didn't turn me off the outdoors.

I lived at Queenstown for five years because my father was headmaster at the technical high school there. So when I was 11, 12, 13 I got to know the West Coast really well. It was a mysterious, wonderful, wet, dark place, a lot of rainforest and the road into the place then, the Lyell Highway, was a narrow, winding road, a dirt road. It was an adventure just to drive from Hobart to Queenstown.

I remember a fishing trip we had on the Gordon River one spring with my father and a couple of other men and we caught ninety large fish, 5 or 6 pound trout, in one week. We kept them in a small creek by staking off a short length of the creek. That was an exciting fishing trip and my introduction to the lower Gordon River.

I've worked for the Forestry Commission since 1966. During the early seventies I was mainly working in the field, but I often had to get away from that routine. Every couple of weeks I'd clear off for a whole weekend with a friend, fishing on the Central Plateau in places where you had to walk for half a day before you could start fishing.

In 1972 a few friends and I from bushwalking clubs and the Conservation Trust put together a proposal for a national park covering the western part of the Central Plateau. I've been working on it ever since. I have also been involved in conservation activities over Lake Pedder and the flooding of the Pieman River.

With an experience of exploring remote country and seeing the threats which disturbed us a pattern started to emerge about what it really was that we were worried about. I wrote a lot of articles. In 1977 I had an article published in *Search* that went a long way towards clarifying my ideas on what it was that I was concerned about. It was the American use of the word 'wilderness' that we picked up over here. Different people mean different things by the word 'wilderness'. So the next step was for me to define 'wilderness'. I defined wilderness as an area of land that had two characteristics: it had to have a certain degree of remoteness and it had to have a high degree of naturalness. By remoteness we meant a certain travelling time from the nearest point of mechanized access. That helped when it came to putting up submissions for wilderness reserves and arguing the case with organizations like the Forestry Commission. It helped explain the importance and value of wilderness to disinterested people.

I appear pretty pedantic in the eyes of a lot of people by getting a bit obsessed about trying to define wilderness. The definition that the Wilderness Society's got is a loose, emotive phrase designed to stir people up and get their sympathy rather than to coldly tell them what we are talking about when we mention the word 'wilderness':
'A wilderness is a large tract of entirely natural country, where one can stand with the senses entirely steeped in nature and free of the distractions of modern technology.'

If you were pretty good at steeping your senses in the feeling of nature you could do it in an armchair. I wanted something that gave specifications of the type of land we should call wilderness. This is important, to show how wilderness contrasts with other environments and adds to the stimulating variety of the total human environment.

My argument for wilderness is from an anthropocentric viewpoint which clashes very directly with what you might call the biocentric viewpoint of a lot of conservationists who believe that wilderness has a right to exist for its own sake, irrespective of whether man wants it or not or whether man exists or not. The biocentric viewpoint is a very difficult one to use when defending wilderness. I can't see any evidence for that viewpoint anyway. There is evidence staring people in the face that wilderness has a value for man. Working in the Forestry Commission trying to communicate these ideas to them I was forced into that sort of thinking.

Bob Brown was in Launceston, active in the search for the Tasmanian Tiger, for quite a while before I met him. He was a good friend of a mate of mine who was active on conservation issues. He said, 'You must meet Bob Brown, you'd get on well with him. Bob Brown is going to make his mark in the world, he's going to change things in Tasmania.'

I did bump into Bob Brown eventually. We had quite a few talks on conservation and the philosophy of conservation and philosophy in general.

By 1976 he was winding up the thylacine search. They'd been at it a long time and hadn't turned up anything conclusive. And Bob was giving up the medical profession to a greater and greater degree to spend more and more time at Liffey philosophizing, trying to write down in a fairly succinct philosophical way what was wrong with the world and what should be done to set it right. Bob was getting more concerned with the nuclear holocaust and less concerned with practical conservation problems such as the thylacine.

He spent some years at Liffey, virtually at a standstill it seemed to me, trying to get together the energy and the inspiration to write something definitive. He wrote lots of bits and pieces but couldn't get it all together. It seemed like philosophical verse at times, quite an interesting sort of style, but the content wasn't really hard and fast enough for me to get enthused about.

Bob wasn't all that excited about the trip initially. I think he agreed to come because it seemed like it could be an issue after Lake Pedder. Obviously the Hydro were going to flood something else and the Franklin was what they were going to flood after the Pieman, everyone knew that. Bob had some appreciation that that might be a significant loss. I had more appreciation of that at the time. I had seen a slide show given by John Hawkins in about 1961 — my father took me to see these slides by adventurers who had been down this wild western river — I could still remember these; it was quite an adventurous epic that I saw then on slides. These guys had taken fibreglass canoes and used blocks-and-tackle and dynamite to manoeuvre their way down the river. They even took a rifle with the intention of shooting the odd wombat or something for food, in case they got marooned down there. There were photographs of them huddled under cliffs for days in the dripping rain while the river roared in flood. It was quite impressive. So I had quite an idea in the back of my mind that the Franklin River was an inspiring place.

Bob was moderately interested. We were able to talk to John Hawkins and John Dean. Dean told us that it was pretty difficult. But it wasn't until we went to see Hawkins that Bob got quite curious about it, because Hawkins had the view that, 'You shouldn't do it, it's too dangerous, the sooner they flood it the better. People will be killed on that river.' The more dangerous it sounded the more interested Bob got.

Hawkins showed us a film. Before he showed us this film he told us about a canyon — it was some miles long with precipitous glassy walls, so smooth you couldn't grab hold of them as you were swept along by the current. You couldn't, of course, climb up these glassy walls. So you couldn't stop yourself and you couldn't climb out as you were swept along. Half way along it there was a hundred foot waterfall. We couldn't get out of him how he had managed to negotiate this hundred foot waterfall. But negotiate it they did.

After Bob heard about this canyon he said to me: 'My God, if it's like that I've got to go down, I've got to see that canyon.' The film stirred Bob up even more because it showed roaring floodwaters in these dark canyons. Bob swore afterwards that it was the Launceston Gorge in flood in this film and not the Franklin at all. Bob was getting a bit suspicious of Hawkins and he wanted to find out the truth about the river.

I've never considered myself the wild outdoors adventure type. It doesn't take much danger to give me quite a thrill. I just like to get away from it all and stretch my legs and feel a sense of isolation and some small sense of danger and self-reliance in being exposed to the elements. People need contrast in their lives, a variety of physical environments, because that arouses and stimulates their interests. Experiencing a less-safe, less-comfortable existence for a short time makes you appreciate the suburbs when you go back to them. I thought the Franklin could be lethal. My wife made me write out a will. And as we waved goodbye to the two people that took us down there —·they were standing on the bridge watching Bob and I sail around a bend in the river — as we went out of sight I said to Bob, 'I bet those bastards think they'll never see us again.'

We'd known that Fred Koolhof and his party had got through on very crude heavy rafts in 1971. We thought their gear was pretty unwieldy and that if they could do it there was a good chance we could do it. We were travelling much lighter and took plenty of care and we went at a better time of the year.

We read Koolhof's account in the Hobart Walking Club magazine. But Dean suggested rubber rafts might be the way to do it. Dean had tried out plastic inflatable rafts with his family on the Mackintosh River and reckoned that they were great fun, that they had a lot of promise. We ended up with one plastic raft and one rubber one. We had a lot more confidence in the rubber one because the plastic one, the more you blew it up the more it expanded.

All we did in the way of preparation was to cart them up to the First Basin in the Launceston Gorge, chuck them in there and put in our packs with about 80 pounds of junk in them, then jump in ourselves to see how they floated and paddled. The cargo in the front steadied them a lot. They worked quite well. We arranged comfortable seating positions with Lilos and inflatable pillows.

There was quite a bit of time involved in selecting the

gear that we thought would be best, but not much time trying it out. But we did spend a fair bit of time constructing the paddles. We had to design them — tremendously long paddles — and that design has persisted to the present day. I was the one that did most of the practical preparations — Bob was offering encouragement and being a good companion.

Once we were on the river, everyday was something you really looked forward to. You were wondering what the hell was down there and you were busting to find out. We thought that there hadn't been anyone down the river since Koolhof went down five years before. But actually about three weeks before there had been a party of Monash University canoeists going down. We didn't know that.

The first few days were taken up with getting used to the whole operation — acquiring skills in paddling the rafts, they were unwieldy; and just getting the gear sorted out took a few days, finding out where the various bits of food were and unwrapping it and wrapping it up again and stowing it in watertight fashion. I think we were physically flat out paddling down the river and learning how to cope with the whole thing.

The weather was good for the first week. It was marvellous. It was tremendous to feel you were down there on your own, that there wasn't anyone else around, and it was pretty well an unknown river. Some rapids you could see down without getting out of your boat. Other rapids, where you couldn't see what was happening and there'd be a fair roar of troubled water down there, you'd think: 'Oh, my god, that could be a problem.'

We operated as a team. One guy would sit in the boat and take it easy while the other guy got out and had a look. If he thought it was okay he'd signal you to go through. You'd throw a few swear words in his direction and off you'd go, hoping it was all right.

When you're half way down a rough stretch of the river

your blood's pretty well up and you're ready for just about anything and you say, 'Right you bastard, we'll give this one a go too.' And off we'd go. At the Irenabyss I think I probably charged off first because I didn't want Bob to have the honour of doing that himself. What I tended to do in situations like that was pull up and make worried frowns at Bob and say: 'We shouldn't go down there should we?' and then I'd charge off. But we were playing it very safe. Just to get down that rough rapid into this Irenabyss looked very dicey. Charging down there, you're bouncing all over the place, and you're hanging on like grim death, hoping as you went over each wave you'd come down in your boat and not in the water. It was quite breathtaking to go down that cascade and get thumped onto this flat water at the bottom; it was amazing to see that come up. We were going down the river with a view to not only enjoying the adventure but to recording it for other people on slide film. And we felt we were exploring the place and so we put a fair bit of effort into trying to think up names like Irenabyss.

As soon as you got around one bend, what was happening there was just so absorbing that you completely forgot about what you'd been through. The two of us would get together at lunch time and try to recall what the river had been that morning.

We spend the odd moment drifting along enjoying the beauty of it. I soak it up in five seconds — I look at it and say, bloody hell, that's impressive — then I brush it aside and I do something else. But Bob really gets immersed in it and drifts off in it. Wallows in it. That's nice, but I just get impatient myself, doing that. I can remember on the second trip, when Sam and Bob and Ric Rolls and Peter Thompson were on the trip, towards the end we were all getting very tired and ragged, particularly   Bob because he was shouldering a lot of the responsibility for the others. One evening on the lower Franklin in the limestone country, as the sun was setting — there was a red glow in the clouds, it was a really peaceful evening — we were camped on this shingle bank and Bob jumped into his rubber ducky and paddled out into the middle of the river and just floated there. There was no current and he floated there looking up at the clouds and soaking it all in, in typical Bob Brown romantic fashion. We thought this was a bit staged and artificial. Thommo couldn't resist pelting rocks at him, deliberately lobbing them short so they splashed him. Bob just sat there ignoring this commotion going on around him. I said, 'For Christ's sake cut it out Thommo, leave him alone.' Thommo wanted to stir him. But Bob needed to get away from the rest of us.

He was very tentative about getting involved in the Franklin campaign. In 1976 he wasn't sure what to do with himself. In that year I was already planning a second trip in 1977 to film a journey down the river by a group of people. I was thinking of using that to kick the campaign along, get it going. Kevin Kiernan at that stage had written one or two articles in conservation magazines about the Franklin and how important it was. Bob Brown and I had made our trip and shown our slides and started propagandizing about it. I wanted to try to get it home to people what it was like to go down that river.

Bob could see that there was a campaign building up. He was most reluctant to get involved in it, he thought there were bigger things wrong with the world that should be corrected. The threat of nuclear warfare for one.

He psyched himself into it. He was most reluctant I think because he realized that if he did get involved that would be it, he'd throw everything into it and he'd be totally consumed by it. Bob was obviously searching for something to throw his whole life into. He'd been trying to write something which would change the world.

I said that the Franklin issue is a practical case that is

right here and happening now. Tasmania's a good place to try to change society because it's small and you can get ready access to Parliament and public opinion. It's relatively easy to become well-known in a community like this and if you've got views which you want other people to share then Tasmania's probably the easiest place to do it, to get real change in society.

I thought that Bob had great potential as a leader, as a public speaker. He was very shy about public speaking at the time but I had a lot of confidence in his ability to develop in that way. Obviously he had leadership potential because he has such a warm interest in people that communicates itself pretty well. Whenever he gets up and speaks at meetings he seems to go across pretty well. All his friends think a lot of him. He has an ability to communicate with all different types of people.

We passed Mt McCall where the haulage-way comes down to the river. Then, half a day past that, we looked back and we could see these corrugated iron huts on the top of the hill back near the haulage-way. That was a bit more of an impact than we were expecting. That depressed us. We had to get into Propsting Gorge and out of sight of that mess before we could forget about it.

Propsting Gorge was a beautiful place, festooned with rainforest and pandani, a really green place compared with the gorges further up which were mostly rock.

We got on really well together, Bob and I. When we got to the Gordon River I felt lucky to be alive. When we hit the last kilometres of the Franklin where it's pretty well all flat and nice, gentle, shingly rapids, I certainly breathed a sigh of relief. I thought, 'Thank Christ, I've come down the Franklin, seen it all and I'm still alive. Bloody amazing.'

We were really fit by then, strong in the arms and shoulders. These clumsy little rubber duckies were surging along like tugboats. We needed the strength because the rivers were wide and long and we had these endless kilometres to cover without much assistance from the current. In fact the wind was blowing against us at times so that if we had stopped paddling we would have gone back the other way. Quite a lot of it was a monotonous slog. The monotony was part of the total experience.

To inspire people to go down there they've got to feel that it's an epic to begin with. If it's only a short trip, say a week, then who cares — you go into it casually, you come out of it casually and then you forget about it pretty well straight away. The beauty of the place — the dark water and the leatherwood petals swirling on the surface — that sort of thing is heightened by the isolation and the feeling of being out there on your own. Whatever the weather does, and what sort of camp site you happen to find, it's all pretty vivid because you're right in there with it and utterly dependent on the environment.

We knew we had to get back there and film it, to do our damnedest to communicate to other people just what it's like to have that sort of adventure. It seemed to us that a film was the best way you could do it. I looked at going down the river more as a *Deliverance* sort of thing — an exciting adventure — Bob looked at it more as a beautiful romantic existence, getting away from it all.

We thought it would be incredibly difficult to save the river. And we thought that it was incredibly irrelevant, how difficult it was. One had to try and if we didn't try we'd be very disappointed in ourselves. All we were concerned about was to have a better go than had been done before with Lake Pedder. Kevin Kiernan was thinking, and we were too, that if we're going to save the Franklin we've got to get in there now, before it's proposed as a hydro scheme. Try and inform people that the place is there and that it's an extremely valuable environment, a wilderness environment.

'I could have quite happily, at any time,
gone home to Liffey and left it to somebody else.'
BOB BROWN

Bob Brown was born into a family of policemen and women on 27 December 1944. He grew up in Trunkey Creek in central New South Wales.

Bob Brown studied medicine at the University of Sydney and has practised in Sydney, London and on ships in between. In 1972 he moved to Tasmania to a small house at Liffey in the country near Launceston. He joined the search for the thylacine, or Tasmanian tiger. As the years passed he spent less time on medicine and more time writing about the future of humanity.

In 1975 he stood as a candidate for the UTG. The following year he rafted the Franklin with Paul Smith. In 1979 Bob Brown succeeded Norm Sanders as director of the Tasmanian Wilderness Society. When Norm Sanders resigned from the House of Assembly in 1982 Bob Brown replaced him in the Tasmanian Parliament.

Without Bob Brown's imagination, energy and compassion the Franklin River would soon be disappearing under dead still water. He has shown all who supported the campaign that the South West wilderness is something to believe in, something worth fighting for.

Bob Brown's inner workings are difficult to describe. He is elusive, or chameleon-like, matching the colour of those around him. He is still noticeable, he is just hard to know.

Some qualities are clear: Bob Brown is very clever, perceptive, considerate, patient. Nothing is too much trouble even though you expect him to be longing to escape, usually from a crowd of people. He is warm, good-humoured, absent-minded. There can be no doubt about his belief in the causes he fights for; he sometimes talks of concerns in an emotive way or with an all-encompassing idealism that would normally make the urban sophisticate cringe, but his absolute sincerity and artlessness leave the audience gasping with empathy and belief.

You look closely at Bob Brown but as soon as you believe you have an impression a new level of subtlety emerges. He looks conservative but is really very provocative and critical of society; he sounds like a simple country chap but is alert to the details of slick city life; he seems slow but his wit and political reactions are quick; he seems gentle but can be very tough and demanding, most commonly with himself; he seems gregarious but loves solitude; he seems open but leaves you groping with few markers in the wide-openness. Talking to a crowd he seems assured but he can still be nervous in front of a microphone. Bob Brown is calculating, disciplined and suppresses his personal feelings systematically.

The most difficult quality to understand is his apparent altruism. What is the ego that drives him? He seems so selfless. But Bob Brown is not simply selfless, he has an acute self-consciousness. He has a sophisticated sort of egotism, a self-interest that goes beyond personal prosperity and pleasure, beyond his family or his country. His ego encompasses all of humanity, his happiness comes from increasing the world's well-being and security. While this would sound corny applied to anyone else, with Bob Brown, as far as I can tell, it is true.

He is very ambitious. He was brought up to achieve in the conventional sense — medicine, a mention of politics — and, when it was no longer sought, he has achieved fame and political success, though he is out of place in the petty, anti-intellectual Tasmanian Parliament. Bob's achievements are not consistent with his upbringing. There was a crucial, total reassessment so thorough that the young Bob Brown seems to have been obliterated and replaced by a man who is still powerfully motivated but heading in the opposite direction.

No-one who talks about a desire for his ideas to change the world is totally selfless. Perhaps that is his hubris. Bob Brown has the unshakeable faith of one who has given up hope, the complete fearlessness of one who has abandoned himself.

Bob always says that any one of us could have been born another but I have never met another like him. He is so remarkable that he defies the mean or cynical standards by which we judge others. He is good enough to be inexplicable, but he is still human, not a saint. Even that explanation is denied us. He has made tactical mistakes, he has misjudged people. But all the while he strived to serve the cause. As he says, more mistakes come from self-serving than from concentrating on the wilderness. In the end Bob Brown is also working for himself because, as for all of us, the betterment of the world is good for each one of us. We should all be so selfish.

Paul Smith actually was the gent who wanted to go down the river and he knew there was a hydro scheme planned for it. He had contour lines on his map showing where it would come to. To me it was all a business of tagging along to give him company. Hydro schemes seemed far away and nebulous, some plan for the far-distant future that didn't focus into reality at that time.

In 1975 there was a meeting at Sam Stark's place in Launceston I remember going to, and a woman there was talking about Kevin Kiernan, whom I'd never met, who was putting forth this idea of the South West Tasmania Committee to try and preserve what was left of the wilderness. In those days there was a strong feeling that even then we were getting to the point where there wasn't any true wilderness left in Tasmania because of the ingress of roads in particular into South West Tasmania.

In July 1976 we had a meeting of the South West Tasmania Action Committee and I offered my place at Liffey for that.

In that summer of 1976 Helen Gee and others had gone down the Jane River on a Lilo trip — they beat us down the lower end of the Franklin by a couple of days. And the same year a large number of people went through the Gordon Splits in rafts and canoes because the Gordon Dam had been closed and was filling up so there was very low water and you could navigate it. You couldn't do that before and you can't do it now. So it just happened that that summer of 1976 saw people go down the Franklin, the Jane and the Gordon River all at one go. Came this meeting in July at Liffey and those people from all those places were represented and Kevin had the idea that we set up a Tasmanian Wilderness Society. Or at least that we change the name from the South West Tasmania Action Committee, which had got a fairly strident reputation — though it had really kept conservation alive since the Lake Pedder days.

You can't give too much credit to those people who survived that period. They had very little support — the Pieman scheme was rushed through Parliament in that period, and forestry was proceeding at a great rate. Kevin and others had at least managed to get the South West National Park almost doubled in size, to include Precipitous Bluff. So they'd achieved a tremendous amount which seems to be forgotten now but was really fundamental.

At that meeting in Liffey we decided to adopt the name 'Tasmanian Wilderness Society'. I remember Chris Bell at that meeting saying that out of this we eventually had to get a World Wilderness Society going — a world consciousness about wilderness. The following month, I think it was 22 August, we had our first formal meeting here in Hobart. I remember we had sixteen people at Liffey, I don't know how many came to the Hobart meeting, but by the end of the year through touting cheap memberships it had gone up to 400. It stayed about that right through until the end of the decade.

Kevin Kiernan worked full time after the formation of the Wilderness Society and after that David Ziegler worked full time as Secretary for a good while. In June 1977 the Hydro-Electric Commission announced plans for a dam on the lower Gordon River with possibly other dams on the Franklin and Gordon. We had our first major advertisements in the new *Tasmanian Mail*, on the front page, and got a tremendous response from that, people writing in to join and to support us. At the end of 1978 I came to Hobart because Ziggy had been burnt out by that. I was here for eight weeks working. We had just a desk in the Environment Centre.

Early 1979 we had another meeting at Liffey. State meetings used to quite commonly be there then. I became Director. In late March 1979 we had a demonstration at the opening of the Lake Pedder scheme. It brought us publicity because it was unexpected. Also, the next day we called for the Governor, Sir Stanley Burbury, to stand aside because he'd said at the opening that there were other rivers running free to the sea to be harnessed. It was a direct intervention in a contentious issue because it was rapidly becoming a big question then in Tasmania: whether there should be another hydro scheme or not. I think that particular day clearly established the Wilderness Society, as distinct from being a conservation group, as a very growing force in Tasmanian politics.

I didn't want to get involved because I was much more concerned by the nuclear issue and by the general dilemma of the human race and I was wanting to stay at Liffey in a huddle and try to write a prescription for an alternative to the way that the human race works. I was very concerned to do that. I realize now that it's been a good thing in a way that I got carted out of there by this issue.

In 1976, October, the *Enterprise* approached Hobart and that had a big impact too because I was sitting at Liffey writing, saying, 'I must stay here until I get my mind together, my thoughts collected, get it down on paper and then I'll be able to, in some way or other, as an individual, wander the countryside and put out this information.' But that was too much for me: knowing the *Enterprise* was coming, bristling with nuclear weapons, with eight nuclear reactors on board, hearing the Premier of the day, Mr Neilson, saying he was welcoming it to Tasmania and various statements from chambers of industry saying, We're going to get $2 million out of this, completely oblivious of the fact that the *Enterprise* is always stalked by Russian submarines and that the whole nuclear horror was being brought to our doorstep without it being looked at. The authorities refused to divulge whether there were any nuclear weapons aboard.

I decided to go and sit on Mt Wellington and fast, while

ever the ship was in the harbour, to draw attention to the fact that people felt strongly about that, much more strongly than their own existences, about the fact that nuclear weapons worldwide — Russian and American and every other nationality that's got them — threaten the human race. It was an interesting exercise because I was very, very shy. The media arrived and I was terribly taken aback by trying to answer questions up on the mountain when obviously they were trying to make out who's this strange person? That's where I met Dr Norm Sanders — he was reporting for 'Nationwide' and did a story which went nationwide and he was very quickly onto the essence of what that was about. He fed himself a line which was the intro to that issue, about the sun coming up, here comes the biggest nuclear reactor, Bob Brown doesn't want that any closer than 93 million miles away — which was a tremendous line. And the sun rose to the theme of *Thus Spake Zarathustra*. That was a significant meeting if ever there was one. Norm Sanders took the job of Director of the Wilderness Society for a period of a year or so before I became Director at the start of 1979.

I stayed on Mt Wellington for a week; it was a fair test on my family and all my conservative background. I got abused as well as people being friendly. It was most interesting that some of the Australians who came up with an American companion to look from the lookout felt compelled to be obnoxious, whereas the Americans were very friendly. They had nothing to lose. And some of them expressed quite openly their fear that when they see a plane go off the ship they think, 'If that ever is for real, my family back in Chicago or Denver is dead.'

The *Mercury* printed one sentence. The *Examiner* printed a double-page spread which wasn't about me — they gave me the opportunity to write a full coverage of why I was doing it. That difference between those two newspapers has followed right down through the

Franklin-Gordon scheme debate. The *Examiner* has editorially been in favour of the *Enterprise* coming and in favour of the dams but it at least has the dignity and the decency to give equal coverage and be reasonable in its editorials, although they're against us. The *Mercury's* had no such editorial even-handedness or gentility.

In 1979 it was clear that we had a big campaign coming up — it appeared in 1976 when the Wilderness Society was set up that the issue would be resolved in 1978 at the latest; it appeared early in 1979 that the issue was certainly going to be resolved that year and it had to be done then.

1979 — I really didn't want to get involved but there I was. I moved to spend more and more time down here in Hobart. We went from having, in Kevin's time, a desk and a chair to, at the start of my period at the Environment Centre, having a little room upstairs where we stayed for the next year before, toward the end of the next year, moving to Criterion Street then the following year moving to 129 Bathurst Street, then last year moving here (*to 130 Davey Street*).

In October 1979 the Hydro announced its Integrated Scheme, $1.3 billion. Within a couple of weeks we had a demonstration with 1500 to 3000 people in Hobart. At the end of 1977 we held a meeting in the Town Hall which was to object to a rise in Hydro prices, thinking that that might attract more people than would an objection to a dam that hadn't yet been announced, and 75 people turned up. In 1979 the Town Hall was packed for a public meeting that two women, who came out of the blue, said that they'd get going. They packed the Town Hall.

Into 1980 we went with a big campaign to get people to bombard, lobby the State politicians. By July 1980 that campaign had reached tremendous pitch with branches vigorously working for it on the mainland and right round Tasmania and 30 000–50 000 messages arriving at Parliament House in Hobart within a three or four-week period before that decision, and a 16–4 decision to save the Franklin at the end of the week, on 11 July. The South West Conservation Area went on the National Heritage List at the start of that week, on 8 July, so it was a momentous week if ever there was one.

The film was fundamental. Paul Smith thought it'd be a good idea to go back and get a film of the area because that was the best way of presenting it. And I remember buying the camera that he used, in West Ryde, while I was on a visit to Sydney in 1976, for $250. He took the first film at the start of 1977. We showed it in Parliament House during 1977 and we bought space for it on television in 1979 — it was shown on both channels, channel 6 and channel 9 — which is really an innovation for a conservation organization to be able to buy half an hour of prime viewing time. As I remember, it was $1800 for both stations. It's hard to believe now that there wasn't antagonism to it; in fact there was a good reception to it and we had no trouble doing that. It wasn't looked at politically even.

We have grabbed ideas from wherever we could. We looked at the way other people who sell cheese and paper tissues, how they do it, and thought if that sells an idea then how much more important that that be grafted by us into saving a wilderness. We had early difficulties with even that — the ethic of using the way in which the commercial world works, to foster something that is non-commercial, that is, the wilderness, and to use our usual community modes of communication to do it, was resisted in different places and it gave all our consciences a tug. I remember a long meeting in the Wilderness Society in Hobart in about 1977 discussing whether or not it was moral to use plastic in car stickers, and if not, whether you should even use paper in car stickers announcing South West Tasmania: World Heritage. I remember similar misgivings when we went to 129 Bathurst Street —

I remember a mainland conservationist coming in and saying, 'Oh, this is a really upmarket place, what's a conservation group doing in a place like this?' As if you should exhibit the fact that you're always beaten and that you're down and out and you should live in a hovel, otherwise you're not true to what you're doing.

The idea of television advertising, and newspaper advertising made a difference to our campaign in the long run. We also innovated. I remember going to the editor of the *Examiner* in early 1979 saying, 'Look, the feeling out there's tremendous. People don't want this dam,' and he said, 'Don't believe it. You get me an opinion poll that says so and I'll put it front page.' And in May 1979 I brought him the opinion poll and he put it front page. It showed that, at that stage, Tasmanians, by 2 to 1, were opposed to flooding the Franklin River.

And a really salient social thing about the present situation is that when that decision was made in July 1980 not one person stepped off the footpath in Queenstown, Strahan, Tullah or Rosebery, or wrote a letter so much as to object to the fact that the Olga scheme was going ahead and it had left them in the cold because it went through Strathgordon instead of Queenstown. It's a tribute to the other form of communication that's used by the Premier and the Premier's media force — the aggressive form of marketing that they've used — that those people now feel so aggrieved on the West Coast. We've never used an aggressive form. Whenever we've got close to that we've regretted it. We've always put forward a positive, non-threatening type of advertising that people can easily digest.

Also the idea of dressing up. It became very apparent to me early in the piece that if, when I went to see politicians, I wasn't dressed in a suit they were uncomfortable and couldn't communicate. It wasn't because I couldn't communicate, it was because they couldn't. It was quite clear that if that was the case then if you had a television camera aimed at you, a lot of the viewers at home wouldn't be able to communicate if people looked strangely dressed or even, in the conventional sense, not fancily dressed. So it was a really valuable lesson to learn. At about that time I remember reading about an anti-nuclear campaigner in Britain who went around in a pin-striped suit, and I thought that fits in exactly with the experience here as well.

Having had a conservative background and a really close observation of and empathy with the way in which our society works, I know instinctively when we're doing something that's going to be outrageous. You get into more difficulty when you're doing something that's always contentious. The blockade presented this problem *par excellence*: how was that going to go down? But when you get to the stage where you haven't got an alternative, then you take risks.

At the back of it all the time — this is with all the people who've been involved — was the very clear recognition that they weren't there playing a game, that they weren't there to push themselves, that we were there trying to save a wilderness area. And I think that we have had a very big advantage there because everybody's got an ego but if your ego gets tangled up with your public presentation you're in trouble. You will start miscueing and misjudging how you should be presenting the case. I could have quite happily, at any time, gone home to Liffey and left it to somebody else, if somebody else had come along.

Just in the last twelve or eighteen months I've got less nervous. The media has been a terrible ordeal; in those early years in particular I had thudding heart and shaky voice and mindblanks — the whole works. That still comes back but it's gotten a lot better and in the last eighteen months I've at least been able to talk to a microphone while thinking about the issue, not being distracted by a tremendous self-consciousness, and also this fear that you're going to say something that's going to be counter-productive to what you want to achieve and to the people that you're representing.

Life is short and really I'm one of five billion people on this planet. As much as I might hate it and be frightened by it or depressed by it, I'm like you — here today and gone tomorrow. There is no hope and deeper meaning to an individual's life, I believe, unless it's tied quite clearly with wanting to see individuals just like ourselves enjoying life here, in rotation, for an endless period on this planet, and getting past this self-preservation, short-term self-interest which is the religion of the times. Materialism is very definitely the religion of the time because it allows people to forget that they're mortal and fragile and are going the same way as everybody else. But it unfortunately breaks the ability of people to relax with their own lives. There is greater fulfilment that comes out of recognizing that sure, yeah, you're going to be done, but there's going to be people who think, feel, look the same as yourself, enjoying in exactly the same way coming after you. Leave it to them, they're part of yourself, even if they're not your direct progeny.

I very often sit and think about the $100 000 a year I could be earning as a doctor and that I could be on the Riviera once a year and so on. I do, I genuinely think about that and it has only been in very recent times that I have been able to accommodate to that. But self-management and giving yourself enjoyment is very very important if you're going to survive just as a mental entity. We often get accused of altruism and it's a very self-deceptive concept to take aboard because we do what we want to because we enjoy doing it and the trick, if you can, is in doing what you want to and to benefit other people as a spin-off. And that's what's happened with the Wilderness Society. People have worked in an unbelievable way, in a way that people outside the Wilderness Society will never comprehend, over these last months and years, but it's not been slave labour. It's been because they recognize that they can achieve something and feel good about that. In feeling good they're actually bringing enjoyment to themselves which is the usual motivation for doing anything, and doing it well, in life.

It's much more easy to say that I've enjoyed the last four years now that the result has come up. At times I've enjoyed it immensely, at times I've despaired of it — at times I've felt good, at times I've felt bad. But by and large I've recognized that if I hadn't been doing it, having known that area, I would be somewhere else feeling deprived of the ability to, in future, face myself and enjoy life. I have been caught between those two things.

I don't perhaps enjoy life in the way that other people do — I'm more reflective about it than some other people are — but nevertheless it's here and you've got to make the best of it with the mental attitude that you have. It's also a fact that people who've been writers or actors or productive people right down through history, haven't necessarily been cock-a-hoop about it all the way through. Very often they've lived in despair and depression.

I haven't done anything to inspire people except to recognize that everybody has in them a very big residue, no matter how outwardly forward they may be, of self-doubt, self-criticism, a fear of being not able to be as good as they dream their potential is — and everybody dreams of a potential beyond where they're at at any given time; and to recognize in everybody else about the place a lot of the things that are in myself; and to not be misled into believing that people who enter with a great deal of confidence haven't, underneath that, a great deal of reservation and fear for themselves; and to recognize that everybody has good and bad periods, and to spend a lot of time talking with people in the Wilderness Society who may be going through a bad patch, as well as enjoying the good patches with them. In talking to them going through their bad patches, unbeknownst to many of them, they've been helping me through mine.

I've sometimes, on occasions, walked the streets wondering who I could talk to because I wasn't going too well on that occasion. But that passed very quickly and people in this organization spot very quickly if somebody's not doing too well. It's amazing how quickly you'll be asked off for a cup of coffee, or a bunch of flowers will land in front of you, or even if you're giving a talk at Wollongong somebody else will bring over a block of chocolate and say, 'This came from Hobart.' That's been one of the real strengths of the Wilderness Society — its own community empathy.

I've picked up on what a lot of other people have put into the organization because I know myself well enough to know that I'm no better or worse than anyone else. And I don't say that to promote any myth about altruism again, that is just a basic fact. I have said before — and I mean it because I really do feel it — born in a different place, given different circumstances, then I could be doing any of the things that other people are doing or have done on this planet and the same applies for everybody else.

Maybe knowing that in the long run I'll be nothing, maybe coming to terms with my own fears about that, and maybe recognizing that there are ultimately tremendous tragedies in store for the human race and that there are hugely cruel and unimaginably dreadful circumstances occurring to other people just like me on this planet at any given second when I stop and think about it, and I think about it every day, makes me recognize that I'm lucky to be here in Tasmania in 1983. To put aside the fortune of life and instead substitute a belief that things that I've been doing or we've been doing are in some way or other a personal attribute that is spectacular and different, would be a deception that I couldn't carry out because I know it's not right.

There's been a conflict all the way through this business, a growing conflict, between media concentration on me as a person, and the personification of the campaign, to a degree, in me, and my recognition that that wasn't so, that this whole campaign depended on a big living group of people who inter-reacted and were inter-supportive. Without those people we would have lost this campaign long ago. The legend of Bob Brown's much larger than life.

The legend of the Franklin River is not larger than life because it can't be. When we've been criticized as portraying the Franklin River and all that wild area as something that it's not, you only have to stop and consider for two seconds the value that that area properly managed can have to millions of individuals in the future, to know that we haven't done that.

There has been a clear recognition that that river had tremendous appeal if only people knew about it, and that that appeal is helped by the way in which we speak about it, the way in which it was named, the way in which it was portrayed on film. But without feeling in any way guilty about that because there isn't any medium which will take into people's households the extraordinary feeling that you can get on occasions by being in that area. There's no way that you can do that. While appreciation of beauty and appreciation of wilderness in particular, because it's got its fears to modern people who spend all their lives in cities or engineering works, varies a great deal, in terms of that being a remnant of a spectacularly beautiful planet, its value hasn't been overstated, it's been understated.

The only legend I would hate to see put forward in my lifetime is the legend of how the world used to be wild but there is none of it left. People who've seen *Soylent Green*, the film, might know about the concept: where you actually have to pay to see a picture of wild places as the last thing that you're allowed to do in life. We won't get to that stage but we can very easily get to the stage where there is absolutely no wilderness left in the planet. We will have made it bereft of the ecologically-intact natural areas that still are there.

I want to get my writing done. I have had to sustain a spirit that isn't necessarily part of my nature over some years now — a spirit of determined optimism even in times of adversity — that has to have its equal and opposite reaction inside myself, and that'll work out in the years ahead. I'm not anything but very acutely aware of the tragedies in store for all of us and that are actually occurring to millions of people right at this moment. Now that takes its toll.

But I want to, more than anything, try to reckon and reason with our existence in the universe, to try and say what I feel about what we're doing here, where we're going to and how we came to be here. I think everybody who has thought about those things has a need, if not a duty, to do that, because the answers aren't there at the moment, in good enough form, for the human race to be cohesive enough to ensure its survival. What's required pretty badly is a philosophy which gives hope to people so that instead of fighting against each other we can really get together to make things work.

*'... Lowe then dug
his own political grave.'*
PETER THOMPSON

In the early seventies Peter Thompson worked in current affairs radio in Launceston. He later joined the ABC in Hobart as compere of 'This Day Tonight'. From 1979 to 1982 he worked as the South West Project Officer for the Australian Conservation Foundation.

Peter Thompson's experience and ability in the use of the electronic media helped increase the public awareness of the Franklin River. In his time it came from being a glint in the eye of an HEC engineer to an issue of interest to politicians thousands of miles to the north.

Peter tells the story of the decline of the Lowe Labor Government. In November 1981 Harry Holgate replaced Doug Lowe as Premier. Then Lowe and Mary Willey left the Labor Party and joined Norm Sanders on the cross-benches. Early in 1982 they voted with the Liberal Opposition to bring down the Holgate Government.

At the election held in May 1982 Robin Gray's Liberal Party won with a landslide. Norm Sanders and Bob Brown stood as candidates for two of the seven seats in the electorate of Denison. Only Norm Sanders was elected.

Shortly after, Peter Thompson stood for the Tasmanian Legislative Council but was not elected. He would still like to work in Tasmanian politics.

Peter was born in Sydney in 1952. In 1981 ACF published his book on the politics of hydro-electric development, *Power in Tasmania*.

I first went to Tasmania in 1972 to work in radio. I was fascinated by the island. I think I imagined it would have some special life of its own, because it is isolated from everywhere else. So I went down there to work. I was reasonably well-informed about Lake Pedder. It was the autumn of the year it was flooded, 1972. I remember attending one or two protest meetings about Lake Pedder, very poorly attended.

I went up to Lake Pedder on the Easter weekend and only spent a few hours there. I went by plane. I was absolutely staggered. I was staggered before I went there

134

that they would want to destroy a place like that, but having gone there ... it obviously changed my life.

It was at least as beautiful as any other place I'd been. And it appealed to me as being unique, because in this mountain environment was an inland lake and beach. There is some sort of spiritual thing wrapped up in that as well.

A lot of other people were there. But I didn't talk to anyone else. I think there was a shared sense of loss. I might have still had this little feeling that it couldn't happen, that the grave error would be seen.

It seemed more and more foolish as the evidence came out. The bloody-mindedness of the local establishment and how stupid it was became obvious when the Federal Caucus got that money. On that afternoon I was doing a current affairs programme on radio and I heard that the money was put up by Caucus. I barely had time to do a few interviews when the Tasmanian Parliament met and Reece danced into the House and said that this — what appeared to be an open cheque offer — was going to be rejected, full stop. There were cheers of congratulations from both sides of the House. That was the end of it. There appeared at the end of that afternoon as little hope as ever of saving Lake Pedder.

Until then I had had no political involvement but a growing interest in politics. I was in a good position because I was running a radio programme which was dealing with current affairs. So I would infiltrate the programme with a fair amount of attention on the issue. I found that people were antagonistic to it: Lake Pedder had been debated to the point of boredom, very much like the situation that developed on the Franklin, Tasmanians got sick of it. Tasmanians have a limited attention span.

As a result of going to Lake Pedder I got more involved in the voluntary conservation movement. I got involved in the Conservation Trust. Once the Federal inquiry came up I gave evidence and wrote submissions.

It was during the time that I was doing that radio programme that I met Bob Brown. 1972 — he was down here at the time for the Tasmanian Tiger expedition. I was going out to interview the guy that was the mainstay of the search but he happened to be away. Bob was holding down the fort and I had to interview him instead. I remember he was extremely nervous talking to a tape recorder. We had a good yarn.

Some months later we both had to go to a public meeting that was put on to discuss environmental impact statements that were to be introduced into Tasmania. We had another talk that night and after that we were friends. We were very good friends by the time I moved away from the place in 1975. I was away for three years. Maintaining that friendship was an important part in my maintaining a close interest in what was happening to the Franklin later.

Bob Brown was a person who was in conflict with himself about what he ought to be doing with his life: whether it ought to be continuing along the conventional lines of medicine or whether it ought to be more socially directed. The conflict was very clear and he'd speak about that but at the same time he would exude calm. That inner calm is a quality that has been a steady part of him all along. And even in those years of difficulty he has been able to exude that feeling of well-being and calm in amongst the tumult.

Bob had the potential to make a profound contribution in whatever direction he went and it was not clear in what way that would be. If anything, it appeared that it would be much more abstract than something as concrete as a conservation campaign.

Philosophers don't have much of an impact on the world. If you can combine philosophy with action it is okay. Which is what Bob has done. The impact of his writing philosophy would have been very small indeed. But by becoming the public figure that he has, the impact of his philosophy in Australia will be promoted.

After Lake Pedder was under, my feelings remained very strong. I had this belief that even if it was a matter of years, Lake Pedder would be restored in the end. And it wouldn't matter how long it took for it to return to its former splendour. I still have that feeling.

I went down the Franklin with Paul Smith and Bob and Ric Rolls and Amanda Stark in February 1977 to make the film, *Last Wild River*. That was a remarkable experience. It was conducted in the most splendid weather. I enjoyed it more than bushwalking. For a start it didn't involve carrying the interminable amount of food that you take on long trips. The boats take that. It was certainly the best outdoor experience that I have had — those three weeks. It was already evident before we went what a change the first trip made to Paul Smith and Bob Brown. A bit like the Lake Pedder experience. They were deeply affected.

After having had exposure on 'This Day Tonight' in 1978 I thought it was an ideal opportunity to make a mark for the Franklin by standing for Parliament. At the beginning of 1979 I resigned from the ABC and went up to northern Tasmania to campaign for the Upper House seat of Tamar for about three months. A very good experience in retrospect. Political campaigning is, day by day, pretty tough, particularly in those parochial small-time electorates. The person who normally wins those elections has been well-known in the area for a long time. I was known only through television and because I'd been working in the north some time previously. I had to set off and, by knocking on people's doors, win over the hearts and minds of the community. The result was fairly satisfactory. It was partly due to the draw on the ballot papers that I missed out in the end.

So I found myself without a job and unsure what to do. Ross Scott was ACF's South West Project Officer in 1978 and 1979. He was one of their more experienced operatives. He was in Hobart and he was going to leave the ACF so there was a job to work on the Franklin campaign.

It was July 1979. I took the ACF job.

It was still a very small campaign. It was operating out of one freezing cold small room on top of the Environment Centre, Hobart. Bob had been involved for almost a year at that stage. There were one or two others. Essentially they were making very preliminary steps in building up a campaign: research to some little extent and trying to get the structure of the Wilderness Society into some more viable state. So it involved the usual demands of meetings and so on, the beginnings of lobbying the Press, trying to get on the media.

I remember Bob was terrified by the whole media experience. The previous year I had had to interview him for 'TDT'. We just sat there in hysterics as the crew became more and more mystified and wondered what was holding up the show. It wasn't live but I had to look the other way as I asked a question.

I suppose what I was able to bring to the campaign was close contact with the Tasmanian media. Getting more and more publicity for the Franklin. One of Bob's first instincts was to commission opinion polls. They were indicating that two-thirds of the community were against the starting of the dam on the Franklin before the Hydro published their report.

We had done a fair amount of work before that report was published in October 1979 in alerting the Hydro and the Tasmanian politicians that there was going to be a fight on their hands about the Franklin. It was quite clear the Hydro was going to recommend the flooding of the Franklin and we tried to do all we could to steal their thunder in publishing details of what they planned. We were beginning to build up our case. We were also beginning the business of publishing photographs: *The Wild Rivers Pictorial* was published at the beginning of 1979. Obtaining photographs, publishing them, distributing, all the usual campaign hack work was starting to roll on.

ACF and the Wilderness Society were working very closely; initially we had adjoining offices. The physical location of the Wilderness Society changed a few times but because of the close friendship between Bob and I we remained in constant contact. We would probably have a long discussion every few days and see each other every day. We were able to feed off each other with ideas. The two of us worked very well together as a lobbying combination and as a thinking combination.

We ranged over a whole variety of things: on the political front, who should be seen next and what our next move would be; on the organizational front, where we should be spending our energy and time and money, how we should be tackling the media, what stories we should be emphasizing, where we needed to do research.

The key to working successfully with the media was to have personal relationships with the people in the positions of influence in the newspapers and television and then talk to them and keep them informed. You were particularly appreciated if you could give them hard and reliable information.

With television it was our ability to present the issue well that was important. Just to come across as credible and in a sense conservative people — people with whom the community would feel comfortable. It was projection of the middle-class environmental front. A lot of environmental issues have been presented by people from whom the community feel separate. Bob Brown's occupation was good — a strange sort of status surrounds a doctor of medicine. And his country roots came across well in Tasmania. He appeared to be a simple ordinary fellow. I had an advantage with my experience in radio and television.

You had to use the media world. That was really crucial in building up political momentum. We had to be taken seriously. All the people involved in the campaign were very sensitive, I think, to the importance of image.

Lobbying and the media work involved being abreast of all the issues, being well ahead of everyone else with whom you were dealing — politicians, bureaucrats and the media. I was constantly digging around for new information, reading what was happening overseas. This is where I got the bulging files on energy systems and energy policy which later became the source of my book, *Power in Tasmania*. That was at the beginning of 1980.

We moved into a new phase after the publication of the Hydro report. The Wilderness Society was now quite active throughout Tasmania. We were building up our lobbying contacts with Members of Parliament — we were in the vicinity of Parliament when it was meeting and that was a matter of some alarm to traditional conservative forces in Tasmania. I don't think it had ever been done in such a systematic fashion before.

Also we realized that we had to take the matter to the community. So we were constantly involved in a round of public meetings — one or two a week — all over the state. As much as possible we would bring in the Hydro-Electric Commission to put their view. That was the major debating stage. It was a time of furious activity but at the same time very stimulating.

Doug Lowe decided he would promote the idea of consensus. Politicians in Tasmania had antagonized conservationists by refusing to meet with them. Soon after he became Premier, Lowe instituted a series of meetings with conservationists. He would meet with us every couple of months. It was quite a good forum. I think he was genuinely hopeful that there could be some sort of consensus decision. He was genuinely prepared to take conservation into account and no-one else in Tasmania's political history had done that.

In the meetings Lowe would unfold his latest scenario on the issue. It was really very fruitful. We were under no illusions about winning the issue but we had a strong sense that there was some process of communication.

The political lobbying was really very intense. It pretty well ignored the Upper House. As we saw it, the major decision-makers were the Caucus group in the Lower House.

In 1980 a number of reports were dribbling out of the bureaucracy in response to the Hydro's report. The Energy Directorate under Nick Evers brought out its report in June 1980. It was a pretty comprehensive document which argued for the Olga scheme and a thermal power station. Then National Parks and Wildlife came out with their report so there was a monumental paper war going on which was difficult to keep abreast of in terms of reading.

Lowe announced a Joint House Select Committee of inquiry would be set up. Our view was very strongly against it, a view that grew out of the fact that we wouldn't have the numbers on the Committee. Much to our relief the Liberal Party decided that they would oppose it, in fact they would not participate in the Committee. They favoured an independent committee of inquiry like we did. We had no illusions — the Liberals were going to come out hotly opposed to saving the Franklin — but it seemed to be a convenient point on which we could agree. Lowe announced the Joint House Select Committee would not go ahead because the Liberals were refusing to participate.

That left us wondering what sort of decision would be

made. The Government was coming under increasing pressure to make a decision to give the Hydro approval. So instead of a delay until after this Select Committee, Cabinet suddenly started preparing to make a decision without any inquiry.

The decision was ultimately made on 11 July 1980 to build the Olga scheme but to save the Franklin. The decision-making process was very deceptive. We appeared to face the very real prospect that they would come up with the Franklin scheme. Doug Lowe himself was see-sawing from side to side. Finally, after three days of Cabinet discussions, we got the so-called compromise of the Gordon-above-Olga scheme.

Bob Brown had gone in to address Cabinet and we were in great excitement and anticipation. In the end the Government came out with a decision which we knew would be hard to fight if it was well-promoted. The Franklin was being saved but there would be a hydro scheme in the South West. We were pessimestic.

The Olga scheme put us in a difficult position of how to respond. In one sense Tasmania had never made a decision for conservation before: the Hydro was being turned down on its favoured scheme. To ignore that after all the fighting that had gone on within the Tasmanian Labor Government to get that far, to say that was nothing, would have been entirely inappropriate. So Bob Brown described the decision as historic.

In the very next sentence, and this is later ignored by the critics of Bob Brown in the conservation movement and the Parliament, we said that the Olga scheme would be a disaster and had to be fought.

It was a mixed victory to say the least. We were now faced with a second Olga campaign. Who would have imagined that after this decision the Franklin might still be flooded? We were only babes in the wood at this stage.

Almost to my disbelief the Hydro made it very clear they

weren't going to accept the decision. I think Lowe then dug his own political grave by not coming down like a ton of bricks on the Hydro. He allowed himself to get into an argument with them. I would have thought Lowe had no option but to sack Ashton if Ashton was going to refuse to carry out Government policy.

We had this extraordinary spectacle of the Hydro men down in the halls of the Parliament lobbying the Upper House against its own Government's policy. They really did believe themselves to be entirely independent of political authority.

The Legislative Council decided to set up its own Select Committee to look at the Hydro proposals. It rapidly became obvious that the Legislative Council was going to come out pro-Hydro in its report. Their recommendation had the most absurd logic. They said that the Gordon-below-Franklin scheme would be environmentally less harmful.

The report came up for discussion in the Upper House and the debate was just a complete farce. These doddering old Members one after the other stood up and asked, How can we stop the Hydro — what a wonderful organization it was; they were eulogizing about the Hydro. It was appalling stuff really — just toadying to the HEC.

Lobbying the Upper House was a hopeless task. I remember visiting a character in his late seventies. Bob and I sat in his office just before the vote and he said, 'Oh, I don't know about these rivers, I've got creeks out the back of my place, I think they all should be dammed. All these creeks, there are plenty of creeks around, they need to be dammed.' It was a comedy, Bob and I started to break up. Later the politician was defeated at the polls and he said at the declaration that no-one under 45 years of age should be permitted to stand for Parliament. These young pups have no experience of life.

So the Legislative Council voted against the Olga Bill.

They insisted on the Gordon-below-Franklin and sent the Bill back to the Lower House. It looked as though there'd be a Constitutional crisis. This was Christmas 1980.

It was a vital period for the Labor Government. It seemed that if the Government didn't get its Olga scheme through then, it might not get it through at all. The Government's credibility stood on its fight with the Upper House. Doug Lowe allowed Parliament to go into recess without the issues being resolved and I think that was disastrous.

Putting myself in his shoes at the time I think if I was determined to get that Bill through I would have put on the greatest song and dance and have refused to allow them home for Christmas dinner and say that Hydro jobs were at stake and so on. But Lowe allowed the Upper House three months breather. There was already division in the Labor Party about the scheme. The months of deadlock created the momentum for Lowe's final undoing.

Early in '81 one of the senior members of the Government, Attorney-General Brian Miller, said that he believed there should be a referendum on the issue. He did that to try to neutralize the opposition to him from the pro-Hydro supporters in his electorate. He was facing pre-selection.

There was as continuing deadlock between the two Houses. For a while we had it both ways with the Lower House stopping the Gordon-below-Franklin dam and the Upper House refusing to pass the Gordon-above-Olga. But we knew that while the deadlock continued the pressure was not *away* from building a dam but *towards* building a dam. The longer it went on the greater the chance that there would be a swing back to the Gordon-below-Franklin. Lowe's position was becoming more and more precarious.

We were using the delay to our benefit in the sense that

we never had a greater number of politicians from Canberra ferried down the river. We had a tremendous success with the media all over Australia. The Franklin really caught fire as a public issue.

But on the domestic front there were grave problems. The push for the referendum grew in the Labor Party as they could not think of a better way to resolve the issue. We were deeply concerned that we wouldn't succeed if a referendum was held.

Another godsend came our way in October 1981 when the referendum was finally announced. We all groaned. On that night the question was put to Doug Lowe on TV, 'Would there be a No Dams option?' He said yes. This inflamed the passions of the pro-dam lobby within the Labor Party — it was still enormously strong in the union movement — and Lowe recognized he had said this without reference to Caucus. Believe it or not Caucus had decided there would be a referendum and then adjourned for lunch! They had discussed for an hour and a half whether they would have a referendum, finally decided they would, then adjourned without deciding what the questions would be. So Lowe decided without consultation that the questions would include a No Dams option.

It was almost the end for him. He went into the Caucus room a week later already recognizing that he would have to back down. He said it would be irresponsible to have a No Dams option: 'I recognize the error of my ways.' And that saved him for another week.

He came out that evening saying he was wrong, had been irresponsible to offer a No Dams option because he as Premier realized there was a need for a dam. How could he therefore offer a No Dams option? It was deeply humiliating for him.

That played right into our hands. We had a complete turnaround. We had a referendum being put to the community which offered no right to say no. A week later, 11 November, Lowe was removed by his colleagues who had been plotting for weeks. The new Premier, Holgate, thought for a day or so on whether to hold the referendum and decided to go ahead with it.

When I think back on the campaign, we were then at the make-or-break point. We had to decide what to do with the referendum; whether to urge people to vote informal. It was really a fascinating time to be part of. There were exhaustive meetings going on amongst all the conservationists day after day. They involved everyone. Everyone felt part of the decision in the end. There was a real concern that if you asked people to vote informal it might be a disaster. Very few might do it. The Olga scheme was the least damaging of the two options given on the paper and perhaps we could fight it off later. Ultimately I have no doubt the right decision was made in asking people to vote informal and write No Dams on their ballot papers.

When the referendum was first being discussed I remember having a conversation with Senator Peter Rae in Canberra. He was amongst the first to suggest that we do a No Dams write-on because there had been an experience in the US where a well-organized lobby had asked people to write on their ballot papers. Nevertheless we were breaking new ground in Australian politics.

We had a frenetic campaign to get the populace to write No Dams. There was a huge flood of the No Dams triangles and people recognized them as an ideal symbol. We spent a lot of money, $100 000, in a combined effort between ACF and the Wilderness Society. We doorknocked the State, which had never been done before — 85 to 90% of the houses. We doorknocked in some of the most remote places.

On the day of the election we manned virtually every polling booth in the state, I think Tullah might have been left off. There was a growing concern about violence. A lot of car windscreens that had No Dams stickers on them had been smashed. The growing hostility in Tasmania was becoming quite unpleasant.

We had our backs against the wall. The Labor Party was half-heartedly supporting the Gordon-above-Olga dam. All the unions, the Liberal Party, the Legislative Council, big industry and all the media were in favour of the Gordon-below-Franklin scheme. And we as a community group were doing our best to win a majority of informal votes. The task seemed impossible.

On the night of the count I think we were somewhat surprised at the result. About a third of the people wrote No Dams and 36% voted informal — which we were later to build up to 45%. That's a good story actually ... The Referendum Bill initially said put a tick in the box which indicates your preference. But some wise man in the Legislative Council said, 'But in Tattslotto you have to put a cross in the box.' So he suggested that to record a formal vote you put a 1 to indicate your preference. That eliminated the need for ticks and crosses and everyone went along with this idea.

On polling day we found a great disparity between polling booths: some were counting 1s and some were counting both 1s and ticks as formal votes and others counted ticks and crosses as formal votes. The Electoral Officer nearly had a stroke. There he was, thinking his reputation was at stake, having provided this awful count.

We barrelled in and said this count does not go along with the Act. So the Government got a legal opinion and found that we were in the right. They had a recount. Informal votes sky-rocketed from 36% to 45%. The Gordon-below-Franklin vote mercifully went down to 47%. It was astonishing that with a 45% informal vote the Government shrugged its shoulders and promptly said it was a great triumph for the Gordon-below-Franklin scheme.

After the referendum the Labor Party was faced with a great drama. There could be a no-confidence motion forcing an election before Christmas. Lowe had moved to the cross-benches and so had Mary Willey. A combined vote of the Liberals and Sanders, Lowe and Willey would have unseated the Government. So when Parliament was about to resume Holgate came up with the smart tactic of proroguing Parliament for three months.

There was a tremendous upset in Tasmania. I remember during the referendum campaign I hadn't seen anything like the political antagonism towards Holgate. Holgate saw that he would have to watch it. His primary consideration was not what to do about the results of the referendum but how to save his own political neck. He had the option to negotiate with the cross-bench but Sanders closed that option when he said flatly he would not negotiate with Holgate.

So an election was looming up when Parliament was to resume in March. Sanders was in a pivotal position to determine whether an election would be held. We had a growing cross-bench and a feeling that conservation candidates would do well in a State election. But very many questions marks.

The Labor Party met in late January 1982 to decide what it could do about the referendum. The numbers were there for the Gordon-below-Franklin scheme and it was passed. But the vote did not compel the Premier to bring on the legislation straight away. That left open leverage for stalling. We knew that as soon as that legislation went into Parliament it would pass and they would start on the scheme. It opened up the possibility of negotiating a moratorium on the legislation in return for a political favour. And that political favour could be that members of the cross-bench allow the Government to survive.

Both Lowe and Willey made it clear they would vote to bring the Government down in a no-confidence motion. Now the pressure was on Sanders who had the opportunity then of saying to Holgate, 'Look, I'll let this Government survive for twelve months as long as you stave off that legislation.' But he didn't say it. It was inevitable that the Government would fall. I think it was a disastrous mistake of Norm's.

On 13 March there was a complete feeling of unreality about the Parliament sitting. They had an afternoon tea party at great public expense with scones, puff pastries and so on. But there was this certainty that the Government would only survive an hour or two. It surprised me that Holgate did not call an election himself. The Public Gallery was packed for the first time in living memory.

The Liberal Party that wanted the Gordon-below-Franklin more than anyone else, and the cross-benchers who didn't want it, worked out a form of words that said, 'Because of the Government's handling of the power scheme this House no longer has confidence in the Government.' They agreed on the form of words but took issue on how the scheme was mishandled. The weary debate went on for two or three hours, the motion was passed and that was the end of the Government. There was to be an election.

The Wilderness Society had been thinking very hard about what to do. There was hope that we might win the balance of power. I decided to stand for the Upper House in the seat of Hobart.

I got involved in the two-month campaign for that seat. There were nine candidates. In the end I topped the primaries and was defeated on the preferences. That was an error standing for the Upper House, crazy.

The Lower House election result was a disaster for us. 15 May represented a complete change. We knew after that

that our only political hope was winning federally, that Tasmania was going to be a virtual irrelevance, that the dam legislation would pass and that, barring some miracle, work would start on the scheme.

Tasmanians weren't prepared to put conservationists in. Both parties ran on this strong plank that conservationists were going to create instability and people don't like instability. Conservationists proved by bringing the Government down what a force they could be. Parties that force an election often get annihilated in the subsequent poll.

Looking back at those years — 1979 to 1982 — everyone involved in the campaign had their lives changed considerably. It was exciting to be involved in an issue gaining momentum, capturing the public imagination and developing into one of the largest public-interest campaigns ever staged in Australia. It felt an important issue not only in terms of conservation but also of democracy — forcing the public will against bureaucrats and politicians. There is a great deal of satisfaction in being involved in something affecting the future of Australia. There was a sense of the hunt. You were out-manoeuvring the people who had a vested interest in the flooding.

I am attracted to political activity but if you are going to get involved in a political game you need to select the match where you have got some prospect of winning. In a small community such as Tasmania there are so many things operating against innovation. There are the Upper House, the Labor Party itself and the union movement — absolutely conservative — and the media owned almost single-handedly.

You wonder if the stakes are worth it.

A Government Changes

*'I'm a member of a
rinky-dink little state parliament.'*
NORM SANDERS

Through the years of the most bitter debate over power schemes in Tasmania, 1980 to 1982, Dr Norm Sanders was the Australian Democrat Member of the House of Assembly. While he was often abused as an interfering American, Hansard also records many of his unflattering reflections on Tasmanians and their representatives.

Before he became an anti-politician, Norm Sanders was the second Director of the Tasmanian Wilderness Society. He has always been a great publicist for the South West.

Norm Sanders was born in Cleveland, Ohio, in 1932. His sense of adventure and his technical skill led him from mountain-climbing and geophysical research in Alaska to oceanography in Tasmania. In 1968 he gained his PhD in geomorphology from the University of Tasmania.

He returned to the USA to teach at the University of California. At the height of the mass-action environment movement in America he led battles against oil drilling, pollution and other threats to the western rivers and coast.

Norm Sanders and his wife, Jill, came back to Hobart in 1975, Norm sailing across the Pacific in a 9 metre yacht. Norm worked as an ABC reporter, lecturer in Environmental Studies and novelist before joining the Wilderness Society.

During the blockade of HEC works Norm Sanders was prominent in Strahan, organizing the camp, Greenie Acres, flying reconnaissance missions in his disposal-store Cessna and maintaining radio communications with the Gordon River camp.

Since the blockade he has turned his rhetoric about the need for labour-intensive, low-energy, design-based industries in Tasmania into action: he manufactures fuel stoves to his own design.

It is axiomatic that you cannot stop a development such as this dam with the local politicians because they are part of it. So you have to go to the next level of governmental authority. If you have got a problem with the county, go to the state. If you have a problem with the state, go to the Feds. Because the local people have their fingers so deeply entwined in these pies and they're getting money under the table, they are committed ideologically, or fiscally. They are either actually getting paid or so much part of the system that they can't see the errors of it.

Of course in Tasmania's case, or in Australia's case, these people are in many cases so naive that they don't realize that they should be taking bribes for what they are giving away. In Mexico, the officials would say: 'Oh yeah! That's worth a lot of bucks. If you want to put a dam in, you know, come across.' These politicians are too dumb to know what they are missing.

Look at our average local politicians. Insurance salesmen, a farm accountant from Victoria, our premier. Small people from small towns and they are impressed with expertise, like the Hydro claims to have. They say, 'The Hydro must know.' And besides it's easier, they don't have to think.

The Hydro says, 'Vote us a million dollars and forget it. Progress forever.' It's an incredible thing in Tasmania where one of the worst examples of state socialism that I have seen has become the Establishment. One of the many paradoxes of Tasmania is that the Libs will embrace something which, if they heard a description of it — a bureaucracy run by the state, which has no input into it by the people, is completely autonomous, is socialistic in its views in so far as it is run by and for the Government — would scream 'Socialism'! But here it is the Establishment.

The Hydro is not the power in this state really. The power in this state is Comalco, ANM, APPM and their local managers plus the landed aristocracy and the newspaper owners. The Hydro merely does their bidding. But it gets its bit out of it too. It's all the old boys club. But what this fight has been about is not electrical power but political power. Who controls Tasmania for what purposes? It's a vassal state. We are supposed to supply cheap labour, give away trees, give away minerals, give away power — to the multi-nationals. It's still a colony purposely and deliberately kept under-employed so they can get a docile work force. The workers in Tasmania strike far less than any others in the country.

The whole tactic as far as I was concerned was to use my presence in the Tasmanian Parliament and the battle in Tasmania to get this out to the mainland. I knew we couldn't stop it locally. I don't care what the *Mercury* ran, the radio said or the 'Dam It' stickers meant — expressions of frustration — I don't care what the Tasmanian people think, it was an international issue and that is where I kept pushing the imagery. The State Parliament gives you a bit of legitimacy from which to launch the policy especially if you are not going with the local line. And if you are speaking the truth. I've worked out people don't like the truth from politicians because they want them to say everything is going to be O.K. The people say, I'm worried about this stuff, but the politician is going to fix it; it is like confessing to a priest.

Doug Lowe had some good ideas and his heart was in the right place but his feet are watery — he can't hold on to a position. He just wants to please everybody. On balance, he was kind of above the rest of them, but he still wasn't forceful enough. If he had been I think he could have succeeded. We got along quite well. We would go out and have coffee together. We had a very good working relationship with Mary Willey. That was the only time the Parliament worked the way it should, when Mary Willey and Doug Lowe and I had the balance of power — that meant we could actually debate things on their merits. In one week we actually got things through that had been hanging around for years. Like the Consumer (Small Claims) Tribunal. The Liberals backed that. They won't do it now, as Government, but they did as Opposition. We had the Government backed into a corner on it until they had to bring it in, then the Government prorogued itself.

It could have survived if I had supported Harry Holgate but it would not have come up with much that was useful. Harry offered me all sorts of deals. He offered these kinds of proposals: 'Look Norm, how about this? We really make a go at this dam, rush at it, build a bunch of roads and then let the Feds talk us out of it and buy us off.' I said, 'You are going to muck up the South West too much doing that.' But that was his proposal to me to keep him in office and then let the Feds stop it, get compensation, and he is off the hook. The Hydro would probably have pushed him further and been more hardline about it. I just don't make deals. I am not a politician. If I were I would probably have done that.

Compromise is essential for the political survival of the person but I don't think it does anything for society. If I had compromised, I would be in the Senate now but I didn't want to. I would not have liked myself if I had. For those couple of years in the Tasmanian Parliament, I found life absolutely awful. I had nobody to talk to, until Doug Lowe occupied the cross-benches. I could talk to him on some issues.

There was fun and games with everyone trying to shoot down Sanders. Poor Hansard. Half the time they could not hear what I was saying because of the uproar — shouting and cat-calls. The Liberals would stand on their chairs and wave Hansards. I met every form of hostility there is, in the House and out. I did not play their games at all. I did not drink in the pubs and I rarely ate in their stupid greasy dining-room. It bothered them because I would not come down to their level. An Australian could not have survived that hostility and ostracism, only an American. The way Australians deal with people is isolating them, because Australians hate isolation — they are herd-animals. Americans couldn't give a damn. As long as no-one was actually beating me up, I could tolerate it. Verbal abuse is neither here nor there. That infuriated them because they couldn't get at me.

I considered the time absolutely wasted. I didn't have to waste three years of my life in that swamp. I could have raised the issue without Parliament, being a good talent and having a good issue. As somebody once said: 'The two best television talents in Australia are Bob Hawke and Norm Sanders.'

But let's face it. I'm 50 years old, I've been in the business for 20 years and I've been in the big time. Your audience is 40 to 60 million people in the US. I was a major figure in California, which has a population about the same as Australia and probably a bigger gross national product. For TV you've got to be a performer; but you also have to have something to say. A performer with a message. But you should make them like you and not be too heavy. Light enough so they can like you. When I went on the Mike Walsh Show against Brian Hoyle, now I did not debate against him on the points of the wilderness. I talked directly to the blue rinse set and they loved it. I was just joking with Mike Walsh, showed him pictures of the river — isn't that beautiful? Hoyle was saying different things — mumble mumble — and I just ignored him, was smiling and just fooling around — I stole the act, stole the whole thing from Mike Walsh. The producer was just appalled. He said it was bizarre.

He rang me a week later and said: 'You know, we got thirty-eight phone calls after that and they loved it.' And they ran that segment when they had the 2000th show of Mike Walsh as one of Mike's best. Making them feel that here's a nice guy, and think, 'Gee, he's working hard to try and save this nice area, the Franklin. Nice people trying to save that Franklin. And look at that other guy, he's just going ugh, ugh, ugh; why's he trying to ruin the Franklin?'

You've got to be warm for TV. You've got to project warmth and not project phoniness. You've also to be able to come across that you're kind of sending yourself up a bit. 'We are all in this together.' And you can't be nervous because if you are nervous you are sending out nervous vibes which is making the audience nervous.

On TV Bob Brown does something I can't do. He has the other approach — he is sincere. He is so sincere you've just got to believe him. He doesn't joke. He wears a funereal suit. You think he is so sincere you've just got to help him. He's good talent but not entertaining talent.

We would have been stopped in the blockade if the media hadn't come back for the second one. We had good media coverage during the first blockade before Christmas and mediocre coverage during the second. And it would have gone right down the drain except the Hydro started to do these beautiful visual things, like bringing a bulldozer down the river. The photos I took — not only could I fly the plane, know the area, take the picture, but I could present them to the media — embarrassed the Hydro. The oil spill for example — first they denied it, then they said it was a chain saw — and the barge with the bulldozer going through the rubber boats — they had those pictures for the evening news and they had no other film of that incident.

I am 50 years old — I've been an electronics engineer, I've been a geophysicist, I've been a commercial pilot, I've been a commercial photographer, I've been a geomorphologist. I'm not easily conned. And if the Hydro said, 'We're the experts,' I would get out the calculator and prove that they are wrong. I reckon, on the Hydro hit list, I'm probably slightly above Brown as I hit them with their own technical knowledge and expertise. In fact, I was the first one to attack the Hydro on its numbers and make it look sick. I was pushing wind power at the time. I proved that it would be cheaper to do wind than hydro power at the time. Ashton, the Commissioner, called me in and said, 'We can talk this out. Why don't you come to us first? You don't have to go public.' I replied, 'I am just trying to make you look sick, that's all.'

The Hydro is a giant bureaucracy and will never be tamed. No. They won't get quite what they want but they will get something else, don't you worry. This could be one of the nicest places on earth but it won't be. Another government may help, but can you see another conceivable government coming along with any sense?

I came to Hobart in 1975 and became a television reporter till 1977. I was specially looking for good talent. That's hard to find. Kevin Kiernan wasn't so good. He was a bit hesitant, wouldn't come out very forcefully.

The first I saw of Bob Brown was when the *Enterprise* came in 1976. I actually fed him some lines. When I met him on Mt Wellington he was good enough but he didn't have good catch lines. He had a couple of good lines. The *Enterprise* was coming up the river at dawn and he said, 'There is the sun, the bringer of life, there is the *Enterprise*, the bringer of death.' That is good stuff. But I wanted to link it with nuclear power. I said, 'Here is a good one: "The closest I want to be to a nuclear reactor is 93 million miles and that is the distance from here to the sun."'

He was good but he was new to the game. He was sincere but he just hadn't picked up all the tricks. On television you have got to relate to an individual not a whole organization, that is human nature. The image of Bob Brown wasn't done consciously, the media did it. I think the media builds up people and it doesn't matter what other people may have done. The media sees the good talent and builds it up.

I quit television when a story was stopped. The Forestry Commission did not like it. Then I started writing my novels. Until someone from the Wilderness Society said, 'We need a name on press releases, you're good with the media, so why don't you become the Director?' So I was appointed, not elected, Director.

In those days the Wilderness Society used to get together on Monday nights and all they used to do was write letters to the editors under everybody else's names — even anonymous — attacking the Hydro, and writing press releases. They were really action-packed meetings. I always maintained the best way to run a group was to have a small group — probably no bigger than three — free to act. You don't have to have a large membership. Now the Wilderness Society is in old age. They can't take any action without a meeting.

I keep telling these people it is time for the Wilderness Society to disband. The Wilderness Society started because the Conservation Trust was so conservative. It is time for a new thing to come up. The bureaucrats in the Wilderness Society were just people — everybody is a potential bureaucrat. People always want an organization to grow, so that they are part of a bigger organization. It's human nature and you have to guard against it. That started while I was Director. It was getting too turgid.

Some people have moved on because they are getting older and want a change. The original activists can't tolerate the meetings. Like geomorphic stages there are three — youth, maturity and old age. When I was in it originally it was youthful, then it reached maturity during the blockade, and now it is senile. Nothing is happening.

There was a meeting at Liffey about 1977 and the worry was that everyone had heard about the Gordon and nobody had heard about the Franklin. We've got to publicize the Franklin. Everyone knows we want to save the Gordon but nobody knows about the Franklin. So it should be: Save the Franklin–Lower Gordon. How do we get the message out? I said, 'Buy an ad.' They had been having raffles for several years and they had $300 in their kitty. I said, 'You've got to put that money out and take a risk, that is what it's for. My first impression of the Wilderness Society was this guy walking around with a bag full of money and a book of raffle tickets. I said, 'The thing to do is there is a newspaper starting up, the *Tasmanian Mail*. It's going to every house in Tasmania as a throw-away — get a full page ad in that saying "Save the Franklin".' They objected saying, 'We can't afford it, we've only got $300.' I said to put a little note at the bottom saying this ad costs $800 and we need money to pay for it. So they did and we ran the ad and got $1300 back, paid for the ad and we had $500 in the Treasury. That moment was the change from the Society being a bunch of nice people, to being an activist organization that was going to put its money where its mouth was, and get into the big time. If I made any one contribution it was talking them into running that ad. When I bailed out, Bob Brown came in.

I went into politics. There were two elections — one in 1979 when I did not get in and the 1980 by-election when I did. The first election when I wasn't voted in I was disappointed. Being a competitor you are disappointed when you don't win the race. I've never really wanted to be a politician, so it doesn't shatter me. Not getting into the Senate this year was a bit harder than that, because we had all the infrastructure set up for getting into that. And not getting into the Senate with Jill not working we had no income. I could have got a job on the mainland but I wanted to stay in Tasmania. To make a living here I have had to move into stoves.

I couldn't stand it in the House of Assembly any more. They were so bad, the whole bunch. The Opposition was no opposition. I remember on my 50th birthday, I was talking to Wreidt in his office. 'I'm 50 years old today and what have I got? I'm a member of a rinky-dink little state parliament.' He said, 'How do you think I feel? I'm 55 and all I've got is this — a desk with a sign on: Leader of the Opposition.'

I can't leave Tasmania because I've got this kid, and you can't move a kid around too much. I like the place, but I can't stand the people, because they are such unaware people, they have no idea they are living in paradise and they are trying to screw it up as fast as possible. They don't travel enough to see how screwed up everything else is. This attitude of derision that the mainlanders have for Tasmania has helped us a lot in this dam fight. They think that Tasmanians all have two heads and are a bunch of half-wits. So they get upset when they think this beautiful thing is going to be destroyed by Tasmanians. If the Franklin were in Victoria it would be a lot harder. That description of Tasmanians is not true of course — Tasmanians are as diverse and intelligent as anybody else.

The Wilderness Society had to take on too many people. It was necessary to take them on. A senile organization has a lot of meetings and accomplishes nothing. It was really essential for this kind of a blockade. I have a lot of friends who are able to handle themselves physically quite well, and who don't take nonsense from anybody. They didn't come to the blockade. This was not a time for direct action. By having all those meetings and days of training, you weeded out anyone with any incentive — they were obedient, patient people, that you ended up with. Anyone else didn't come in the first place or they left. Consensus decision-making kept anything from happening. It also meant that the *agents provocateurs*, which I am sure the cops had because they tried everything else that was amateurish, couldn't do anything. The cops admitted to us, 'We are trying to find out what you guys are doing. We just can't break it.'

My basic role on that whole blockade was trouble shooter. And I could sense when things were starting to go wrong. We tried to get the Aborigines to move into Greenie Acres. Joyce Davis had been a camp manager in many places. Greenie Acres was entirely because of her. She found the land, she organized the camp, she got it all going.

They were having one of their eternal morning meetings and I had been trying to get the Aboriginal people to come to Greenie Acres. They had been down on West Beach and they were getting hassled. I said, 'Move in with us. We'd just love to have you.' You know about the rift between the Wilderness Society and the Aborigines. 'Move in. I'd love to have you and I'd like to talk to you about the area.' I talked to them for days and finally they were coming. They loaded their trucks and then they wanted to drive down into the camp. And I said, 'No we don't allow cars down there. But I will get you twenty people to carry your things and allow you to set up.'

The morning meeting there at Greenie Acres had a good 200 people and I went up to the facilitator, a meek looking little girl. I explained to her that I had to help the Aborigines set up and they needed twenty people to carry their things. We've got to all work together. She said she would put it on the agenda. I said that that wasn't good enough, I need the people now. She said I can't interrupt the meeting. So I stood up and said, 'The Aboriginal people are here and they want to move in. We need twenty people to help them set up. Come over to me if you want to help.' Of course the people were overjoyed to get out of the meeting and this body of people got up and came over. I got twenty people and the facilitator was livid. She said, 'You can't do that.' I said, 'I just did, Lady!'

Without Greenie Acres we would not have had a blockade. It was essential to the whole operation. Furthermore Greenie Acres had to run perfectly. We had health inspectors running around and they thought we had a perfectly healthy set-up.

People are attracted to the Wilderness Society because it is a goal. It is a religion. They are religious freaks. Not Jesus-freaks. But wilderness-freaks. Bob Brown is God. Jill and I said to Bob, 'The biggest danger about this blockade is that a lot of people are coming here because of you and a lot of people may get hurt or killed because of you; it's on your head and your conscience.' He said he had to go ahead. The river was bigger than that.

He needs mothering, he is all alone in the world. Bob is so homeless. We need a God, we can't do without a God.

*'From that moment I knew
my days as Premier were numbered.'*
DOUG LOWE

Doug Lowe was the Tasmanian Premier who tried to save the Franklin River from flooding. His government proposed the Gordon-above-Olga dam as an alternative to the Gordon-below-Franklin. The Gordon-above-Olga scheme would still have scarred and flooded large areas of wilderness including the Gordon Splits.

Doug Lowe's compromise pleased neither the conservationists nor the Hydro-Electric Commission. Unable to placate the former or control the latter he lost the confidence of his party. He was replaced as ALP leader and Premier in November 1981, shortly before the referendum eliminated the Gordon-above-Olga, his preferred option.

With his Minister for National Parks, Andrew Lohrey, Doug Lowe created the Wild Rivers National Park, which included the Franklin. He then nominated that park and two others, together called the Western Tasmania Wilderness National Parks, for World Heritage listing in 1981. International recognition of those parks by the World Heritage Committee late in 1982 enabled the Commonwealth Government to use its power to stop the Gordon-below-Franklin dam.

Doug Lowe was born in Hobart on 15 May 1942. He was an electrical fitter before becoming Tasmanian ALP State Secretary in 1965.

He entered Parliament in 1969, became Minister for Housing three years later and Premier in 1977. He led the Labor Party to victory in the 1979 elections. Since his removal as Premier and resignation from the Labor Party he has been an Independent Member of the House of Assembly.

Doug Lowe is an intelligent and principled politician.

I am the only Member of the House of Assembly who has ever spoken in opposition to the flooding of Lake Pedder. That was back in 1971. I'm a Senator of Jaycees. As a result of a number of trips into Lake Pedder that various chapters of the Jaycees sponsored I had formed the opinion that there was a significant case against the inundation of Lake Pedder and that it could have been avoided.

The first time I went there was quite fascinating; the second time, because of the high usage of the tracks into the area, the impression I was left with was that it was a hell of a mess. It brought home the important point that not only should we preserve our wilderness but that we manage it and make sure that we don't allow it to become polluted with evidence of human presence.

I took over as Premier on 1 December 1977. As we moved into the period when we knew the Hydro-Electric Commission would be bringing forward its next major recommendation the thing that I stressed as Premier, and which the Government generally accepted, was the need to not be faced with a *fait accompli* by the Hydro, which conventionally had handed down a recommendation to the Premier of the day who immediately took it into the Parliament as Government policy.

I took over the Hydro-Electric Commission myself in April 1978. There was sufficient bias and distortion in information provided by the Hydro-Electric Commission that I realized I did need a separate, objective and competent group of people to advise me on the complexity of energy policy matters, not only power development but conservation strategies and all other related matters. I established a separate Energy Directorate within my own Premier's Department which would test all the advice that was presented, whether it was the Commission, National Parks and Wildlife, Forestry or Mines. I made sure that everything funnelled into the Directorate of Energy. It would then do an objective appraisal of the information or advice provided.

The Hydro-Electric Commission was very upset by its existence and spelt out that opposition very firmly to me privately. Obviously, by comments that were made by the Opposition, those concerns had been transmitted to other people as well.

Under the Labor administrations of the past the

Premier had normally been the Minister for Energy. Because of the very close personal contact between Reece and Knight as Commissioner, the Commission had a very high influence on the Premier of the day, Premier Reece. It was my opinion that Knight as an individual was far more than just a head of the largest and most influential government instrumentality, the Hydro-Electric Commission. He, in many instances, personally advised Reece on matters of government policy that were totally unrelated to power development. Whereas I established a specific facility within the Premier's Department for policy research and analysis across the full spectrum of policy matters, I think it is true to say that during the Reece premiership that function was carried out basically by the Premier of the day in consultation with but a small group of influential public servants including the Hydro-Electric Commissioner, the Under-Treasurer, the Director of Mines and one or two other people.

Sir Allan Knight, in 1971, when the legislation for the Pieman River Power Development was presented, mentioned at the briefing that was given to all Parliamentarians that the Integrated Power Development would probably be the next phase after the Pieman, the Integrated Power Development being the completion of what was started with the Gordon River Power Development Phase One. At that stage he spoke simply in notional terms.

When I took over as Minister for Energy in 1978, the first thing that I said to the Hydro-Electric Commission when they had briefed me on the stage that had been reached was that I expected them to present to me not only their recommendations on the Integrated Power Development but also all other alternatives. I said: 'I believe I've got to put it to you that you cannot accept that the Government I lead is automatically amenable to a scheme that will flood the Franklin.' And the response from the Commissioner was: 'Well, if that is your instruction, so be it. But any scheme that didn't involve the inundation of the Franklin would have to be seen as irresponsible.' I knew then what the underlying conflict was.

As Minister for the Environment, I had always kept an open door policy, not only for the conservation movement but all people who were involved, including industry itself. Some substantial improvements were made. I think the general atmosphere between industry and the Department of Environment during that period improved because of the consultative and consensus approach that is fundamentally my own personal philosophy.

When I later took over the portfolio of Energy I was anxious to use that same open-door policy for all sides of the argument and from that time on I established a regular three-to-four-monthly meeting with all the conservation groups, and I met individuals within those groups more frequently.

At the end of the debate I hoped that we would come up with a strategy that would enable sound economic development for the future. But the most crucial thing was the permanent and perpetual preservation of the South West and Wild Rivers National Parks which included the Davey catchment, the Olga catchment, the Franklin catchment and the lower Gordon catchment.

I thought if I could get those into a national park and have it registered nationally as part of the national estate and internationally as part of the world's heritage that would be secured for all time. Whatever happened in surrounding areas, in forestry development or mineral development or whatever, would not intrude in any way into the area that had been permanently preserved. Then, because of the sensitivity and the international recognition of that area, the management plans that would be required would be of such a nature that we could be reasonably confident that there would be no permanent devaluation of the area in total. That strategy evolved in the period 1977–78, following the Cartland Committee Inquiry. The Commission was very well aware of that. The thing that we were all aware of in Cabinet was that the Commission itself was doing much, without any consultation with Cabinet or even its Minister, in investigative work around the area that ultimately was to form a major part of its recommendation for the Gordon-below-Franklin power scheme. As the decision on the next major power development drew closer we knew, and the majority of Cabinet knew, that we had to act fairly quickly.

The Commission had thought, right to the last, that once it brought me its report it would probably be adopted, given the attractiveness of their presentation. In 1979 it brought its report to me.

I informed the Commission that I would table it for publication and forward it to all government instrumentalities that were directly or indirectly related to the proposals and I said I would also throw it open for public analysis. From that time onwards there were a number of forces, both within and outside the Labor Party, who were very anxious to see adopted the procedure that had occurred in the past, of automatic acceptance. Eric Reece was one of the prominent people in that move and he contacted a number of members of the Parliamentary Labor Party saying that there was no real need for all this public discussion — the Hydro-Electric Commission was a world leader in this field and surely it should know what it was about. So it started.

The Commission, in my judgment, leaves for dead many of the large transnational corporations insofar as its ability to marshal forces and organize to gain its will. When I took over the Energy portfolio in 1978 one of the first things that I was anxious to do was to bring the Commission under Ministerial control. The Commission told me very firmly and directly, when I informed them of my objective, that the Commission was totally opposed to Ministerial control. It engaged the services of Mr Ken Gifford, a QC from Melbourne, and spent a lot of money trying to point out why it would be most undesirable for the Commission to come under Ministerial control. When the legislation was finally approved in the Parliament it was only a shadow of what I had set out to establish. Direct approaches were made to influential Members of the Legislative Council. That indicated to me just how effectively the Commission itself could move if it wanted to. The events of 1980 and beyond were a complete confirmation of that.

The Hydro Employees Action Team (HEAT) was established in mid-1980, if not with the public urging of the Commission, at least with its private support. Its objective was to represent the self-interest of the Commission and the Commission employees. It was a potent force because it encompassed not only some of the senior people in the engineering field but it also encompassed a lot of the blue collar workers who in the past had formed the base of traditional Labor support. The network grew to encompass trade unions — the HEAT philosophy filtered through into a number of the metal trades unions. Through contact at the top the Commission had direct linkage with business. The Chamber of Industries combined to form a substantial lobbying network to try to press for the implementation of the Commission's viewpoint. You also saw during that period the hitherto-unused public relations approach, where some very experienced and skilful people who had accounts representing individual businesses, started to provide an overview of strategies that should be pursued in lobbying the non-Cabinet Members of the

Parliamentary Labor Party and some Cabinet Ministers. And moving to use the forces of the Legislative Council if necessary to reverse the Government's decision.

I thought that the package of decisions that were taken in July 1980 were very comprehensively discussed, within the Party and the community, and very justifiable.

In July 1980, immediately prior to commencing our considerations, we allowed Bob Brown to address the Cabinet. The reason we did that was because it was recognized that the Hydro Electric Commission's senior officers were going to be before Cabinet during the deliberative process; therefore we thought it was at least reasonable that the conservation movement, as represented by Bob Brown, should be able to put its viewpoint.

The conservation side was generally fairly responsive. They knew that their only hope of saving the Franklin was to carry through with the process that I'd established of full public analysis. In July 1980, when the decision was taken to proceed with the Gordon-above-Olga, the conservation organizations had said: 'We're not going to come out and publicly support a Gordon-above-Olga scheme but if you can save the Franklin we'll be well and truly happy that that has been achieved.'

The unfortunate thing was that so quickly after we'd taken the decision to save the Franklin conservationists became so publicly opposed to the alternative. I'm sure that one of the major excuses that the pro-development group had to become as volatile as they were was the public impression that nothing would satisfy the conservation movement.

If there had been an expression of rejection but a preparedness to go along with the Government's policy then I think that it would have limited the acceptability of the opposition to the Government's programme on the part of the hawks — the Commission and its supporters.

When the Wilderness Society said, 'We're opposed and we're going to go in and obstruct work on the scheme,' it gave the very excuse that the pro-development group were looking for to really come in heavy against the Government. It brought together this quaint composition — former Labor leaders, former Liberal leaders, big business, the Hydro-Electric Commission and the Parliamentary Liberal Party, and unions. It brought them all in against the Government of the day. I was never under any delusions that the conservationists would be in opposition to the Gordon-above-Olga scheme but to me it was either that or lose the Franklin.

The two considerations that were taken to the Cabinet were two major hydro developments — one, the Hydro-Electric Commission recommendation, two, the alternative recommendation of the Olga. The Commission says that it didn't really put forward that as a second alternative but if you read their report they did. At a crucial stage, at about two-thirty on the first afternoon of our discussions, the majority of Cabinet went into that meeting very much with open minds, they didn't really know what the final judgment would be, because it was a fairly complex matter and they had a large body of information before them. Then at about three-fifteen Michael Barnard asked Russ Ashton, following a number of questions relating to the employment implications, something about the larger employment that would be involved in the Gordon-below-Franklin scheme. And Ashton said: 'Well, wait on, that's not strictly correct, the Gordon-above-Olga is just as employment-intensive as the Gordon-below-Franklin.' Bill Gaskill intervened and said: 'Rather the Gordon-above-Olga does employ marginally more people over a longer period than does the Gordon-below-Franklin, because it is a labour-intensive programme. That ought to be clearly understood.' From that moment I think the majority of members of the Cabinet believed that that had answered the one reservation that everyone had — employment.

We asked the Commissioner and Mr Gaskill to provide by first thing next morning a specific flow-sheet of employment levels. But when that Cabinet broke up at about five o'clock on that Monday afternoon, firmly in my opinion, and I think the rest of Cabinet, was that we had been given the answer that we had been looking for. It meant that we would be able to proceed with power grid expansion in accordance with our needs at least and that costs were marginally higher than the Gordon-below-Franklin but only marginally higher. We also felt that there had been a substantial understatement of its output by the Commission, but the fact that it was going to provide more jobs over a longer period made us reasonably sure that the Olga was the answer. The Commission had not stated in any documentation that the Gordon-above-Olga was more employment-intensive.

When I went that same day to the film evening for the launching of *Manganinnie* there was a call to save the Franklin just as I was about to introduce the Governor and then a spontaneous round of applause. It was impressive, it's true, but it was not the catalyst that caused me to change my position.

The following morning the Commission brought back the diagrammatic information that confirmed what had been stated the preceding afternoon by Messrs Ashton and Gaskill. The decisions that were taken were not just power development. There was the energy conservation strategy, the wilderness conservation strategy — seven or eight specific points. Each had to be seen as interrelated with the others.

The Wild Rivers National Park was agreed in principle back on that Monday and Tuesday in July 1980, and that was confirmed by the Parliamentary Labor Party on the following Wednesday and Thursday. But then it was up to Cabinet to determine the implementation of the entire package.

We decided, so as not to be provocative to the Legislative Council, that we would withhold the World Heritage nomination until after the legislation had gone through. But then when the Legislative Council was, at the encouragement of all the pro-development lobby, obstructing the legislation, I convinced Cabinet that then was the time to play what I saw as the crucial card in the whole exercise: that was to short-circuit the availability of the Franklin River by forwarding it for nomination for World Heritage. We had a meeting of the Parliamentary Labor Party in May 1981 and I convinced the Parliamentary Labor Party that it was right and I went out at two o'clock to an Executive Council meeting at Government House and that's where we had the formal proclamation of the Wild Rivers National Park, and from there I sent an immediate letter to Mr Fraser calling on its nomination for World Heritage listing. The Wild Rivers National Park was specifically surveyed prior to its formal nomination in November.

During the course of 1981, with the pressure building up from within the Party itself, one by one there were defections from the group of supporters for the Government's policy, the Gordon-above-Olga scheme, to the Hydro-Electric Commission's policy. As I saw that diminishing support I stressed that I believed there was no need to panic — the fear with many of the members of the Parliamentary Labor Party was that ultimately the Legislative Council would withhold Supply and force us to an election. Our policy had not been determined lightly and its implementation was really fundamental in determining the relationship we really had with the Legislative Council in the long term. We were not even midway through the term, an election was not due till

July 1983. I called on the Parliamentary Labor Party to buckle down, support the policy, and if the Legislative Council endeavoured to change the Government's scheme we'd just withdrawn the legislation and resubmit it next year, or the year after. In my judgment and on all the advice we had there was no pressure that we had to have any additional power scheme before the turn of the decade.

One of the people who was a reluctant acceptor of the Olga decision was Brian Miller, the Attorney-General, but he was always loyal to the Government's policy. In February 1981 he saw a referendum as a means of resolving the confrontation between the Government and the Legislative Council. Key people were being privately lobbied by the pro-development forces, some of them even having their pre-selection threatened. The option of a referendum to those people seemed attractive. In the end it was inevitable that the numbers were going to be there to support a referendum.

When finally the matter of the referendum was considered by Cabinet, as I expected Cabinet made the decision in principle to have the referendum as a means of breaking the deadlock between the Houses, then we went to the Parliamentary Labor Party with the Cabinet recommendation. I was specific in indicating that the wording of the questions was something that we would consider at a later time. The decision in principle was approved.

That afternoon members of the Parliamentary Labor Party who were on the pro-development side had gone out publicly saying it was a victory for the pro-development element and under no circumstances would there be consideration of a No Dams option: there's going to be a dam. The Press in the late afternoon came to me and I decided to call a press conference early that evening where I said: 'Look, this is going to be a genuine referendum not an artificial thing. There is going to be an opportunity for every shade of opinion to be expressed, including No Dams.' It was printed next morning: No Dams option to be available in referendum. By the time I hit my office my phone was absolutely inundated by those members of Cabinet who were on the pro-development side, and particularly Holgate who phoned and said that he was going to insist that my stance was reversed and that he had the support of the majority of the backbench and the affiliated trade unions.

I called an immediate Cabinet meeting because I could see there were real problems. I got to Cabinet; the majority were really hostile. I think six of them said: 'Look, no No Dams; because if No Dams comes up ahead of the rest what do you do? We've got to accept it. But we aren't going to be in that position so it's no No Dams, right?'

At a special meeting of the Parliamentary Labor Party, no No Dams was confirmed. There were five who voted against that. It was from that moment on that I knew my days as Premier were numbered. It was the first major vote in the Parliamentary Labor Party and in Cabinet that I had not been able to get through. I may have over-estimated my ability but I think it was just a case of increasing pressure on key individuals in the debate who were starting to find that they couldn't tolerate the pressure of opposition for much longer.

That's where the seeds were sown and those who hold power within the ALP, which is not the trade unions as such but a narrow spectrum of them, they started to work very deliberately against me and they were putting pressure on backbenchers, threatening preselection. When Geoff Pearsall was replaced by the Liberal Party for matters relating to his personal affairs it simply gave those who were my opponents in the Labor Party the one excuse they were looking for. Can the Liberal Party criticize us if we get rid of our leader the same week that they got rid of theirs? The two things happened within twenty hours of each other: Pearsall at 4 o'clock on the Tuesday afternoon and me at 11 o'clock on the Wednesday morning.

When I was removed from the Premiership on 11 November 1981, there had been a poll taken by the *Bulletin* preceding my removal and it was found that the Tasmanian Labor Government had 51% support from the community while the Liberal Party had 35% support. So even though there was a major body of criticism against the Government we were still getting the message across and the people realized the plight we were in and they were still supporting us. One of the disappointments was that when we had that level of support unfortunately the majority of the members of the Parliamentary Labor Party went to water.

The Hydro-Electric Commission would say that they were not involved in my removal and I have no doubt that that is a true statement. But the course of opposition that they chose to mount and the methods that employees of the Commission and trade unions that have members in the Commission chose to embark on, very much at their encouragement, led, undeniably, to my removal.

The power debate is the only area where Eric Reece has been able to attract any real influence. He has been able to establish an alliance between the conservatives of the Tasmanian business community, the metal trades group of trade unions which predominantly has sat on the left of politics within the Labor Party and a number of groups of self-interest that comprise technical and professional people from within the Commission itself. Drawn together you've had this conservatism, radicalism — not that they're ever radical in Tasmania — and self-interest combined to form a very significant body of influence that was very carefully used to bring pressure to bear on the Legislative Council. There are very few families within

Tasmania that don't have some relative somewhere working within the Hydro-Electric Commission. That network has been very effective.

Eric Reece's influence on some people within the Labor Party was very significant, particularly those who held views pro the development of the Integrated Power Development scheme. A matter of four or five days prior to my removal he was visited by a person who, within the Parliamentary Party, had been one of the strongest supporters of the conservation of the Franklin River but who ultimately voted against me in the leadership challenge and who, as a result of that, became a Minister of the Crown. The general message that was being given was that I was a liability to the Labor Party.

I think that Mr Reece was grossly disloyal because I had given him unstinting loyalty for the period of our association in the Parliamentary Labor Party, even on occasions voting at variance with what my own conscience would dictate simply because he was the leader. I regret very much that he didn't render to me that same code of loyalty in my moment of crisis. He always said to all those who would dare to oppose him on a viewpoint when his Government was in trouble that the time when the Party most needed the loyalty of its members was when the Party was under challenge. The Party could never have been more under challenge than in the period leading up to and following the power decision of the then Labor Government.

You never forget what's happened in the past and it would be foolish to do so, nor must you ignore the lessons of the past. But at 41 years of age I still believe I have a role to play as a Parliamentarian and I cannot be effective if I'm going to live in a sea of hate regarding those people. So though I resented what happened at the time nonetheless we are working to establish a better future for a rising generation of people and those who will follow them. I have to work with those people and it's better if we work in an atmosphere of friendship and understanding.

In order to try to achieve the preservation of the South West, compromises had to be made that were at variance with what would be one's personal selection. But that's the democratic process. Total inflexibility may well be counter-productive. There will always be something less than perfection in the final judgments that are taken. But that again is humanity itself.

Particularly in a position of leadership you have to justify decisions that were against your own personal selection. That is the role of leadership. When I found that I'd reached the untenable position, that I was expected to accept I no longer had the support of the majority of the Parliamentary Labor Party but the logical consequence was that the policy that I had worked so hard to implement would be reversed, then I had to say: 'No more, I have compromised to my limit, I will compromise no more on that issue.' And I left the Party.

One of the ironies is that I still happen to be in keeping with the Federal Parliamentary Party's policy.

On the power debate in particular because I had for so long had to carry the acrimony of suspicion and misunderstanding simply because of the role I had to play as leader of the Parliamentary Labor Party, I was relieved to be able to clear the air on those matters. I do appreciate the opportunity that is now available as an Independent Member to be able to follow my own conscience on the wide range of issues that come before the Parliament. I would be less than honest if I didn't say I still very much miss the opportunity of being able to directly affect the day to day affairs of government as I did for ten years as a Minister of the Crown.

*'I suppose I had some faith
in the system.'*
ROBIN GRAY

Robin Gray was born in Melbourne in 1940. His father was a Labor-voting church minister, his mother a Liberal. He left school at 16 to work as a clerk in the Victorian Public Service and later studied agricultural science at Melbourne University.

In 1965 he moved to Deloraine in northern Tasmania to establish an agricultural consultancy. He became a Liberal Member of the Tasmanian House of Assembly in 1976 and Leader of the Opposition five years later. After the Liberal Party won the State election in May 1982, Robin Gray became Premier. Conservationists were devastated.

Like most Tasmanian politicians Robin Gray has championed the HEC's Gordon-below-Franklin dam. Since he became Leader of the Liberal Party he has been so convinced of the popularity of that scheme that he has resisted all inducements to consider the alternatives. He fought for the dam till the bitter end in the High Court on 1 July 1983.

Robin Gray does not have fixed political ideas other than the notion that doing what is most popular is the way to succeed. As he says, he supported the dam because the majority of Tasmanians wanted it. Robin Gray appreciates the pragmatism of National Party leaders; in the 1983 Queensland election he campaigned for the Premier, Joh Bjelke-Petersen, rather than his own Liberal Party.

In this, as in his pastoral interests and intuitive conservatism, Robin Gray is like the former Prime Minister, Malcolm Fraser. Many Liberals, such as the present Federal Leader, Andrew Peacock, suspected Malcolm Fraser of being closer to the Nationals than to true Melbournian Liberalism.

Malcolm Fraser and Robin Gray have an affinity, if not a friendship. According to Robin Gray, Malcolm Fraser's only mistake was to have misgivings about the dam and for that Gray blames the Prime Minister's advisers. In return Malcolm Fraser could well blame Robin Gray's intransigence on the dam as a major reason for his loss of the Prime Ministership. As Peter Bowers, the national columnist for the *Sydney Morning Herald*, said on 15 October 1983:

'Robin Gray became the catalyst in Malcolm Fraser's defeat on March 5 by scorning Fraser's compensation offer not to build

the dam, thus delivering the environmental vote across
Australia to Labor.'

As a Member of Parliament you are obviously interested
in how we are going to supply our future electricity needs.
That interest grew as we moved into discussions about the
next power scheme and the Gordon-below-Franklin, and
the lead up to the Liberal Party making its decision about
whether it would support the Gordon-below-Franklin.

It was a question of evaluating all the options. We
assessed the need for electricity, we assessed the expected
demand and we looked at the options. The only economic
option, the only sensible option that we saw from an
environmental viewpoint, was the Gordon-below-
Franklin. It's a cheap hydro-electricity scheme, it's a clean
scheme, it's the only resource which Tasmania has to
offset the disadvantages that we have in other areas, such
as isolation.

I've always believed that the HEC has done a good job
for Tasmania. I believe the majority of Tasmanians
support that. They've opened up vast areas of Tasmania
which would have never been opened up to all
Tasmanians, in fact any visitor who wants to come to the
State. Without the work that they've done, this State
would have been very, well we would have been half the
State that we are. We wouldn't have had the industry,
wouldn't have had the employment, we wouldn't have
had the population, we certainly wouldn't have the
tourist facilities ... So I've always believed the HEC is of
great importance to Tasmania.

I haven't seen much of the South West. I don't think
many Tasmanians have. There are a few nature-lovers
and bushwalkers who've been to the wilderness areas but
apart from that it was the odd bushman, the old miners,
the people of the West Coast who really knew the South
West.

I love the bush just like anyone else does; but there are thousands and thousands of square miles of wilderness down there and this power scheme wasn't going to harm that environment, it would have opened up the South West to a lot of people. Most of the beauty spots would have been left untouched.

Were there any particular beauty spots he would single out as being attractive?

Oh no. There are all the well-known spots . . . We live in a state which is very lucky to have the great beauty that it's got. There has to be a balance between conservation and development. You can't have total preservation, just as you can't necessarily have development totally at the expense of the environment. You have to have a balance.

It should not have been necessary once we had a majority decision expressed amongst the Parliament of Tasmania for there to be any further question about it. A decision had been taken, it was acknowledged that there was going to be some sacrifice but by and large the majority of Tasmanians believed that the power scheme was the best development for Tasmania.

And that should have been the end of it. We became concerned about the mainland and we ran an advertising campaign so that people on the other side of Bass Strait understood why it was that we wanted this development. But money goes nowhere when you start trying to win a campaign of that sort.

I think people ought to accept the majority decision. As far as Tasmania was concerned it was a majority decision. If it had been the other way then we would have accepted it. We believed it was a matter for Tasmania; people living distant from it really couldn't make a judgment about it. It's easy to say it's a dreadful thing to dam the river, when you don't know all the facts. That's what happened across

Australia. The people in Tasmania who had the opportunity to hear all the points of view had made up their mind. On the mainland there were certain sections of the media, particularly the *Age* and the *Sydney Morning Herald*, who didn't want the facts and who misrepresented Tasmania's position.

Would he adopt the position favoured by the majority, even if it conflicted with his own views?

I think you've got to take note of what the people want. You govern on their behalf. If you're not responsive to their wishes then they're entitled to put you out and they will put you out. Doug Lowe would still have been Premier if he'd been right. But he wasn't.

There was never any doubt in my mind that the right thing was what was wanted by the majority of Tasmanians. I believe that as time has gone on all Tasmanians have come to support our view. Now obviously the scheme has been stopped and we have to accept that. I have accepted that it's not going to be built. But no-one can tell the future . . . You've got to remember that 70 per cent of our unused hydro-electric resources are now locked in that World Heritage area.

In January 1983 Malcolm Fraser offered Tasmania $500 million to fund a coal-fired power station as an alternative to the Gordon-below-Franklin dam. Earlier he had suggested to the Premier that Tasmania abandon the project.

I think it was unfortunate that Malcolm didn't come out with a statement on the issue right at the start. Really what Malcolm should have done was stand up and say, 'This is a matter for the Tasmanian Government and we're going to support the Tasmanian Government. We understand the views of the conservationists but the reality of the situation is that it's Tasmania's decision.' That's what Doug Anthony in the end said. Malcolm should have accepted that this was the right decision for Tasmania, as he has said since, and allowed us to get on with the job. Had he stood by the Tasmanian Government, gone out to bat for us, put our point of view, I don't believe it would ever have become the issue that it did. By prevaricating and indecisiveness they allowed it to become an issue.

Robin Gray knocked back the Prime Minister's offer as soon as it was made. But wasn't he in a better position, then, to negotiate with Malcolm Fraser, than to gamble on a High Court case that he was advised Tasmania would lose?

I suppose I had some faith in the system. I thought common sense would prevail. I think Tasmanians would have been justifiably disappointed if I had accepted that sort of offer. They wanted the dam to be built, they still want the dam to be built. For the majority of Tasmanians that was the best solution — we don't want compensation.

I think the High Court decision is very worrying. It means the end of the Federation as such. Quite clearly now the Commonwealth can assume powers over a vast area which before this was considered to be the responsibility of states. The tragedy of that is that small states like Tasmania are going to get scant attention and consideration from Canberra.

Most people agree that the people best able to make decisions in the interests of the people in a certain area are the local people themselves. That's the basis of Federation. The people of Tasmania are best able to make judgments about their needs, the people of Western Australia are best able to make judgments about theirs.

That's what really is the great tragedy of this decision. I'm sure the Founding Fathers never envisaged such a situation occurring.

The HEC will continue to be the energy-producing authority for this state. They've got tremendous resources of expertise and experience. Their role is in construction, reticulation and supply, and administration. The Government should be in control of planning.

Working closely with the HEC I've found the Commission responsive to the views of the Government, the needs of the Government. We have a happy relationship.

Occasionally talk-back radio reveals something of the way the world works. In January 1983, a few days after Malcolm Fraser's $500 million offer, radio station 7EX in Launceston offered the chance to see into the relationships between those who rule us. The amiable, some might say laid-back, Robin Gray chatted to his home-town crowd. He told a joke about his Liberal colleague, the Prime Minister at the time, Malcolm Fraser. At first I thought he was serious.

I hope he's not listening. (Laughter.)

You know he's a great fisherman and of course he's spent a few days over here this week fishing. When he arrived up there this time he got his fishing gear and got his best fishing lines out and headed off to the nearest lake. Unfortunately he picked a fairly soft spot, waded in and before he realized it he had walked into some very unstable edge of the lake and started to sink in. He's a big man, Malcolm. And bit by bit he started to go in.

Just as he was about to go under the water, fortunately three kids came along on their BMX bikes and saw him in trouble and threw out his fishing rod to grab hold of and bit by bit they managed to pull him back to the shore.

Malcolm was of course overcome with appreciation for their kindness and he said to the three boys, 'I really do appreciate it and if there's anything you'd like at all that I can grant you just tell me what it is.'

The first kid said to Malcolm, 'Well Prime Minister,' he said, 'You know that big motorbike you ride around Nareen, could I have a ride on that?'

He said, 'Yeah, yeah, sure, I'll organize that. You can come over and ride around all weekend if you like.' So the kid was tremendously pleased.

The second kid said, 'Well Mr Fraser, you know that VIP jet of yours, could I fly in that? Could I sit up next to the pilot?'

Malcolm said, 'Yes, sure. When I go back to work you can come with me and I'll get the pilot to give you a spin.'

The third kid said, 'Prime Minister,' he said, 'I'd like a state funeral.'

The Prime Minister looked at him. 'A state funeral,' he said.

'Yeah,' said the kid.

'What would you want a state funeral for?'

'Well, it's like this Malcolm, when I get home and tell the old man what I did today, he'll murder me!'

The National Stage

*'Clearly the State Government
has responsibility.'*
MALCOLM FRASER

Throughout 1982 the Franklin campaign concentrated on one person, the Prime Minister, Malcolm Fraser. In January 1983 he responded to nation-wide concern, making a $500 million offer to Tasmania to stop work on the dam. Earlier he quite deliberately helped conservationists make the Franklin into a national issue. This contradicted all his rhetoric about the matter being a State responsibility. It also helped bring Malcolm Fraser down.

The former Prime Minister is a man of contradictions, sometimes seeming to be quite perverse. For example, there is no doubt that he cared for the wilderness of South West Tasmania and did not want the Gordon-below-Franklin dam to be built. He loves landscape photography and fishing in the Tasmanian highlands. However his few public statements emphasized the State's right to build the dam and defended Tasmania's claim that it needed the power from the dam. By speaking in this way Malcolm Fraser concealed what many of the country's voters would regard as his better nature, concern for the wilderness.

Perhaps he believes Australians prefer a leader with a tough, arrogant persona. In person the man is very shy and sensitive. His handshake is gentle, almost weak. Unlike most politicians he is uncomfortable with strangers, relying on his wife, Tamie, to circulate at social functions. He prefers to argue than agree. Shyness is transformed into haughtiness intended to inspire sufficient fear in the other to protect himself. One senior public servant described Malcolm Fraser as 'The most fearsome man I've met.'

He also has the loner's ambition to prove himself, to have people respect him, not for his social skills but for his power. The separation of private from public personality is probably more rigorous and more schizoid than most politicians.

Malcolm Fraser was born in 1930 in Melbourne. He studied at Oxford before becoming the Liberal Member for Wannan in western Victoria in 1955. On 11 November 1975 the Governor-General, Sir John Kerr, appointed Malcolm Fraser Prime Minister in place of the popularly-elected Gough Whitlam. The Liberal Party won the election that followed. In March

1983 they lost the Federal election and Malcolm Fraser's Prime Ministership came to an end. He resigned from the leadership of the Party and left the Parliament.

I spoke to Malcolm Fraser in his Melbourne office but he did not wish his comments to be recorded. The Franklin issue caused him great political problems which he could not satisfactorily resolve and I can only guess that he does not want to discuss his failure publicly. He has always preferred attack to defence. What follows is an account of his vital role in the battle based on conversations with people who, unfortunately, can only be described as 'sources close to the former Prime Minister'.

Even before the Tasmanian election in May 1982 Malcolm Fraser was conscious of the Federal political consequences of the South West struggle. First the Senate had established a Select Committee to examine the controversy in September 1981. Then the dam versus dam referendum in December 1981 stirred the national doubts about Tasmanian justice because the choices did not include a No Dams option. In answer to a question in the House of Representatives on 23 February 1982 the Prime Minister said:

> Clearly the State Government has responsibility ... The referendum might not have helped the State Government very much, nevertheless, it held the referendum and it made certain decisions ... Irrespective of whether those decisions are good or bad, it is the State Government that needs to be responsible for them.

This less-than-enthusiastic support was for the Labor State Government of Harry Holgate.

By the time of the May election Malcolm Fraser knew that he would have to deal with the Franklin issue. His officials were working on ways of stopping the dam. He contacted the Liberal leader in Tasmania, Robin Gray, to tell him not to back himself into a corner, to leave an escape route in case the dam could not be built. Robin Gray, believing that Tasmanians wanted absolute commitment after years of equivocation, refused to take his Federal leader's advice and promised the people of Tasmania that, if they elected a Liberal Government, nothing would stop the Gordon-below-Franklin dam. Although Holgate's Labor Party promised the same thing the Liberals won by a landslide.

With a Liberal Government in Tasmania the Prime Minister's statements had to support Robin Gray. At the National Press Club on 2 June 1982 Malcolm Fraser said that the building of the dam

> is entirely a matter for the State Government. Robin Gray made it very clear before the State election and I would have thought that as a result of the State election it is very clear that the people of Tasmania as a whole have made their view very clear.

Privately however he was discussing the merits of the dam with his Ministerial colleagues and others and saying himself that it was not needed. In Parliament his Minister for Home Affairs and Environment, Tom McVeigh, answered questions about South West Tasmania in a way that provoked anger in Robin Gray. As Tom McVeigh recalls it:

> You had a Premier who said, 'McVeigh is a disaster, he is wet behind the ears, I wouldn't talk to the bastard — he's a conservationist.'

Such reflections indicate the Premier's declining confidence in the Prime Minister who chose his Minister. And after Robin Gray's request for withdrawal of South

West Tasmania's World Heritage nomination, Malcolm Fraser had to publicly differ with his Tasmanian colleague.

In October 1982 Robin Gray so doubted Canberra's resolve to 'let Tasmanians decide' that he toured the mainland justifying the dam before a backdrop of Tasmanian Government/Hydro-Electric Commission advertising on its benefits.

Shortly before this tour confidential legal advice prepared by a senior official of the Commonwealth Attorney-General's Department, D. J. Rose, was leaked to the newspapers. The Rose opinion argued that the Commonwealth had the responsibility to protect the South West under UNESCO's Convention for the Protection of the World Cultural and Natural Heritage. The opinion concluded:

> Any decision not to intervene must therefore be based on political grounds, not on any constitutional impediment.

The publication of the Rose opinion undermined the Prime Minister's statements about the South West being solely a Tasmanian decision. It forced him to consider two difficult alternatives: to intervene in Tasmania in spite of the Liberal Party's abhorrence of such centralist attacks on 'States' rights'; or not to intervene despite legal and, increasingly, public opinion.

The public wanted action to save the Franklin. Opinion polls showed massive support for the conservation cause, with particularly strong votes in Victoria and New South Wales.

At the end of October Malcolm Fraser had to face the growing Franklin forces: the Democrats introducing a World Heritage Properties Protection Bill into the Senate with Labor support promised, Mr Gray speaking at the

National Press Club in Canberra and members of his own Government publicly criticizing the dam. If he was going to call the early election that he had been planning since the Budget in August he would have to swiftly deal with the issue. On 31 October he hurt his back and the nation saw a grey-faced old man loaded into the back of an ambulance on a stretcher. There would be no Federal election in 1982.

The next two months almost sealed the fate of the Franklin. No doubt Malcolm Fraser would have liked to play a more active part in his Government's decisions than by telephone from his sickbed. But his absence from the Prime Ministerial office also gave the Government a way of testing its footing on the issue. In a technique employed earlier in the year Doug Anthony, as Acting Prime Minister, could make the running on a contentious issue, taking the most-favoured line. If, as in the case of an increase in Parliamentary salaries, Doug Anthony's solution arouses too much public criticism, then Malcolm Fraser can return to the Cabinet room and retract the original bungle saying he had nothing to do with it. Salaries were cut to much acclaim. The technique did not work so well with South West Tasmania.

On Saturday 4 December a Liberal, Peter Reith, campaigning on an anti-dam platform with Malcolm Fraser's tacit support, won the Flinders by-election in Victoria. The victory was interpreted as support for the Government's policies. Doug Anthony ignored the 40% of Flinders voters who wrote No Dams on their ballots.

At the same time as the Flinders electors voted No Dams Tom McVeigh was secretly flying 'as Tom McVeigh the guy, not Tom McVeigh the Minister' over the Franklin in a helicopter. He says:

I think it is just the rugged terrain that grips you, fascinates you, and then that fascination gives way to astonishment because of the sheer beauty and peace of it.

On the following Monday in Cabinet Tom McVeigh was fighting for the Franklin's life. He was outnumbered by those who would flood it but a final decision was delayed until Wednesday. In the meantime all the State Premiers came to Canberra for a Premiers Conference. The conservative Premiers of Western Australia, Queensland and Tasmania all told Doug Anthony to stay out of Tasmania. This suited his own inclinations.

On Wednesday 8 December, after 'agonizing and traumatic discussion', according to Tom McVeigh, and some balancing of the electoral gains and losses, Cabinet decided not to intervene in the Tasmanian dam dispute. Tom McVeigh announced the decision to a packed House of Representatives that afternoon. Conservationists, newspapers and ordinary Australians reacted to his statement with unprecedented outrage.

Although Malcolm Fraser had been in constant telephone contact with both Tom McVeigh and Doug Anthony he had not exerted much sway over the Cabinet. He was later angry with the Acting Prime Minister for handling that matter so insensitively. However, because he had not publicly participated in the decision, he could come to the rescue later. If Doug Anthony had got away with his non-intervention decision he would not have needed to. But he wanted to do more.

During early December Malcolm Fraser took a great interest in the coming World Heritage Committee meeting in Paris. He regularly telephoned the Australian delegates without any real purpose other than to urge them to do anything necessary to get the South West on to the World Heritage List and to gather news.

The message reaching conservationists indirectly from the Prime Minister was: 'Wait for the World Heritage listing; once the South West is on the List we will be able to do something.' This seems to have been his sincere hope — that listing could assist in Tasmania.

The listing itself, while a great morale boost to conservationists and ultimately essential for the dam-stopping High Court decision, was, at the time, of ambiguous political value. The Tasmanian Government desperately and with some success argued that since the listing had been made with the World Heritage Committee knowing that the Australian Government would not stop the dam, then the Committee itself had sanctioned the dam. While this was obviously opposite to the intentions of the Committee, the argument has some logic. Listing did nothing to solve Malcolm Fraser's predicament. Tasmania would not voluntarily stop the dam-building. He would have to intervene.

Conservationists anticipated a grand gesture when Malcolm Fraser returned to work. Back in Cabinet in mid-January he managed to convince the grown men and woman who had ditched the Franklin a month before to support an offer of $500 million to Tasmania to save the river. This offer was to be his tactical retreat from Doug Anthony's position, his secret weapon.

The idea of an offer to Tasmania occurred to Malcolm Fraser before the Tasmanian election. Cabinet discussed it in June 1982. Superficially the offer to fund an alternative source of power seemed to satisfy both requirements of a solution: to be seen to be doing something about the Franklin but without coercing Tasmania. However it would not be easy to find an alternative that would wean the Tasmanian Government from their desire for the dam; the offer would need to rival the dam in electoral imagery as well as in electrical efficiency. As one Liberal Member with a low estimate of the Tasmanian electorate's visual acuity put it: 'It has to be big with flashing lights on it.'

The offer was postponed. That may have been a mistake — early negotiations with a less-confident Robin Gray, even if they ultimately failed, would have helped defuse the issue at Federal level. But Malcolm Fraser's style is not pre-emptive, he would rather let a dispute develop as long as possible before committing himself at a time when he can decisively resolve the conflict.

While he was in hospital Malcolm Fraser refined the idea of an offer. Officials prepared cost estimates for different sorts of power stations so that when the Prime Minister returned to Canberra an offer could be drafted. He called for legal and energy advisers to prepare a Cabinet submission. I do not know whether he persuaded Cabinet by reference to public opinion in the lead-up to an election or by assuring the Cabinet that there was no chance of Tasmania accepting the offer. But they authorized him to negotiate to a limit of $850 million.

Next he went to Tasmania 'fishing'.

He was indeed fishing at Lake Augusta on the Central Plateau when a helicopter containing the Minister responsible for Tasmania, Kevin Newman, picked him up. They searched the wild Central Plateau, which is dotted with small lakes, for good fishing spots before heading off towards the Franklin.

On the way they flew to the partly-completed Pieman scheme. The HEC engineers set out to impress the Prime Minister with their dams and workers. But he was rather disgusted by the unnecessary mess their works had made of the countryside. As the party flew on he said of the self-satisfied engineers. 'They must think I'm a _____ idiot.'

Malcolm Fraser and Robin Gray met at the HEC camp at Mt McCutcheon. Mt McCutcheon is a windy high-point on the road to the Franklin. Named after a bulldozer driver, the area had been cleared and scarred by the Hydro-Electric Commission. The two leaders took a walk. Along the way Malcolm Fraser offered $500 million to Robin

Gray. This was just the opening bid but Robin Gray rejected the offer so adamantly that the Prime Minister did not prolong the bargaining. Once the money had been refused Malcolm Fraser set about trying to extract some political value from it. On 19 January 1983 he made a statement declaring his hand and excusing his failure to stop the dam. He could not intervene:

> The Commonwealth does not have a specific power to order that the damming of these rivers should not proceed.

However it did have, as the Rose opinion had argued, powers that were non-specific, powers that were later used by the Hawke Government to stop the dam.

Within hours of the Prime Minister's statement the Tasmanian Premier stated his rejection of the offer. When it was discovered that the offer had been rejected before it was made public, conservationists accused Malcolm Fraser of insincerity. They said the stand against the Government would continue until the dam work stopped. Robin Gray's immediate refusal of the offer reduced its political effectiveness. Even if there had been some pretence of negotiations delaying the final rejection Malcolm Fraser may have looked good. But within weeks his $500 million gamble, if it was remembered at all, was remembered as a sham.

Anyone who has to read Tasmanian papers could have predicted that the Tasmanian Government would not contemplate any alternative to the dam. But if Robin Gray had surprised us all then Malcolm Fraser would have been pleased for both political and environmental reasons. Instead he was stuck with the stigma of Doug Anthony's decision to let the Franklin be flooded.

Within the limits of his perceived power, defined by Liberal ideology and party pressure groups, Malcolm

Fraser did what he could to stop the dam. He failed. Some believed that a Labor Government would do no more, that Federal intervention would not be tolerated. Bob Hawke showed that with the imprimatur of the High Court the community could accept, even demand, that a government should go further.

Malcolm Fraser went into the March 1983 election with the blockade of HEC works continuing on the Gordon River, with the ALP promising to stop the dam and with the National South West Coalition of conservationists campaigning for the Labor Party and the Democrats. Everywhere the Prime Minister was confronted by the issue — a silent vigil stood outside the site of his campaign launch in Box Hill in Melbourne, No Dams triangles and placards surrounded him in the television coverage of his walks through Bendigo and other marginal seats. He could not produce any new South West initiatives, he was on the defensive at public meetings and in interviews.

On 5 March voters concerned about the environment voted for Bob Hawke and Don Chipp. Malcolm Fraser lost the Prime Ministership, resigned as leader of the Liberal Party and took up the life of a grazier and one of the world's former leaders.

During the High Court battle he used to ring Robin Gray to offer him encouragement. It would have been the voice of a lonely man, lost without power. Malcolm Fraser the politician who has not completely retired would probably attack the Hawke Government's final resolution of the Tasmanian dam issue as a violation of unwritten 'States' rights'. But this would be in spite of his other self, the one that is pleased to see the Franklin secure. However the man we know from public life, the man whose harsh actions voters have rejected, would never admit such softness to us.

'So I taught myself about electrical power supply systems.'
GEOFF LAMBERT

In October 1979 the Hydro-Electric Commission recommended the construction of the Gordon-below-Franklin dam. Geoff Lambert's exhaustive critique of the case for the dam uncovered the most powerful economic argument against its construction: the power was not needed.

During the early stages of the campaign Geoff Lambert produced detailed submissions attacking the HEC case and presented them to committees of inquiry. Later his relentless logic, applied to political strategy, helped securely guide the more public phase of activity.

Dr Geoff Lambert is a neuro-scientist who researches the nature of migraine in Sydney. He has been the major force in the South West Tasmania Committee of New South Wales since he started as 'the chief cook and bottle washer's offsider' in 1977.

Geoff Lambert was born in Queenstown in 1946. He is a fourth-generation Tasmanian. His father was a miner on the West Coast.

The South West Tasmania Action Committee in New South Wales was formed on 13 November 1974. I am not exactly sure who initiated it, but there was a group here called the Wilderness Protection Committee. I think they pressured Roger Lyle into becoming the convenor of the South West Tasmania Action Committee here and it was one of seven branches, we even had one in Darwin. They kicked it off with a big film show here with slides of the Gordon Splits — it was all bushwalkers at the time. A group of people got together every Monday or every second Monday night and discussed the threats to South West Tasmania but discussed them in the light of bushwalking experience down there. There wasn't a lot of activity but there was enough. We sent people to Tasmania to make submissions and gather information, do research in the library.

We kept the name 'South West Tasmania Committee' even when the Committee in Hobart changed its name to the Wilderness Society in 1976. By that stage there were only the two groups, the Sydney and Hobart. That was a bit surprising in view of the fact that the Lake Pedder campaign was centred on Melbourne and Hobart. From what I have been told there was virtually no Lake Pedder campaign in Sydney, but for some particular reason our group just kept bubbling along.

I got shanghaied into it here when I subscribed to the National Parks Journal and saw an ad for a film night and Judy said, 'We should go to that,' and I said, 'Well, maybe we should.' We went and they wanted volunteers, so we got roped in and have never been able to get out since.

I haven't lived in Tasmania since the late 1940s. I only lived there for the first three years of my life. But I am still a Tasmanian. I still call myself a Queenstowner. It gives me a real advantage in arguments. I got into an argument one day with a woman when we were down haranguing Tamie Fraser during the election campaign. She said, 'I'm a Tasmanian.' I said, 'I'm a Tasmanian, I'm a West Coaster.' She said she was in favour of the dam and I said I was against the dam. It carries a little bit of weight because you are not seen to be an outsider.

When we lived in Melbourne my father kept reminiscing about this place on the west coast, Trial Harbour. We went down to go fishing there one year and I was fascinated by the scenery and the old railway lines I found there. I started going back year after year, round the west coast, tramping around these railway lines.

We just sort of stumbled along up here, I suppose, until 1979; it was a kind of holding operation. We were there, we had an office, we had weekly or monthly meetings. Once a year we had a big film night that was a regular feature. Everybody knew we were there and it just reinforced the feeling that something was happening. We sold calendars and a few books and so forth, but we didn't ever really do much apart from that in the first two years.

Then the HEC report came out. It happened that there

was more expertise in technical matters, or more interest in them up here than there was in any other Wilderness Society branch, so we put in a submission to the Evers Committee and we were really delighted with the response. Bob Burton called me up one day and said that the Department of the Environment had called Hobart TWS to find out who the hell were the people in Sydney who had written this tremendous report! If you look through the Tasmanian Department of the Environment's submission to the Evers Committee, there is page after page after page where it is verbatim from ours. They didn't acknowledge it but that didn't bother us. So we figure we probably had a reasonable sort of impact on the Evers Committee, which in turn had a very good impact on Doug Lowe.

Before the HEC report came out I had developed an interest in demand projections for electricity in Tasmania. I compiled as much information as I could and I decided that so much hinged on predictions of demand being correct that we ought to examine the question deeply. So I taught myself about electrical power supply systems. I started off at the most basic level I could find which was the *Encyclopaedia Britannica* and worked upwards. I had access to a good library at the time at CSIRO. I compiled all the data I could get from the HEC reports. We have always subscribed to as many journals and reports as we could get. The HEC was actually quite willing to make stuff available to groups like ours. They still send us free copies of *Cross Currents*.

When their report came out in 1979 I went up to the post office and collected it — it was 2000 pages long! I thought: 'Shit! How are we ever going to answer this?' But when you sat down and looked at it, the whole report was just so full of errors and contradictions that a really comprehensive answer was called for — and possible. In fact there were so many things wrong with it that it was difficult to know where to get a lever on it. But the power demand was the really critical one. It is talking about the future which no-one can be sure about. All we can do is say, look at the past, look at the mistakes they made in the past, look at the assumptions they have made to get their predictions. Then when we are three or four years down the road from that original prediction we can also say: 'See, they made that prediction and now it is wrong.' It is so absolutely crucial. Politicians, even technocrats, tend to gloss over the importance of correct demand projections.

It is a matter of self-education in all of these things. I had to teach myself about thermal power systems; I had to teach myself discount cash flow analysis. There is an advantage in having a research background and having access to good libraries and knowing how to go about chasing information. I have always, since I got into research, really enjoyed trying to put arguments together in a logical sequence, so I could say such and such a proposal is or isn't true, or a conclusion follows or doesn't follow from a particular premise, and therefore the case stands or doesn't stand. The fact is proved or disproved. That HEC report and the answer to it were a really beautiful exercise, a challenge in that respect. The HEC uses a chain of reasoning and you only need to break one link in the chain and you have ruined the whole argument ... but the most important ones to break are the ones at the start. They are the ones that we devoted most attention to.

I have often seen in the campaign that the arguments failed to meet head-on. The government might put up a particular argument based on economics or job creation or power, and the Wilderness Society or the conservationists would say: but, what about the platypuses or whatever? What about the world heritage? But nearly every argument that was put up in favour of that scheme could be countered. Some of our counterarguments may depend a little bit on subjective interpretations but so many of them can be objectively justified and just stopped dead. It's a tactic that worked well in the Pedder campaign — it drove the HEC to distraction. There would be an ad, counter-ad and counter-counter-ad, day after day in the newspapers.

We produced *Free Currents*, which was a critique of the HEC's October 1979 *Cross Currents*, which was a summary of their report. It took the HEC to task in a manner that I have mentioned, meeting every argument head-on to the extent that we reproduced the HEC magazine on the left-hand page and our answers on the right, in almost identical format, so that people could really lay those arguments out side by side. We produced 3000 of those and distributed them free around the country to all members.

The way I presented the idea to the Senate Select Committee was that the South West of Tasmania is such a magnificent place, beautiful and valuable place, that it doesn't matter what you want to do there it is highly unlikely that you would ever be able to find a justification to do it. But leaving aside South West Tasmania, the arguments for a power scheme are entirely unsatisfactory and unsupportable, so it doesn't matter where you want to build the power scheme, you shouldn't build it.

By mid-1980 there was a Legislative Council Select Committee, so we re-wrote our Evers submission, even though it was sure to be a bit of a profitless exercise. We knew before we went down there that we weren't going to get anywhere — there was a terrible antipathy towards us. The first question I got was, 'Why are you, from New South Wales, coming down here to tell us what we should do with our rivers?'

That was at about the time of the 1980 Federal election and we could see the value, not the urgency at that time, but the value in bringing it more into the political arena.

We started to say that the Franklin was going to be a major Federal issue, only have believing it ourselves.

The Lowe by-election in Sydney in March 1982 really proved to people that you could achieve something. I think the 12% No Dams write-in knocked the politicians back a bit. Neville Wran said, '12%, you can't ignore that.'

My theory is that people see parallels between the river and their own lives, parallels that they don't see between other threatened areas. A river is much more of a living thing, it is alive, it progresses from youth to old age. And when you dam it you are killing it in a way that people will relate to much more than if you flood a lake or a button grass plain, or if you chop down a forest. I think people saw that ... and felt empathy.

Bob Brown reckoned that the two weeks down on the Franklin were the best two weeks of his life. The 1983 election campaign here was one of the best three weeks of my life. It was tremendous, absolutely tremendous, really exhilarating; so many things to do, so many things happening, seeing all those people here working together, developing an organization and actually having an impact on people — very exhilarating to find that you had power to influence something.

Our day was usually about 7.30 a.m. to midnight. I was doing co-ordination mainly, getting stuff out to electorates, seeing that jobs got done, looking after the finances, printing leaflets and so forth, distribution of materials. I always have been a dogsbody just sort of pottering about in a co-ordination job.

In the early days we were all pretty politically conventional and I think the Wilderness Society didn't really have any basic philosophy from which the concept of conserving the wilderness arose naturally. It had prior assumptions about why you should preserve wilderness, but they were based mainly on the wilderness itself. They were not fitted into a social, economic or political framework. So earlier on we were just a sub-section of the general community, scruffy bushwalkers perhaps, but otherwise not too different from everybody else. But soon there were a lot of idealists drawn into the campaign, idealists who saw a much wider struggle going on. They invigorated the Society and, not being bound by convention, moulded it into a rather unconventional conservation group. But to achieve our aims we had to operate in fairly conventional political patterns. With having to run a Federal election campaign, the end result of our success in it is, in a sense, that we have legitimized the political system. There may be a danger in that we have seen that political process works and in many cases the cause of all our trouble was that political process. We have just turned it to our advantage rather than changing it so that it never works to our disadvantage. That lesson has been learned though, and we are now trying to work at a more grass roots level.

In the middle of this campaign, 1977 or 1978, I said to myself: 'When we have won South West Tasmania, got it reserved as a national park, the South West Tasmania Committee will be quite happy to fold up its tents.' But there are two things that have happened: the Society has raised tremendous public support and a reservoir of skills and knowledge, and it has also built up the expectation that it can go on to bigger and better things. Now I don't want the Wilderness Society to fold up at all. If there is no South West wilderness to fight for, I think we have got the opportunity and the resources to help in other areas. If the Wilderness Society was going to fold up and disappear, then there would be a tinge of sadness about it for me. Then I would look back and think: 'Gee, those were the days.' In the Wilderness Society we have looked upon each coming year as 'This will be the crucial year, this will be the end of it', and each year the campaign gets bigger and bigger and bigger. Some people still think we are going to go down hill from here, but the past does not justify that expectation. I think we are going to go on to bigger and better things. I don't think we have reached the good old days yet. They are still to come.

*'It's like losing something
that you love.'*
KAREN ALEXANDER

Since 1980 Karen Alexander has led the Tasmanian Wilderness Society in Melbourne.

She first went to Tasmania in December 1967 with the Monash University Bushwalking Club. In 1970 she went to Hobart and later lived with the King family, tin-miners at Melaleuca in the far southwest of Tasmania.

During the Lake Pedder campaign Karen wrote letters and attended public meetings. On her trips to Lake Pedder she found the wilderness littered with photographers, at different times meeting Olegas Truchanas and Peter Dombrovskis.

Karen Alexander was born in Melbourne on 22 April 1948 and has studied mathematics, science and land use management.

It was July 1979 that TWS started in Melbourne. There was a meeting at Melbourne University. I came back to Melbourne from Tasmania later in July. Somebody asked me to give a talk on the South West for the first meeting of TWS in Canberra. So I went to Ross Scott, and I said: 'What's been happening?' He had just finished working as Project Officer for ACF then, so we went up to ACF and I read all through these files, and I went to the Canberra meeting. There were seventy people there.

In Melbourne there were monthly meetings. The first Wilderness Society demonstration I remember here was the day in October 1979 when the Hydro released their report. Nobody had seen it but we all went down to the focal point then which was the Tasmanian Government Tourist Bureau — I must send them a bottle of champagne, they've always been good — because they represented Tasmania here. We went down there and handed out leaflets, and talked to people about it and tried to get them to sign petitions and generally had a minor demonstration that didn't get any press. There would have been twenty people there.

Then there was an obvious need for displays, so the first big thing we did was making displays and going out to stalls. One of our big successes was to go down to City Mall, which at that stage was pretty much of a mess, and sell T-shirts, badges and stickers — we didn't have much of a range then. But that stopped within about six months: we were told that we weren't allowed to go there because we were competing with Myers and Coles.

In April 1980 we decided to open an office.

The first of our public meetings was planned for 1 May 1980. Ross Scott organized that. That gave us our first feeling for what the public reaction was going to be and everyone was petrified about it. We had hired a hall at RMIT which could hold something like 600 people. We had a Tasmanian friend staying with us and as we were setting up the decorations in the hall she said, 'You'll never fill this, it's huge. You're holding a meeting about South West Tasmania, people here aren't very interested.'

The meeting was at 8.00 pm. By 7 o'clock people were starting to arrive and by 7.30 the place was almost full. At a quarter to 8 we had to put a sign outside saying 'Full' because you could not fit any more people in. There were people jammed down the aisles, jammed up the back and right down the stairs so they couldn't even hear. I remember Ross, everybody was just so ecstatic. To get 800 people way back in 1980.

That was a clue — even though we had hardly felt it in any way and there hadn't been much in the papers in the way of letters or anything like that — but there was a very strong body of support in the community already, a base level of support, which I partly put down to the Lake Pedder campaign.

In the Lake Pedder campaign there was certainly a campaign in Tasmania but its strongest base of support was here in Melbourne. People just worked terribly, terribly hard for the Pedder campaign and there were big meetings about it and it was a big election issue in 1972. People knew about it.

What happened after that was that there was a very strong campaign mounted — this grass roots campaign — to get people to write letters to Lowe and that Tasmanian Labor Caucus, to get them to save the Franklin. We would have meetings up at the Melbourne University of anywhere between 60 and 100 people. They'd be there writing letters and getting other people to write letters. God knows how many Doug Lowe received. That public telex machine was just going constantly in the week up to that July 1980 decision.

When the referendum came up in 1981 people started to feel that we had no say in what happened in Tasmania. Apart from the fact that it was totally unfair, even if it had been fair we still had no say in it. By that stage I think people had some fairly emotional involvement and it wasn't enough to leave it to the Tasmanian Government or even the Tasmanian people. It was *our* concern. What about us?

It was in the middle of that year that we started saying, 'Right, who are our local Federal Members? We want to lobby these people. This is a national issue.'

As far as organizing people and getting people's enthusiasm directed in a certain way I think that was relatively easy. What was easier here was that you didn't have the pro-dam contingent. And the media: the *Age*, through Tim Colebatch, was on side a long time ago and that's been a real key to the campaign. The ABC, through certain people there, were sympathetic enough to put things on. They would try to be balanced about it, as 'AM' said, 'We did try to find a pro-dam song but there isn't one.'

I was naive about campaigning: we'd send off letters to the papers but we didn't go and visit anybody and make sure they're informed. Ross got together a press kit and saw a few people. What helped fuel their enthusiasm was that someone was in the office nearly all the time to answer calls and the mail, and just keep the information flowing. I was at the office full time from late 1980. It became a really big job.

I can remember going home after a meeting and saying I can't take it any longer, there's just too much work, we've just got to find someone else to be in that office regularly, and a week later Michael Fogarty turned up. Michael came in and said, in his glorious way: 'Ah, I'm really interested in helping,' and I said: 'Wonderful, what would you like to do? How much time have you got? Would you like to work in the office here?'

He's still there. He just came at the right time. That freed me to do other things like organize political lobbying, letters to the paper, and a whole series of meetings.

April 1981 was a really big public meeting where we got well over a thousand people. That was the first time we'd had politicians. We had Don Chipp, Stewart West and Peter Rae. I think that was a really critical time because that pushed it into the Federal arena. And Peter Rae, being a Tasmanian Liberal, saying, 'I don't think that dam should go ahead,' swung quite a few people.

Very early in the piece we sent out letters about the issue to all the ALP branches, offering them speakers. Then in 1980 we tried to get a motion through the ALP State Conference. Some of us went out there and got it through that day. It was a fairly strong policy and it went through fairly easily. That was built on at each ALP Conference after that. That was crucial lead-up, keeping those people informed.

There was a really strong push to try and get to the Liberal Party branches the same way. But it's just about impossible; they refuse to let branch lists out.

So we had to concentrate on the upper echelons — which is probably the right level to go to in the Liberal Party — the Members and the power structure and the people who are making decisions, rather than the branches that have no sway compared to the ALP.

Market research was first suggested by two advertising people who had offered their services. They had seen some of our ads and didn't think they were terribly good and rang up and said, 'We're happy to help you.' The first thing they suggested was to be totally professional about it. 'You're trying to sell a product and therefore you must do some research in order to find out what it is that people want, how they see it. Because you see it one way does not mean that the general population does.'

That research was incredibly valuable. One thing it told us was that people had an understanding of what World Heritage was which most of us didn't believe. The other thing that it told us was that it wasn't the beauty of the place that they were worried about losing but the fact that it was rare, it was unique and it was irreplaceable. The other thing was that they had no idea what a wilderness is, no concept whatsoever.

That meant that we could concentrate on particular aspects of the campaign and particular arguments that we'd been using which would get through to the people in the middle class in those eastern suburbs which was our power base. They were the marginal seats. Long ago we identified the marginal seats — they were the ones that were going to be crucial at an election — and they were fortunately our power base as well. That was where the majority of members were, probably because they've got the time to think about those things, the education to know about them, and the money to travel.

Alex Dumas got involved in the referendum campaign. He brought in that very strong streak of professionalism in terms of the artwork and the copy. Before that the things we produced had been good, but they hadn't had the same flair. That really pushed the standard up and was followed through in nearly all the advertising.

It's the difference between someone looking at a newspaper ad or a magazine ad and not looking at it. You either waste your money or you make the best use of it.

It was that first summer, February 1968, when we had a long trip in the South West. In those days you could do a long trip along the South Coast, up to Lake Pedder, across to Mount Anne, down along the eastern Arthurs to Federation Peak and out along the Pictons, all in four weeks in which you met maybe a handful of other people, you crossed no roads, there were no planes. One of the things that did intrude was a helicopter from the HEC. You can't do that trip any more — Pedder's gone, the road goes down to Scotts Peak, there are very few places along that route that you can't see some intrusion by human beings. From 1968 to 1983 is less than a generation and that wilderness area has decreased by half. I guess that's what got me stirred up about it.

I'd heard much about Lake Pedder before I went there, although it was long before the campaign got under way. On that first trip we approached Pedder up the Port Davey Track. The first place you could see it from was a little saddle between Mount Solitary and the end of the Frankland Range. You could get up there and see the lake and see the beach and all the vegetation of the dunes. It looked so serene.

It was late afternoon we first saw it, classic shots of the light coming down through the clouds from over the top of the mountains and highlighting the beach. It was the end of a long day, I remember being tired and wanting desperately to get there, and coming out onto this magnificent beach — you just feel as if you've been totally renewed. You could keep going forever, this place was so wonderful. Now I miss it incredibly.

The first time I went to Lake Pedder I met Olegas Truchanas. That was a momentous thing. I didn't know who this person was but he was obviously an extraordinary character: he was climbing up a tree over Maria Creek and diving into the creek. There was this barrel of a man — he was short and very strong.

One day, after the floodwaters were well and truly up and the lake had gone, I was going up on to Mt Anne — it was beautiful, an absolutely glorious winter's day, clear sky, snow on the mountain — and Peter Dombrovskis was up there taking photos. I decided to go back with him instead of going on with the others. Walking down the ridge late that afternoon — the sun again was there, coming from the clouds behind the Franklands — Peter said: 'I wonder what it would be like on the beach now.' The full realization of that loss suddenly hit home. I remembered what it was like and that it was gone, never to be there again. You feel empty. It's like losing something that you love.

What's awful is when you try to convey to somebody that something's beautiful, it's unique, it's utterly irreplaceable and they're like a stone wall. It's terribly hard to argue with somebody like that. You realize that it's not until enough people feel that way in the community that you can save these sorts of things.

It's awful that we have to have one incredible loss, or, in the case of the Franklin, you have to get to that stage where there is destruction in the wilderness, through that rainforest, before it's brought to people's notice. It's not till you actually reach the limit, the crisis, and the destruction has actually started, before you can stop it. Logically we should have been able to save the Franklin way back in 1979. It should just be perfectly obvious it's a World Heritage Area, it's unique and therefore you don't flood it. In fact we should go back to the stage before that and say, 'What areas are there in Tasmania and the rest of the country that should be kept?' It's the decision-making process in Tasmania, and nationally, that's got to be reviewed. That's got to be changed.

*'I went in boots and all
when Butler was appointed.'*
JOHN MULVANEY

Professor John Mulvaney holds the Chair of Prehistory in the Faculty of Arts, Australian National University. He is a prominent scholar in the field of Australian prehistory and is author of *Prehistory of Australia.*

Though he was not involved in the archaeological investigations on the Franklin River, John Mulvaney made archaeology an issue in the dam fight. With Rhys Jones he declared the significance of Kutikina Cave and the other archaeological sites in the region and organized international statements of concern about its proposed flooding. By the time the Western Tasmania Wilderness National Parks were inscribed on the World Heritage List the cultural value of the area was recognized as being of similar importance to the natural value.

John Mulvaney was born in Victoria in 1925. He was a member of the Australian Heritage Commission from 1976 to 1982. In December 1982 he resigned from the Interim Council of the Museum of Australia to protest against the Fraser Government's decision not to intervene to stop the Gordon-below-Franklin dam.

My own involvement with Tasmanian prehistory is older than Rhys Jones'. I was down there in 1962, the year before he came to Australia. It was on my recommendation that the Australian Institute of Aboriginal Studies set apart a research grant for Rhys Jones to commence Tasmanian fieldwork, prior to his arrival in Australia. I actually published in 1961 two major reviews of the state of Tasmanian prehistory, emphasized our lack of knowledge and the problems that needed to be looked at, before Rhys Jones arrived in Australia.

We didn't know how the Aborigines got there in those days. It hadn't been established that Bass Strait was dry in human times. It was clearly a tremendously important problem to know where the Tasmanians had come from and how long they'd been there. As they possessed this very simple material culture which differed from the mainland, it really was an interesting problem. Evolutionary-minded people of course have claimed that it was because they were more primitive. It isn't that. Isolated in Tasmania in very small groups, there wasn't as much incentive to change.

In 1960 I did some excavations in southern Queensland, at a place called Kenniff Cave. We now know its occupation goes back for 19 000 years. It was the first site where Ice Age (Pleistocene) dates were found in a stratified deposit. I got those dates in 1962 from the 1960 excavation.

What we seemed to be finding in the lower layers of this site were Tasmanian-like stone implements. This has become a standard doctrine ever since: that in early deposits in Australia, such as Lake Mungo (*an archaeological site in the Willandra Lakes World Heritage area in western New South Wales*), you get implements that match up well with Tasmanian specimens. So that even if we didn't have the knowledge about the land-bridge and sea level changes I think archaeologists would claim without doubt that the Aborigines got to Tasmania across the mainland, simply on the basis of these stone tools. And of course that's what they've got now in the Franklin as well.

I've been to Tasmania a lot over the years. I've been interested in Rhys Jones' work. I've gone down as a 'tourist' for a few days in every little while, so I've visited a great number of the sites in Tasmania. When I joined the Australian Heritage Commission in 1976 I became very interested in historical structures. Port Arthur became one of such places. For a while I was campaigning for the preservation of Port Arthur.

When I was on the Heritage Commission, in 1977, I was on leave in Britain. The World Heritage Convention was meeting in Paris to draw up the criteria for the World

Heritage List. At that stage the Australian Government said that there was not enough money to send anyone from Australia to attend it, and they intended sending a cultural attaché from the Australian Embassy in Paris. As I was in England, I offered to attend at my own expense. Then at the last minute the Government said they would pay my expenses, so I then went as the official delegate, along with the Embassy officer. So I've been in at the beginning, because in June 1977 this meeting framed the criteria for putting places on the World Heritage List. I've felt a very deep personal interest in World Heritage matters since.

I found from the start that the Canadians were the best delegation there. We tended to work together. And the Americans, in the period of President Carter, were an enlightened group. We had a lot to say in framing the cultural criteria — making them more realistic so that they would have more universal applicability than just to apply to French culture, French buildings or the like.

For the natural criteria the IUCN people had a very well formulated series of criteria. I felt at the time that the meeting was so over-represented for culture, as against environment, that it worried me. Canada, the United States and Iran were some of the few countries with genuine environmental experts present.

The first couple of occasions when I spoke, I said that culture seemed to be dominating; what about the environment? By lunchtime the Canadians assumed that I was an environmental man, so I felt very flattered!

I maintained my interest in World Heritage matters. I was on the Committee which organized the World Heritage meeting in the Sydney Opera House in 1981 and attended it as an Australian delegate.

I was on the Heritage Commission in 1981 when the Tasmanian Government nomination of South West Tasmania came in. At the time very little was known about the archaeology of the region, although it was referred to. It was evident that Kutikina Cave was of tremendous importance. It was at that stage, when it came up for World Heritage nomination, I began to realize its importance. As I'd never been to South West Tasmania, I decided that it was high time that I read the 1979 Hydro-Electric Commission Report on the dam proposal.

It's shocking that I hadn't read it previously and I accept the criticism that the HEC makes, that the archaeologists were a bit late in the day. But I read it in October 1981, and then I realized that it was an appalling document. In fact I've said, on oath, that if some of the things that were said in that report were written in a university essay, we would fail the essay. There were *non-sequiturs* all over the place. I found out there were only sixteen lines on the Aborigines and their past.

I decided that in all conscience, as a prehistorian, I would need to do something about it. I decided to write a submission to the Senate inquiry. It was dated 7 December 1981. It contains some minor factual errors but I'd still stand by 95% of it.

Rhys Jones was overseas for a few weeks at this stage and as soon as he came back I said, 'Rhys, you must make a submission.' Subsequently his submission was much more definitive than mine.

Rhys Jones is the one who's done the fieldwork and publication, although I'm emphasizing where the evidence fits in world terms. But Rhys is the one who did the work along with Tasmanian people like Don Ranson and Kevin Keirnan, whose role is beginning to be acknowledged but probably was rather under-acknowledged in earlier times.

That was where matters stayed for a while. We on the Heritage Commission didn't expect that the Government would do nothing.

In February 1982 the Heritage Commission met at Port

Arthur. At that meeting I was Acting Chairman of the Commission. We concluded that under the terms of the Australian Heritage Act we had a right to advise our Minister that he should cause an inquiry to be held into environmental impact aspects of the dam. That was all we could advise him to do under the Act.

Now by sheer chance the next day, when we went to Hobart, Harry Butler was appointed by the Premier. (*Harry Butler is an environmental consultant and former television personality who was appointed in February 1982 to minimize the environmental and electoral impact of the Holgate government's decision to go ahead with the Gordon-below-Franklin dam.*) He was brought to Hobart and as I sat in my motel room I saw him being interviewed on the news. He made a statement that he had a lot of experience in archaeology and that there would be no problem in salvaging the area. I nearly exploded!

Because I was Acting Chairman of the Commission, and they knew I was there, the media asked me for an opinion. Had it been anybody else they might have been more temperate. But I gave my opinion and the next day's *Mercury* front page headline reads: 'Expert warns Butler off South West Caves comment'.

I went in boots and all when Butler was appointed; that's what turned me on. Otherwise I don't think I would have got so deeply involved. Through the appointment of Butler and his archaeological comments, the Tasmanian Government got itself into public statements with a deep PR flavour. I just felt 'Damn this, it's not good enough.' As I wasn't a public servant and thereby restrained, I decided to give my opinion. I continued to do so, giving a few lectures to learned societies and attempting to stir them up a bit. I also spoke from the back of a truck in April, at a rally outside Parliament House.

Penny Figgis (*the Australian Conservation Foundation's National Liaison Officer in Canberra*) organized a meeting here in my office, following which Rhys and I drafted a letter. It had been agreed that if we raised enough signatories the ACF would do something about publishing it. This letter was sent to overseas scholars whom Rhys and I knew — archaeologists, anthropologists and geographers — about thirty-five people in all. I believe that, by July, twenty-three of them wrote to the Prime Minister, sending copies to us. Some of them were very powerful letters. Through Penny we got this advertisement published in the *Australian* on 4 September. We held a press conference which was the first such conference that either of us had experienced. From then on I just regarded myself as dedicated to the cause of saving the Franklin.

In early December 1982 I was in the House when the Minister, Mr McVeigh, made his terribly misleading speech about salvaging the archaeology. My term had expired on the Heritage Commission. The only Government body under his control of which I was a member was the Interim Council of the Museum of Australia and the next morning I hand-delivered my resignation. I was probably discourteous, because I delivered the letter and on the same day, through Penny and Senator Chipp, I arranged a news conference. Apparently Mr McVeigh took it as a personal insult that I acted like that, but I believed that his government was doing far worse.

I'm afraid it was the discourtesies that went on all round that got me offside. I believe that the Prime Minister never acknowledged these overseas scholars' letters; Mr McVeigh, I suppose, was forced to make the statement, but the ham-fisted things that he said, together with his attempt to accuse archaeologists of being obstructionist: these things really incensed me. So did the fact that the HEC simply ignored the new archaeological data. I believe in a fair go.

Early in 1983 I spoke at election and other public meetings and I suppose at that stage I was being 'political'; but in 1982 I felt that I was being a thoroughly responsible academic. If you analyze what I said and wrote in my submission, what I am talking about is academic-level material. It is my honest conviction that the caves are important. What has worried me is the fact that Rhys and I were voices in the archaeological wilderness for some time. We've got everyone behind us now. I think many of my colleagues thought that I was making statements that were unduly political.

I regret very much that a lot of other scientists did not come forward in this. But scientific bodies generally seem to claim that it's not their business to enter politics.

My response on this is that we're not talking about politics. There are political aspects, but if this area is destroyed, and the scientific world just lets it happen passively because it's not their point to make political interventions, I think they're just abnegating moral duty. This is how I see it.

I do intervene at the time ill-informed politicians say erroneous things about my discipline.

I have seen Kutikina Cave twice. When we held the Heritage Commission meeting in Hobart we chartered a plane and we flew over the cave area. In March 1982 Rhys Jones was working at Kutikina Cave. They were getting a supply helicopter in and the Parks Service very kindly offered me a seat on it, so I flew in. I only had several hours there and that was all.

It was superb. Having seen it, it confirmed everything that Rhys Jones had said about it and more.

I got involved in the 'Blainey View' programme on television, and so the ABC paid for me to go down to Tasmania again in May 1982. It was a very short trip because it was wet and the helicopter had to lift out again.

I've visited archaeological sites in many parts of the world in my life. I've visited them in every state of Australia and there are very few important archaeological sites I haven't seen. So I was very happy to go on oath to say that I do consider that site to be absolutely outstanding and among the best sites, not only in Australia, but in the Pacific region, for its potential and for what it actually contains.

Also for what it symbolizes. It's a tremendous testimony to the human spirit. These are the sort of sentiments that don't sound like 'science' and send the Hydro-Electric Commission or politicians 'up the wall', but I sincerely believe in such values. And that's what the World Heritage Convention is all about.

It is a symbol that *Homo sapiens* was, of all living species on earth, so adaptable that they could reach Australia from the tropics, say 40 000 or 50 000 years ago; they could move right through Australia, across all those tremendously different environments; they could develop art forms and technology in Arnhem Land that merits World Heritage registering by 20 000 BP; they could get to Mungo in the semi-arid belt and adapt to a totally riverine, freshwater situation, develop burial rituals; and also, before 20 000 years ago, when there were glaciers all around them, they were living at the most southerly penetration of the globe. Now that's tremendous testimony to the human spirit.

We happen to have better preserved in Australia than on almost any continent evidence for the period 40 000 to 15 000 BP. We have it uniquely preserved in Australia because this place wasn't developed by agriculturalists; it hasn't been dug over by peasants digging caves out for the rich soil to throw on paddy fields; it hasn't been urbanized. For all those reasons the evidence remains, and we happen to have a continuity of Aboriginal culture which has changed over time, but nevertheless it's the same culture — it's unique in world terms.

I believe that the three cultural places we have on the World Heritage List all inter-relate. One is tropical, one is semi-arid and the other is cool temperate. There are aspects of each one which are unique and yet there are common aspects to all three. It seems to me that if you're going to preserve something for the world's heritage, those three places are fine.

The other point about the Tasmanian places is that the combined moisture and the limestone are preserving organic materials so that pollen and fauna are preserved in a way that doesn't occur on the other sites. There also must be human remains preserved. One might find rock art engravings, I don't know. But to destroy that potential seems to me vandalism against humanity.

*'It was unanimous
that it should be listed.'*
MAX BOURKE

Max Bourke was the Director of the Australian Heritage Commission from its establishment in 1976 till 1983. The Heritage Commission has supported the conservation of South West Tasmania with a vigour and lack of equivocation unusual for government authorities. It prepared the nomination of the Western Tasmania Wilderness National Parks for World Heritage listing and then prosecuted the administrative measures needed to stop the dam once listing was won.

As an executive member of ICOMOS, the International Council of Monuments and Sites, Max Bourke worked to have that body recommend the Tasmanian parks be listed for their cultural qualities. He then attended, as an Australian delegate, the meetings of the World Heritage Committee in Paris on 14 December 1982 when the parks were inscribed on the World Heritage List. The listing almost failed to happen when the French said they did not want to list a property Australia was about to destroy.

The Australian Delegation, headed by Professor Ralph Slatyer who is also Chairman of the World Heritage Committee, consoled the French and averted crisis.

On 18 December 1941 Max Bourke was born in Sydney. He studied agricultural science at the University of New South Wales and has worked for the NSW Department of Agriculture, the ABC, the CSIRO and the Commonwealth Department of Urban and Regional Development. He now works for the Department of Home Affairs and Environment.

The Commission's been sounding off about South West Tasmania ever since it was established. The Commission took steps in 1976 to include the South West on the Register. Following a request we agreed to wait until the State's South West Advisory Committee Inquiry established boundaries for the South West. We were faced with the question: what is the South West? Which area should be on the List? After the Committee reported, the Commission put the whole of the South West Conservation Area on the Register.

The Commission was actively involved in the World Heritage process right from its establishment. We asked the Prime Minister to write to all the States. In 1977 he wrote explaining what the List was, and asking them for nominations. There was a pretty deafening silence for a while and then a couple came from New South Wales, eventually Queensland put forward the Great Barrier Reef and the Commonwealth, because the Commonwealth owned it, put forward Kakadu.

The principle had been established that the nominations had to come from the States. I can remember meeting Doug Lowe at a function in Hobart in about 1979 and he was saying then that he wanted the South West to go on the World Heritage List. He announced that he was going to nominate it for the List on the day the World Conservation Strategy was released.

That was late 1981. The National Parks Service of Tasmania and ourselves were involved in writing and rewriting the nomination to get it right, making sure we'd covered all the aspects. We pushed the need to put in more about the archaeology because at that stage there really hadn't been much done down there but there was evidence coming out, literally as this was happening, that there were important archaeological sites there.

It went off just in time for submission in that group of 1981. The World Heritage Bureau recommended its listing. We raised at the Bureau that the officials of UNESCO had clearly overlooked the fact that this place was nominated as a cultural site as well as a natural site. We said: 'Look, you'd better make sure they send this off to ICOMOS, the International Council of Monuments and Sites, because they're supposed to cover the cultural aspects.' As it turned out the IUCN made a few comments about the archaeology — I don't know that they're all that competent but still they said it was significant and it certainly is.

ICOMOS, of which I am an executive member, had the nomination but they had some difficulties because they got the thing very late, something like November 1982. There was some delay in UNESCO. They were given a very short amount of time and they have certain rules that they must assess these places scientifically. But there was no published literature about these sites at that stage. The only publications were newspaper articles in Australia and an article in *Hemisphere*. So it really was, as the French would say, *territoire inconnue*, unknown territory. It was very difficult for them to do the right thing — to reach a rational scientific judgment. The first scientific paper was published in *Nature* in 1983.

I attended the ICOMOS meeting in November to try to get the thing agreed to.

ICOMOS is a slightly Francophile organisation. It's Paris-based and the French and the French-Belgians played a central role in its establishment. But like the World Heritage Committee it is now an international organization with about 70 member countries.

The archaeology of the South Pacific really is *territoire inconnue*. The best people working in the field are, without any doubt, Australians. It's an area where knowledge has exploded over the last 15–20 years. And whilst there are some French who've worked here — ranging back two centuries, there have been Frenchmen working on the anthropology of the Pacific — they haven't kept up with the Australians. Mulvaney and his offspring, as it were, are the founding fathers of the new archaeology of Australia.

Unfortunately ICOMOS had to try and come at a judgment. They didn't want to use people who come from the country to assess things but there aren't people outside Australia in a position to assess it.

They'd had some bad experiences being lobbied in the

past. They feel they're technical assessors and they didn't have the evidence. I took with me, courtesy of Rhys Jones and John Mulvaney and other people, the documentation they needed and they agreed it should go on the List. I was a bit concerned that ICOMOS might not take a position at that time. They might have argued for deferral. I felt their support was pretty important.

The World Heritage Committee have only been listing places on the World Heritage List for three years. They're now starting to ask avery tough questions. This year they've knocked back over half the nominations. That's good. There was a danger — some countries were putting up every national park in their country; France put up every historic chateau in a whole region, this huge list of chateaux.

Australia has always felt that the List must be selective. It should be a list of really outstanding places. Mr Fraser pushed very hard for South West Tasmania's listing.

He gave unequivocal instructions to the delegation in Paris to get it on the World Heritage List, full stop. We had to do that in the face of very intense lobbying by the Deputy Premier of Tasmania. He put their case to not have it listed to a number of countries in a fairly sophisticated lobbying campaign.

As against that was the TWS. I had to try and get a map at one stage so I rang up the Friends of the Earth, which is Les Amies de Terre, in Paris. In the week prior to the meeting when you rang that telephone number in Paris it was answered 'Tasmanian Wilderness Society' which was quite a strange experience.

The day the conference opened was just fantastic. It was this awful, midwinter drizzle and grey — a terrible day. We arrived in a big black embassy car and there in front of UNESCO's headquarters with all their banners and placards and guarded by the gendarmes was this wonderful group of demonstrators. There weren't all that many of them — perhaps fifty altogether, of which quite a few were Australians. They held up placards and were handing out things to rather bemused-looking employees of UNESCO, of whom there were thousands trotting through the front door of their building.

The delegates to the Convention couldn't believe it — they kept coming up and asking, 'What on earth's this?' This sort of lobbying, which is standard in Australia, a lot of them had never seen. It had been done the year before in Sydney. There had been a small protest about uranium mining in Kakadu which went on during the Prime Minister's opening address — a group stood up and held a banner aloft. And they handed out material to people coming into the conference.

You're not allowed to argue your own case from the floor of the meeting. You are allowed to answer questions. Indeed Professor Slatyer did answer some questions that were raised in the debate and read a statement out from the Prime Minister. I think it was quite important that delegates heard that the Prime Minister of the country wished to have the place listed and was going to endeavour to protect the site. I think that swayed the delegates once they heard that.

The actual debate on the floor was about whether a place ought to be listed if it was going to be damaged. Should they immediately put it on the World Heritage in Danger List?

The debate was quite lengthy. Most places, by the time they get to that Committee, have been totally agreed on or disagreed on by technical recommendations, and most of them went through in a matter of a few minutes. You get the odd question raised — there were questions raised about a couple of Yugoslav sites. I think we intervened in a couple of cases to get some sort of assurance that places were going to be protected. But South West Tasmania went on for an hour and a half.

There was no debate about the significance of the site. But various countries expressed views about whether places ought to be listed if they were likely to be flooded, or severely damaged. One delegation raised the question of whether or not UNESCO should become involved in domestic politics. The dam was perceived as a domestic political issue. It was in danger at one stage of being adjourned for lunch. They might have deferred it till another year. The French were saying: 'Maybe we ought to defer this for the time being. Really it looks like it's under threat and we'd better work out whether it should be on the World Heritage in Danger List.'

At the end Professor Slatyer read out the statement from the Prime Minister and the vote was held and it was unanimous that it should be listed.

I felt delighted, elated. It was terrific. We were sent there to do that, and it went through. Quite obviously I had a very strong personal view of it going through. I can remember my colleagues on the delegation being very thrilled. One didn't want to carry on too much in this terribly formal atmosphere. But we were all very celebratory afterwards.

I've been going to South West Tasmania for twenty years. I first went in 1963. I love the area. It's a wonderful place, it's a frightening place, it's a very beautiful place. I've had some wonderful experiences down there, both thrilling and exhausting. The closest I ever came to dying in more than twenty years of bushwalking was in South West Tasmania: caught in a snow storm in the summer on the Ironbound Ranges.

One of Australia's lesser-known landscape painters, William Charles Piguenit, is a painter whom I have admired for many years. He was a surveyor who worked down there, born in Hobart. He was full of this Edmund Burkean philosophy of the sublime and the beautiful.

I put in a private submission to the Senate inquiry in which I argued for the preservation of places of beauty. People are terribly coy about that but I can't understand why it isn't legitimate to argue for a beautiful environment. I know everyone says, 'That's soft and woolly and it's not hard-nosed.'

Our world is the only world we've got and if we can't enjoy the beautiful places in it ...

In the 19th Century nearly all the Australian immigrant painters — Chevalier, Buvelot, von Guerard — even some of the early native painters — Roberts and McCubbin and Conder — were absolutely imbued with this philosophical theory of the 18th Century about the nature of beauty and the sublime: the notion that you needed forces that were powerful and 'terrible' — terrible in the sense that they used it in the 19th Century, not in the pejorative sense that we use now. Piguenit's paintings capture the sentiment of the wild and terrible environment.

In the cultural environment, tastes change quite rapidly. Maybe in a hundred years' time people will say, 'Let's take that off the Register of the National Estate, that's rubbish.' And maybe that's a valid thing to do. Society will change and it will say, 'That's not worth protecting and that is.'

Over the centuries the notion of conservation has waxed and waned quite dramatically. At times it is a very powerful force. Conservation has the same root as the word 'Conservative'. As Hugh Stretton points out in his book, *Capitalism, Socialism and the Environment*, in the main, conservationists are extremely conservative people. They are looking back and I think that has always got to be tempered with looking forward. I'm not a Luddite. I don't believe that we should preserve every historic building in Sydney or Melbourne.

World Heritage Day in Canberra
ROGER GREEN

Tuesday 14 December 1982 was the turning point in the campaign to save the Franklin River. The week before, on 8 December, the Federal Government, led by Acting Prime Minister Doug Anthony and under pressure from the conservative Premiers of Tasmania, Queensland and Western Australia, decided not to intervene in the dam dispute. The campaign had reached a new low.

Tom McVeigh, the Minister for Home Affairs and Environment, read a statement to the packed House of Representatives explaining the Cabinet's decision. That night McVeigh, who had fought against the decision in Cabinet, looked very uncomfortable on television trying to justify it.

The reaction to the decision was unprecedented — the next day newspapers were full of reports and angry letters, the Australian public was outraged. Local Members all over the country received a barrage of protests from their constituents. Professor John Mulvaney resigned from the Museum of Australia pouring scorn on McVeigh's suggestion that the Aboriginal artefacts by the Franklin could be salvaged.

Malcolm Fraser, convalescing in a Melbourne hospital after his back operation, must have been wishing he had held an election months before. He had now allowed the South West conservation issue to build up so much momentum at the national level that he would have to find a solution.

On 14 December four events occurred that must have convinced him of the need to act.

In Tasmania, the blockade of HEC works on the Gordon River began. Police arrested fifty-three people for trespassing on HEC-controlled land. News and pictures of the arrests flashed into living rooms all over Australia.

In Canberra, nineteen Government backbenchers, given courage by the public outcry over the Cabinet decision not to intervene in Tasmania, protested to the

Acting Prime Minister about the decision and the way it had been made. It was the last day of sitting for the House of Representatives for 1982. Anthony promised a full party-room airing of the Franklin issue at the first Party meeting in 1983, aware that an early election would probably stop such a meeting taking place.

In the Senate four Government Senators crossed the floor to vote with the Australian Democrats and the Labor Party. Together they passed the Democrats' World Heritage Properties Protection Bill. A few hours later the Bill was introduced into the House of Representatives. No Government Members voted for the Bill to be debated.

In Paris, a few minutes before that vote, the World Heritage Committee inscribed the Western Tasmanian Wilderness National Parks on the World Heritage List.

In Canberra in late 1982 the politics were as arid as the climate. Stories of an early election had sustained the Press for months. When the Prime Minister, Malcolm Fraser, injured his back even those stories evaporated.

I had been fruitlessly lobbying Ministers and Government members to stop the flooding of the Franklin River. On 8 December they all trooped into the House of Representatives to hear Tom McVeigh announce the Cabinet decision to allow the dam to be built. Opposite me, just out of reach on the Government front bench, sat all the Ministers I had been trying to convince. I stared at them.

I picked out the ones who had offered hope. They avoided my gaze. As McVeigh drily read his statement I felt sad, not yet angry. I couldn't believe it. How could they be so heartless?

After that show of Government solidarity in the House Tom McVeigh was soon left alone to defend the decision. On 'Nationwide' that night he did an unconvincing impression of a minister supporting a Cabinet decision.

He virtually admitted that the Government decided not to intervene in Tasmania on the calculation that they would thereby secure five Tasmanian seats in the House of Representatives. Mainland MPs would have more trouble selling the decision to their electors.

Within a few hours conservationists were determined that the public reaction would be so strong that the politicians would be forced to change their minds. Changes came sooner than we expected.

On Tuesday 14 December I walked over to Parliament House to talk to Government backbenchers. Ministers were little use now. They were all bound by the Cabinet decision.

I started early because it was the last day for the House of Representatives for 1982. It had been a long, arduous Budget session dominated by the Treasurer John Howard and his retrospective legislation on tax avoidance.

I climbed the Parliament House stairs into King's Hall, my office. Behind the friendly men in the House of Representataives' enquiry box, on the wall of the main thoroughfare to the men's toilet, is an internal telephone. Lobbyists who don't have special access to Ministers' offices or a modern building in Barton use that phone to make appointments. We have to take our chances with speeding tourists who've spent too long on the coach.

During the Budget session I had spent many hours standing at that phone with my list of Members' extension numbers in hand trying to explain to Honourable Members and Senators why they should see me.

In December they weren't hard to convince. They were becoming interested in the Franklin River, an interest born of anxiety. There was likely to be an election as soon as the Prime Minister's back healed. The good result for the Government in the Flinders by-election on 4 December would only encourage him.

And community support for the saving of the Franklin was growing. Members as far from Tasmania as North Queensland and Perth weren't just getting respectful letters, they were having to answer delegations demanding action. In Flinders, an electorate on the Mornington Peninsula near Melbourne, 40% of the voters had written No Dams on their ballots.

Into this setting of uncertainty about an election and massive community concern for the Franklin River came, on 8 December, a clear decision by the Federal Government to allow the HEC to build its dam, a policy which contrasted with the ALP's 'No Dams' position. This frightened Members in marginal seats. They wanted to talk. They didn't want conservationists to campaign against them.

I spent the morning urging Members to challenge the Cabinet decision, to argue for its reversal. If they could not get the decision reversed they should prepare to cross the floor to vote with the Labor Party when the World Heritage Bill came into the House. The Bill was likely to pass the Senate that day.

David Connolly, the intelligent and respectable Member for Bradfield on Sydney's North Shore, wanted to be assured of company if he crossed the floor. He didn't see any point in challenging a Cabinet decision if the Bill still failed to pass. I told him there would be other Liberals with him.

Most of the Members in the safe Liberal seats on the North Shore supported the conservation of the South West wilderness. One of the most persuasive arguments that can be put to a backbencher is the suggestion that all his or her colleagues in neighbouring electorates support a certain view. Conservative MPs seem to have little idea what their colleagues think on subjects outside the parties' accepted doctrines. But they can respond to a convincing trend.

The anti-dam backbenchers' motives ranged from personal ambition to a sincere belief that the wilderness should not be flooded. Those most concerned about their political future were torn between the need for unquestioning loyalty to a Cabinet decision and the need to extract every possible vote from their constituents to retain their seats. There were no votes on the mainland in supporting the dam. The ambitious had the additional challenge of trying to second-guess Malcolm Fraser — there were rumours that he was anti-dam so a strong stand taken on the issue could win his respect and suggest that the forthright Member may be ministerial material.

Those inclined to accept in principle the arguments why the dam should be stopped were not usually motivated by the ideal of saving wilderness for its own sake. Most of them questioned the dam's economics and the indirect subsidies that mainland taxpayers would have to pay for it.

There was no debate about the significance of the site. But various countries expressed views about whether places ought to be listed if they were likely to be flooded, or severely damaged. One delegation raised the question of whether or not UNESCO should become involved in domestic politics. The dam was perceived as a domestic political issue.

It was in danger at one stage of being adjourned for lunch. They might have deferred it till another year. The French were saying: 'Maybe we ought to defer this for the time being. Really it looks like it's under threat and we'd better work out whether it should be on the World Heritage in Danger List.'

For the World Heritage Bill to pass the House of Representatives eleven members of the Government would have to vote with the Opposition. Ewen Cameron wasn't going to be one. Cameron, from Indi in Victoria, was very sympathetic but didn't see much chance of

241

changing the Government's position until after an election.

I continued the round of those Members known to be onside or seriously considering their position. During the preceding months Chris Harris and Vince Mahon from the Wilderness Society and I had drawn up lists of Members and Senators and where they stood on the issue. Chris Harris had begun the process when he established the Wilderness Society's Canberra office early in 1982. In November, when the others returned to Tasmania, our form guide had four categories from interventionists to States' righters.

Soon after midday I was in my wood-panelled passageway busily making calls when I heard the cries of a large crowd of people outside the building. I had forgotten about the lunchtime rally. In front of Parliament House 1500 people stood in the sun with Save the Franklin banners and placards. It was a heartwarming spectacle. A few months earlier we had fifty people.

Don Chipp gave a rousing speech. Labor's Stewart West and Susan Ryan and the poet Judith Wright McKinney addressed the enthusiastic crowd. Everyone was excited and, for some reason, optimistic. I walked around the perimeter soaking it in.

At the front of the crowd Colin Mason, the Democrats' spokesman on the environment, discussed parliamentary tactics. He was confident that his World Heritage Bill would pass within a few hours. The Victorian Liberal Senator, Alan Missen, told the assembled politicians, office workers and students that he would cross the floor to vote for the Bill. The crowd's applause echoed through Parliament House.

During the afternoon Government backbenchers also became more excited and, perhaps, rash. Jack Birney from the seat of Phillip in the eastern suburbs of Sydney was just about ready to cross the floor. Sandy MacKenzie, the

National Party Member for Calare in central NSW wouldn't cross yet, but he was preparing. Stephen Lusher, another National from the neighbouring seat of Hume, was drafting a motion reversing the Cabinet's decision of 8 December.

I went to visit Alan Jarman, the Member for Deakin. All the Melbourne Liberals were clearly onside except the Minister for Communications, Neil Brown. Alan Jarman was keen to do something. His son was the President of the Young Liberals who had long been urging the senior party to take action on the Franklin.

Jarman and I had a drink and talked about strategy. Then he rang up Alan Missen and Michael MacKellar, the former Minister for Health from Sydney. MacKellar had been hot and cold on the Franklin. This day he was very critical of the Cabinet decision.

While MacKellar and Jarman hatched a plan I went on my way around the corridors. David Jull from the Brisbane electorate of Bowman said he would see Jarman.

The Western Australians were getting interested. John Hyde, leader of the so-called Dries or Economic Rationalists, had always doubted the economics of the dam. He believed that free market forces, if allowed to operate, would prevent the construction of the Lower Gordon scheme. Unfortunately such forces didn't operate.

Peter Shack, the Member for Tangney south of Perth, was concerned and thoughtful. However he was sensitive to the notion of States' rights. Many Liberals were torn between their concept of federalism and their criticism of the dam. At 5.30 Peter Shack had to rush off to a meeting.

In a quick ring around, Jarman and MacKellar had found nineteen Members who wanted to express their discontent to their leader.

Meeting in Doug Anthony's office at the front of Parliament House, the backbenchers complained about the Cabinet's hasty decision-making and the likely electoral backlash. Doug Anthony and Tom McVeigh placated the Members, assuring them that the matter would be given a full airing at the next party meeting in February and urging them not to do anything reckless before the House rose.

Outside the temperature was dropping from the mid-thirties. A weak south-easterly change covered the sky with cloud. Lightning flashed in the distance. But no rain fell. It was just another false hope for a thirsty country.

After the meeting was over I found out exactly who had attended. The names were those I had expected, those who I had contacted that day.

I began leaking details to the Press. At the *Sydney Morning Herald* Patrick Walters and Paul Kelly were already on to the 'backbench revolt' and wanted names. Furious phonecalling began.

At 6.30 the World Heritage Properties Protection Bill passed the Senate. It was supported by the Democrats, the ALP and four Liberals — Alan Missen, Peter Rae from Tasmania, Neville Bonner from Queensland and the South Australian Robert Hill.

At the same time the first pictures of the blockade were shown on the television news. Protestors at the dam site, police in boats, the stunning backdrop of river and rainforest — the first five minutes of the ABC's 7 o'clock news was full of action in the wilderness. The timing was perfect. I've never enjoyed the news more than in the *Sydney Morning Herald* office that night.

Back in King's Hall there were urgent conversations about how long the World Heritage Bill would take to be printed and how soon it could be introduced into the House. Stewart West, Labor's spokesman on environment, had his speech ready.

The evening began to stretch out with waiting: the Bill took ages to print and there was no word of World

Heritage listing. We knew the World Heritage Committee in Paris had begun its deliberations. I repeatedly dropped into the AAP office to see if there was any news.

In King's Hall I breasted an anxious Peter Falconer, Liberal Member for Casey on the outskirts of Melbourne. He was one of the Government's most sincere and reliable supporters of Franklin River conservation. How many were going to cross the floor? He was hesitant. He suggested it was too early for floor-crossing. He said little but it was obvious that Mr Anthony's promises had broken the rebels' resolve. Falconer believed that there would be an early debate in the House and that he would then have a chance to air his views.

At about 10.30 the news from Paris came through: the South West national parks had been listed. World Heritage! There was a new surge of adrenalin. In the newspaper offices telex machines chattered out confused details. But there was no mistake — the rivers were on the List.

At last we had been dealt the card we needed. With World Heritage listing there was now little doubt that the World Heritage Convention could be implemented in Australia and, if the Federal Government wished, the dam could be stopped. For months we had heard Mr Fraser say, 'Wait till it's on the World Heritage List.' Now it was.

Only a few minutes before he entered the House, Stewart West heard the news of the listing. At 11.20 the World Heritage Bill was officially received from the Senate. West rose to oppose the motion to adjourn debate on the Bill. He cast aside his speech and for ten minutes attacked the Government for not preventing 'the very heart and soul being torn out of the South West by the damming of the Franklin River'.

He made out the case against the dam and described the plight of Government Members in marginal seats. 'People are being gaoled down there right now because of actions of conscience. I suggest that honourable members oppose the motion so that Government supporters will be seen quite clearly as the environmental frauds they are.'

The Government was unmoved. John Howard, the most senior Minister in the House, pointed out that the motion was procedural and thus not to be opposed by any pre-selection-fearing member of the Government. Then the question was put. The Opposition called for a division and the adjournment motion was carried on party lines. In spite of cat-calls from the Opposition none of the anti-dam Government Members crossed the floor. The House rose for the summer.

Unfortunately for Members like Falconer and Jarman and MacKenzie and Birney, the House did not sit again before they lost their seats in the March 1983 election.

After the House rose I went with Alan Jarman for a drink in his room and then down to the Non-Members' Bar. This bar is an austere box with a few pillars and a bar just long enough to enable decisions or, at least, observations of great national significance to be made.

Alan was very friendly. He introduced me to some smart young Liberals on the rise. I introduced him to the Melbourne *Age*'s Simon Balderstone. Balderstone had made the running in the Canberra Press Gallery on the South West issue. Alan Jarman tried to explain his difficult position to him — why he hadn't crossed the floor that night. He would later. Stewart West joined in, very earnestly. He was keen to make the point that the Labor Party was conservationists' only hope. The debate dissolved into the alcohol and cigarette smoke that filled the dreary bar.

At 2 a.m. the night was still warm. It was a great, wide, open Australian summer night. As I walked down the drive I looked forward to the morning's headlines.

*'We would have been sitting on the
King River Bridge and their first bulldozer
would have forded straight around us.'*
CATHIE PLOWMAN

The blockade of HEC works over the summer of 1982–83 was the biggest conservation protest ever held in Australia. With 1440 people arrested it constituted a major act of civil disobedience.

The blockade's main action occurred near the dam site on the Gordon River between 14 December 1982 and 1 March 1983. There were also many arrests on the access road to the dam site, the Crotty Road, also known as the Kelly Basin Road, and in the West Coast fishing village of Strahan. The blockade was organized by the Tasmanian Wilderness Society and, in particular, Pam Waud and Cathie Plowman, a psychologist and a psychiatric nurse.

Cathie Plowman was born on 25 September 1958 in Sydney. She was brought up in country New South Wales before becoming a nurse at North Ryde Psychiatric Hospital.

She was a member of the South West Tasmania Committee of NSW in 1981 when she decided to go to Hobart to help in the referendum campaign. She soon became involved in blockade planning.

Non-Violent Action, or NVA, training was the mass organizational technique used during the blockade. NVA involves gathering people into small, tight-knit 'affinity groups' and then making decisions, by consensus, on what action the group will take.

There have been disagreements between NVA trainers and other activists over the ends of political action and the means of achieving them. While many pragmatic conservationists were prepared to do almost anything to stop the dam, NVA advocates believed the opportunity of the blockade should have been used to attempt to fundamentally change society's decision-making procedures.

In November 1981 I accidentally sat in on an NVA meeting. The three people were having a fishbowl exercise and talking about hassle-lines; a fishbowl exercise is used to develop an awareness of group dynamics, a hassle-line is a type of role play used to prepare for conflict situations — the scenario we used repeatedly was a row of greenies sitting in front of a bulldozer being confronted by a row of Hydro workers.

I thought that this was a rather odd sort of meeting and then there was the 'sharing'. The sharing was when everybody said how they felt generally, or how they felt about the meeting, or about the people in the room, or about what they'd had for tea. I was a bit dubious about it all but everybody else seemed pretty positive about it. I thought that it was just that it was new to me and that sooner or later I'd get 'it' too.

I think that for some people who got involved in NVA training it was really valuable in terms of their becoming aware of and considering other people. But I think that the procedures are rather threatening and that there is a lot of pressure placed on people in the group meetings. I felt it was invasive. Often people were embarrassed or intimidated. I know that there were people who were alienated because they questioned or didn't conform to the NVA procedures and others who didn't get involved in the blockade because of them.

A non-violent blockade was essential and it was an excellent blockade. We got what we wanted: worldwide attention and support. We had extensive and generally supportive media coverage right across Australia, not just for days but for weeks on end. I didn't agree with the way NVA was used but it did provide a means of control. People were hammered into the group structure and the group enforced acceptable behaviour, squashing ideas and actions that were considered to be destructive or dicey. It has been said that the consensus process hampered initiative because people could be easily 'consensed' out of acting. I think that is true. Perhaps the greatest benefit of NVA for the Franklin blockade was that potentially violent, dangerous or dubious actions usually weren't allowed to happen. Over 2000 people took part in the blockade and no-one really did anything that proved disastrous, although there were some close shaves.

There were some positive results of NVA techniques. I know there were some very close and strong affinity groups formed. These certainly provided support for their members who may have been in miserable weather blockading machinery, or possibly being harangued by pro-dam people, in prison or maybe doing some of the many unglamorous but essential chores that kept it all happening. Still, affinity is not achieved by moulding.

In the pre-blockade months I spent much energy agonizing over NVA and how it was being utilized. By the time the blockade began I was too busy to worry about it.

To me NVA was another tool to be used in the most effective way to save the wilderness. Maybe accepting the tyranny of it was the price to be paid for ensuring a successful blockade. To some people perfecting NVA techniques became the goal. Because I didn't embrace totally the NVA approach and philosophy I was somewhat rejected by the trainers, though at one stage I had been a trainer myself. I know that a few other people were in a similar position. It's sickening really, this division shouldn't have happened — much energy was wasted; more positive things could have been done with that energy.

In late 1981 we thought that a blockade would be necessary after the referendum in December. It was all very unrealistic at that stage. We thought that we'd bring hundreds of people from I don't know where since we hadn't told anyone but ourselves about the blockade.

After February 1982 Pam and I started co-ordinating things and that's when it took off. Pam had more idea in the early days just what was going to be involved; Pam had the initiatives and I did a lot of the running-around jobs. I guess it was like that all the way through the blockade. Despite a few problems I think Pam and I made a good combination.

It was a long year; the preparations were often pretty repetitive and tedious. Though there were some exciting moments — secret missions into the field, making plans, doing reconnaissance, stashing food and equipment, marking routes — all had to be done inconspicuously with tracks covered. Tim Walsh collected the bulk of the equipment — cooking gear, plastic buckets, rubber duckies — we could never get enough of them and they all needed to be checked and repaired. Paul Dimmick worked for months designing and building radio equipment. Someone else organized a benefit tour by Redgum, but it hardly broke even. Money was a problem right from the start.

We had plans for a camp for 200 people at the King River bridge on the Kelly Basin Road. We'd fix them easily. The plan was that we'd beat the first bulldozer there and that we'd just occupy the bridge. We had visions of a bulldozer driving down the road.

It didn't happen that way at all. First of all a couple of cars of surveyors went down — we had our spies sitting in the scrub watching what happened on the road. First of all it was survey pegs and tapes, then chainsaws; it happened very gradually. The bulldozers came much later. If we had used that plan we would have been sitting on the bridge in July '82 and when they took their first bulldozer in they would have forded straight around us. They forded the King River below the bridge and then ploughed through the huon pine reserve there, right where we would have been camped. It would have been pretty cold and as we had only announced the blockade plans that month we wouldn't have had any people.

We were very reluctant to concede that we needed contingency plans for the Gordon River. I guess it was because our bridge blockade plan seemed so easy and river blockades seemed impossible. We were very naive.

I think people might have had illusions before they

went to the blockade that they'd stop those bulldozers physically by being there. Close to the time even I felt the same myself, that you could actually stop a bulldozer by sitting in front of it. What stopped them was the tremendous publicity and support we had right across Australia and the world which we took into the election campaign. Those people who went there played a large part in stopping those bulldozers in the long run.

When we announced direct action we did it with a major press conference. That was 26 July 1982. We invited a lot of conservative-looking people along to sit in the audience so that they'd come on the TV cameras. I remember sitting there with Pam, heart thumping away and thinking, 'Well, this is it, we're in it now.'

During the first few days of the blockade we were all tense and tired. There were hassles with the boats, there were always hassles with the boats because so many people wanted to go on them and there was never enough room. There were many problems with trying to get 53 people on a boat and away at the right time and fixing up supplies.

In the first stage everyone just wanted to go up the river and get arrested. In fact there was this arrestomania. People would come into the Information Centre and say, 'I've come to be arrested tomorrow;' and I'd say, 'Well there's no boat tomorrow.' And they'd say, 'Well I want to get arrested tomorrow.' 'You can't get arrested tomorrow.' Arrest was coming first — it was described as the ultimate sacrifice in the field — arrest was the all-important thing.

I was having to worry about kitchen cooks and things like that. I was doing camp co-ordinating, boat co-ordinating, I was looking after equipment and supplies, I was doing media interviews, I was doing first aid — there were very few doctors and nurses around, I was doing all the liaising with the People's Park caravan caretaker where we were staying and I was collecting everybody's camp fees. I was doing a zillion things.

It was a really long week. We were hardly eating, healthy food came about once a day. We survived on the adrenalin. By the end of the week we were pretty tired. Doug Hooley flew Pam and me back to Hobart for Christmas. Somehow we managed to keep it up for 2½ months.

'There were three policemen
between them and us.'
PAM WAUD

Pam Waud was working at the Wilderness Society but feeling 'a bit useless' when Bob Brown suggested she think about NVA. That was November 1981. For the next sixteen months she was consumed by the task of organizing thousands of people into a blockade.

Pam Waud was born on 2 May 1949 at Preston, Lancashire. In England she studied photography and travel brochures. She landed in Sydney in 1973. At the University of New South Wales she studied psychology — 'rat torture and statistics'. After graduating she moved to Tasmania.

On the first reconnaissance mission in my old Volkswagen, the muffler fell off down the Crotty Road. It must have been about January 1982. We were doing a lot of reconnaissance. The Crotty Road in those days was just a one-lane, quartzite, ex-railway line and we just drove down that. We drove to the King River bridge where we decided our camp would be when we were blockading. We were looking for some really good blockade sites, and there were some very deep cuttings in the road, with steep cliff on one side and a steep drop on the other side. That was where we were going to blockade.

We just had no comprehension of how enormous it would end up being, at the beginning. I have got a copy of a letter which I wrote to Karen Alexander in January, when I started taking over, saying I hope we can get 100 people. If we can get 200 we will be lucky. We just had no idea what we were doing, what we were getting stuck into. Of course it just grew and grew and grew and grew. We have got a budget there that I worked out for $16 000 for two months' blockading. It ended up being $180 000 for nearly three months. We had to work in secrecy. Cathie and I used to take files home with us at night.

There was always a lot of nervousness in the Wilderness Society about actually doing that sort of thing. Right until the very day it proved successful, people were worried about it, putting it off and putting it off just because it was a departure from the regular campaign. In those days we thought it would really adversely affect things like the State elections if the world knew that we were planning something illegal like that, so we kept it quiet. We need not have bothered really. When it finally was announced, we didn't lose any members. In fact a lot of support came forward because of it.

We had meetings in someone's house until we went public. We sort of vetted people before we invited them to come along — not vetted them but we checked that they were on side. Somebody had to know them. They were not just open to anybody, those meetings. Really, looking back on that it was all a bit silly. It is a pity we did it that way.

Always it was never going to happen. It was the most frustrating thing about the entire blockade organizing, that I was working for a year full time on something I didn't think was going to happen.

The rest of the Society were very busy in their other campaigns that were going to prevent the blockade from happening.

We had to exhaust other channels first and that was what everybody in the Wilderness Society decided. That was pretty obvious. It was also obvious that summer was the right time to do it, because then you could get the people who had their holidays and then the weather in the South West isn't so terrible.

The Gordon River brought in enormous tactical and logistical problems. We finally decided we would have to have a base camp in Strahan. Without the people of Strahan we couldn't have done the blockade the way we did it, because there was so much they gave us — the land for Greenie Acres, the boats, the moral support, amazing.

Transport was an enormous logistical area, transporting people to and from Strahan. The gear, the food — all food had to be transported from Hobart.

We tried to liaise with the Hydro. We made one attempt. Emma Gunn and I went to see John Knight of the Hydro-Electric Commission public relations and told him — this was after the blockade was public — that we were peaceful and hoped there would be no violence. He hoped so too, but he was not very impressed with Emma and I sitting there telling him and his assistant that we were going to stop them. I can't remember exactly but he was a little bit angrily bemused, you might say, at these two women in their best clothes sitting there.

I think all along people like the Hydro and the police couldn't understand what we were on about; they just couldn't. It was just bewildering to them that we were doing it so openly.

We had a vigil which started in September after the land was vested in the Hydro-Electric Commission and that vigil stayed there at Butler Island until the blockade started. Norm Sanders flew over every week on a reconnaissance flight to see how the road was progressing.

The blockade was deadly serious right from the beginning. One of the things about it was that I was scared about what would happen. I could see bloodshed. So could everybody. That was always on the cards. That it didn't happen is due to the long planning and the training. Training is absolutely essential for this type of operation. You can't have people going into dangerous situations or stressful situations unless they have been part of the decision to go into it, absolutely crucial. I have a lot of respect for that training; absolutely crucial to the blockade. The trainers have suffered a lot of flak for what they were doing from people who disagreed with them.

During the blockade I didn't do anything else at all. I just became a functioning part of the blockade. I stopped seeing myself almost as a human being. I stopped feeling like a human being. I stopped having any human emotions. I didn't take any interest in men, for example, or in anything else really.

There were three aims that we worked out. The first one was to generate enormous publicity, which was very successful. The second one was a show of commitment, strength, determination — that was shown very clearly by all the people being arrested and put in gaol. The third one was to slow down and hopefully stop work but of course that has to be a political decision in the end, that work stop. What we are doing in blockading is putting pressure on the politicians. It is a very strong form of lobbying. So that is how we stopped work in the end, not physically, although we did slow down things while the eyes of the world were on the river.

Some of the people who spent a lot of time upriver had really good relationships with the Hydro. Some of them were really nice, easy-going people. No problems. There were two bulldozers up there for a long time, there were just two: and the driver of one was not to be trusted — he'd squash you as soon as look at you — and the other one was really good and easy-going — he'd talk to you.

Some of the heavy-handed tactics like the eviction, making it illegal to camp in a national park, I was absolutely amazed that they didn't bring in months before, because it was so much more difficult for us once they had done that. We wouldn't have been able to build a large scale organized base camp if they had done it a couple of months earlier. It would have really taken the wind out of the river blockade. But they didn't.

Some of the things they did were just amazingly good publicity for us. That advertised G-day beautifully, our eviction. That brought the media running back when they had gone. It brought them back and they stayed for G-day. It was marvellous. As often as not ignoring us would have been the best tactic they could have adopted, or some way of discrediting us. Any kind of violence, no matter who started it, would have produced a backlash against the blockade.

That was what terrified me about G-day. We were so close to things happening when the OTD (*Organization for Tasmanian Development*) came out. There was a great long row of them, jeering, throwing peanuts and washing powder over us, it looked like they were chomping at the bit to get into a fight. There were three policemen between them and us; we were all on the verandah singing and playing music. One moment I though they were all going to come and leap on us. The whole of G-day would have been ruined because the story would have been violence and not that 228 people had been arrested. The headlines would have tied the blockade in with violence.

On G-day we planned a large Strahan action. But when the OTD arrived in their large numbers at Strahan wharf we had a big meeting to discuss whether we would still do a Strahan action. The Strahan Action group decided to postpone the action till the next day. They didn't get any publicity for it because it was the blackout period for the elections then. But we didn't want any high tensile chain (*which the protestors used to attach themselves to fences and machines*) left lying around the office in Hobart — we wanted to use it.

Cathie seemed to be able to concentrate on the here and now and what was happening at a precise moment and how to sort it out. I worried more, and concerned myself more with the long-term and the wider effects of it. And the big hassles between various groups in the blockade and the overall scheme of things. I was known to everybody and could keep things intertwined. I had an idea what was happening in all the different places. Cathie and I formed what I think was a pretty reasonable team.

It was the most stressful period of my life — the year

planning it and then the tension and stress mounting as it became more and more inevitable and reaching a peak the day before. Then getting used to living with that kind of stress — there was no escape from it when you're there — 7 days a week and 12 or 14 hours a day. Oh, I can remember that stress, unbelievable stress. But I'm delighted that I was part of it. It has really been an amazing experience for me. It changes you, that sort of experience. You become far more confident in your own abilities. If you're one of the main organizers of something that goes so well, that is so successful and so big, it gives you a lot of confidence. You know you can do things. It teaches you all about yourself too — you know how you operate under that kind of pressure. You learn about your own weaknesses, and strengths.

The disadvantage is that after doing something like that it's very hard finding another job in the Wilderness Society. It really got hold of me, organizing that blockade, it gripped me and enthralled me for so long. What can I follow it with now?

'We told him we'd be campaigning against the Government at the next election.'
MURRAY WILCOX

Murray Wilcox is one of Sydney's leading barristers. He has a long history of involvement in environmental defence cases in New South Wales including cases on mineral sand mining at Myall Lakes and The Entrance, the logging of rainforest, the construction of a stadium in Parramatta Park and the preservation of the Old Treasury Building in Sydney. He was the foundation President of the Environmental Law Association of NSW.

Since 1979 Murray Wilcox has been President of the Australian Conservation Foundation. He has spoken on behalf of ACF on South West Tasmania, met leaders of the Tasmanian and Commonwealth Governments and drafted the Democrats' World Heritage Bill that passed the Senate in 1982. He chaired the December 1982 Tullamarine airport meeting of conservation groups from around Australia, convened by the ACF.

Murray Wilcox was born in Sydney in 1937. After a boyhood in the country and study in Sydney he became a solicitor in Cooma. He went to the NSW Bar in 1963 and became a Queen's Counsel in 1977. He served on the Law Reform Commission from 1976 to 1979. In 1983 he conducted an inquiry for the Victorian Government on the possible introduction of poker machines into that state.

We talked in his chambers in Phillip Street, Sydney.

The period of the Franklin campaign has coincided largely with the period I have been President of ACF. The HEC presented its proposal to the Tasmanian Parliament in October 1979; I was elected in November. The very first interview that I did as ACF President was with a Sydney television station about the Franklin and what it was like. They asked me to go down to the Botanic Gardens to film me in a scenic backdrop. So I talked about the importance of South West Tasmania, which fortunately I had visited a couple of years before on a family holiday.

Literally every ACF Council meeting and executive meeting that's occurred since then has had as a prime matter on the agenda the South West. Almost all the time there has been a prospect that the battle was going to be won relatively soon, but it kept going away.

There was a tremendous amount of effort on the part of conservationists to persuade Tasmanian politicians.

Doug Hill was going down to Hobart every two or three months and talking to Doug Lowe and some of his Ministers, and also the Opposition, and achieving something as far as Lowe was concerned. ACF had also done a lot of work in preparing alternative strategies and submissions, both at the Federal and the State level.

But when the Liberals got in with a clear majority it was hopeless. The only thing was to concentrate on the Federal arena. We were not going to persuade the Gray Government to back down.

The Koowarta case was a constitutional battle to decide whether the Commonwealth or the Queensland Government had the power to make laws on racial discrimination in Queensland. The High Court decided in May 1982 that, because Australia had signed an international treaty outlawing racial discrimination and because such discrimination was a matter of international concern, the Commonwealth had the constitutional power.

The Koowarta case was the most significant precedent for the Tasmanian dam case. The Hawke Labor Government's World Heritage Properties Conservation Act was the domestic implementation of the World Heritage Convention, which Australia ratified in 1974. The World Heritage Act and the regulations made under it were drafted to stop the Gordon-below-Franklin dam. On 1 July 1983, on the strength of the international convention, the High Court judged the World Heritage Act to be valid.

Before the decision of the High Court was given in the Koowarta litigation I had thought about the external affairs power but it wasn't really very clear how far the High Court would be prepared to go in a situation where the whole of the action necessary for implementation of a treaty was within Australia. Koowarta was the first case where the High Court upheld legislation under the external affairs power which required action only within Australia.

Given that judgment and given the fact that we were being driven to look at the Commonwealth power, obviously I started to think about that. It so happened that about that time Doug Hill asked me if I would put down on paper what I thought was the Federal power.

So I sat down and prepared something which was sent to Tom McVeigh, the then Minister, and I think copies were fairly widely distributed around Canberra, which argued that there was an external affairs power.

It was about the same time, the middle of 1982, that the Federal Government started getting its own advice on this matter and my views got some publicity: so it generated a bit of interest in the Federal political arena. Then we were all hoping that the Federal Government was going to decide to intervene and again there was this mirage of success not very far away.

Then the Democrats decided to introduce their own legislation. There was a rally organized for Sydney in October 1982 and it turned out to be a very wet day. About four or five thousand hardy souls turned up. It got enough publicity.

About a week before that David Campbell, Don Chipp's private secretary, contacted me and asked if I would be prepared to assist the Democrats in preparing a Bill. I said yes, and a meeting was arranged which took place in this room after that march. Lincoln Siliakus was also here. Anyway we sat around and discussed what were the powers and how it could be done. I made a few notes for it and said I would try to draw up something. I then did a draft and I sent it down to a friend of mine who was a former Parliamentary draftsman in Canberra, Noel Sexton, and asked him if he'd have a look at it.

I had to be in Canberra — I was asked to go down to give some evidence to the Senate Select Committee on South-West Tasmania, with Doug Hill — in late October. I arranged to see Noel Sexton early one morning — I went out to his house and spent an hour or two with him — while we settled the form of this Bill between us.

We picked out as the heads of power to rely on, the external affairs power, the corporations power and the interstate trade and commerce power. Now of course the eventual High Court decision upheld the external affairs power and the corporations power so I think in terms of selecting the powers we got it right. We didn't include anything about making laws for the Aboriginal race. We didn't think of that.

We prepared that Bill and the Democrats introduced it in that same form and of course it went through the Senate after a series of debates in November and December.

All the time that that debate was going on I'd had a feeling from vibes we'd been getting that the Government was going to intervene. I first learnt that it was otherwise when I was here one night about 7 o'clock and I had a ring from a reporter from the *Sydney Morning Herald* who asked me for a comment on the decision. I asked: 'What was the decision?' and he told me.

That was 8 December. Debate was going to be resumed in the Senate a few days later and in the ultimate they finally dealt with the Bill on the evening that Parliament got up. They got it in the House of Representatives about half past eleven. I can remember the excitement of that getting through the Senate — Colin Mason rang me and told me. And then it went to the Representatives and they didn't deal with it which was a very great disappointment.

Then they got up for Christmas and they would resume

in February. In the meantime work had started on construction, the blockade had started, the area was on the World Heritage List and we were facing the prospect that a lot of damage would be done before Parliament would resume.

I decided that I would try and get to some of the senior Ministers to persuade them that, before Parliament resumed in February when the Bill would have to go to the House and where we had some chance of putting pressure on some of the Government backbenchers, the Government itself should take the initiative in the meantime by reconsidering it. I had in mind that when the Prime Minister came back with a different view a different result might be obtained.

The first thing that we did was to get a public opinion reaction to the decision. This was useful. There was a poll taken in three marginal electorates — Casey and Chisholm in Melbourne and Phillip in Sydney — and Bennelong, Mr Howard's electorate. That showed a high degree of awareness and a high degree of disapproval of the Government's decision.

About a week before Christmas I saw John Howard in his office down in Martin Place. I had about an hour with him on it, and I argued the thing in terms of principle. I didn't get very far with him on that. I also told him about the public opinion poll and I thought he was much more interested in that. But in the end I got no more than a promise that Cabinet would be looking at it again, during January, and that he would pass on what I had said.

About the same time we'd been trying to organize a meeting with the Acting Prime Minister, Doug Anthony. I remember I went down to Canberra two days before Christmas, Thursday the 23rd.

That I found a very unsatisfactory meeting. I felt he had no perception of the degree of public interest in the matter and was very much inclined to denigrate the ability of the conservation movement to persuade people that this was a matter that should influence their vote. Frankly I felt he was out of touch. He made it quite plain that there was no possibility that he would support any review of the decision on intervention. He also made it plain that that was a result of pressure that had been put on the Government by Queensland and Western Australia.

So that was a fairly dispiriting meeting. I felt there was some confusion, even in his mind, about the difference between the Constitutional power to intervene and the political decision as to whether you should exercise that power. We kept going round in circles, talking about power and whether the Government could, in political terms, intervene.

Tom McVeigh was at that meeting and he took me back to his office and we had a talk there. It was pretty obvious that Tom McVeigh was very upset about the decision that had been taken. He also gave me a run-down on what had happened at the World Heritage Committee meeting from which Professor Slatyer had recently returned.

It happened that I had arranged to go to Tasmania with my family immediately after Christmas to walk on the South Coast track. We did that and then went to stay with some friends in Launceston. Whilst I was in Launceston, through the good offices of my friend, I got to talk to Kevin Newman, the senior Liberal Minister in Tasmania, and I had an hour with him. He indicated to me that he personally was opposed to building the dam, but nonetheless he was going to fight to the death for Tasmania's entitlement to make its own decision. He also made it pretty clear that he would wish the problem to go away.

That was a common theme — that was the theme I got from John Howard also. I don't think Anthony regarded it as a problem. In the Liberal ranks there seemed to be an awareness that it was a potential problem for them electorally, in an election which obviously had to be held during 1983 sometime.

As it happened I knew from some years back the editor of the Launceston *Examiner*, Michael Courtney, and whilst I was there I gave him a ring and went and had a talk to him to see whether he thought that there was anything that could usefully be done to influence the approach of the Tasmanian Government. I also asked him about publishing an article in the *Examiner* about the alternatives to the Gordon-below-Franklin dam. I subsequently wrote it and the *Mercury* published it too, in late January.

Courtney organized a discussion with Gray. Doug Hill and I went down on 17 January. This meeting was only arranged with some considerable difficulty. But he did agree to talk on the basis that we kept it confidential, and we didn't tell anybody we were going. And so we didn't. I haven't publicly revealed it till now.

We went down on 17 January. At that time we weren't aware of any offer from Fraser to Tasmania. It was later that same week that it was announced that Fraser had offered goodies to the tune of $500 million and that Tasmania had knocked it back. When we saw Gray on the Monday he had had the offer — because apparently it had been made on the previous Thursday, the 13th — but we didn't know anything about it.

We spent two hours with him and we had a very amicable discussion about the whole thing. I got the impression that he wished nobody had ever thought of damming the Gordon below the Franklin. But he said to us that he felt that it would not be possible to change course because the people of Tasmania would not buy it.

The burden of what we said to him was that we had talked to a number of senior Federal politicians and we said that there wasn't any doubt at all that the Federal

Government would dearly like to get rid of the problem and that our reading of the situation was that they'd be prepared to pay almost any price to do so. So that he was in the position where he could write himself a cheque if he decided to abandon the project. We said to him that this would probably be the best chance he'd have because if there was a change of government — we told him we'd be campaigning against the Government at the next election, that decision had been made in principle at the meeting of conservationists at Tullamarine airport on 19 December — we told him that if the Labor Party got in then he'd be in a mendicant position, as of course he now is. We suggested that he'd be well advised to talk while he still had something to sell.

I also made so bold as to say that if the Liberal Party Government was returned perhaps that'd be the worst thing that could happen to him because if they actually built the dam, spent the money and couldn't sell the power he'd never get any compensation. But he was prepared to take a chance on that, that was a long-term problem.

Anyway this meeting really achieved nothing except perhaps to open up communication between him and ACF. And then it was later on that week that I learnt that even as he sat there talking to us he had available to him Fraser's offer. Fraser's offer did provide evidence of what we'd been saying — that the Federal Government was desperate to buy him off.

Gray locked himself into starting the dam before it was necessary and then of course it's very hard, once you've got men at work, to pull them off, unless you've got immediate projects to put them on to. I think, frankly, he handled the thing very badly, as have successive Tasmanian Governments. All three of them — Lowe, Holgate and Gray — have made very bad mistakes.

It's a very unsatisfactory situation. Very early in 1980,

shortly after I was elected ACF President, Geoff Mosley and I went to see Bob Ellicott, who was then Minister for Environment, and we pointed out to him the situation that was coming and we reminded him of Fraser's 1975 policy when they said the Federal Government should make special arrangements for South West Tasmania. And I can remember saying to Ellicott: 'Now is the time to talk to Tasmania, before it becomes a live issue, and try and come up with some constructive alternatives.'

Ellicott's position was, very simply: 'They know where we are.' The problem with that was that when Doug Hill explained that to Lowe and said, 'Well, why don't you talk to the Feds?' the attitude was the same: 'They know where Hobart is.' And so the two governments went on for years simply being unwilling to make the first approach. It seems to be a travesty of the idea of co-operation between governments in a Federal system. People who complain about the ultimate decision being destructive of federalism really ought to think about what an indictment of federalism the whole thing has been.

All my contacts with Liberal-National Party politicians can be summarized in two statements: one is that I've been given a very friendly and good hearing, and two is a total absence of result from that hearing.

Conservationists had arranged another meeting at Tullamarine for the first weekend in February. It was on the Thursday before that meeting that the double drama occurred of Hawke succeeding Hayden as leader of the Labor Party and Fraser announcing an election. The timing was fortunate for us because we had organized this meeting and there we were: knowing that an election was on, knowing who the leader of the Labor Party was going to be — we couldn't have got off to a better start.

That was the meeting where Barry Jones came out and said: 'Give your votes to Labor in the Lower House,' and a representative of the Democrats said: 'Give us your Senate votes.' Fortunately they were in substantial agreement and we were in substantial agreement in the movement and so that's how it was done.

I think the mechanism of the National South West Coalition was a good idea. Had there been more time it would have developed even more and become even more impressive.

Given the fact that we went into it at such short notice, and given the fact that there were people all over Australia involved, I think it was really remarkable co-operation. But for the fact that there were a few people in Melbourne keeping tabs on it, it could have been a financial disaster — we could have lost hundreds of thousands of dollars.

I had come to the conclusion some time ago that the Liberal-National Party conservation record was lamentable. Anybody who was at all concerned about the natural environment had to be very critical of what was done. We wouldn't have gone political but for the Franklin and the complete disavowal of responsibility by a national government.

The big moment of euphoria, as far as I was concerned, was election night, because I expected Commonwealth legislation would survive the High Court. Once there was a change of government that was that.

After the election there was the question of the form of the Bill and the main problem about it was that it was restricted, in that it could only apply if there was a proclamation of an area and the area could be de-proclaimed without any Parliamentary oversight. So that if there was a change of government the Liberal Government could just remove the proclamation and the Tasmanian Government could start again. There was no provision for anyone other than the Federal Attorney-General to take legal proceedings. These were quite significant departures from the Democrats' Bill. We'd been promised during the election campaign a Bill such as that, only better. I wrote a letter to Senator Evans, the Attorney-General, setting out these complaints.

We worked out what minimum changes we would press for. Then I subsequently had a late night conversation with Gareth Evans. I'd been trying to get him all day and all evening — he rang me about eleven o'clock one night (2 May) — the poor fellow sounded absolutely worn out. It must have been about the time they were dealing with this security crisis thing. Anyway, he'd been very very busy setting up the new government. He told me they were prepared to widen standing, they were prepared to accede to our wishes regarding deproclamation, they were not prepared to make it apply to all areas because they felt that they shouldn't do that without consulting the States and they hadn't had a chance to do so.

They amended the Bill in the House and I had some contact with Senator Chipp and Senator Mason about what the Democrats were going to do in the Senate. In the end they decided they wouldn't move further amendments because they wanted it to go through the Senate quickly and be available to the High Court. I suppose that was the right judgment, given the unwillingness of the Government to accommodate all our needs.

So it was duly enacted, it went to the High Court and I didn't have much role thereafter. I followed what was happening and I chatted to barristers about what the prospects were and what were the likely heads of power that would appeal to particular judges.

Then the result came out. So that was the saga.

I hope it will lead to a Commonwealth-State plan of management for the area which will enable the establishment of a park which will be not only world class for its natural advantages but which could be a model for other places.

I also hope that it will open the way for a real attempt to

look at alternative employment opportunities in energy creation, ideas that we've been talking about. It seems to be an ideal opportunity for a wind farm and to provide jobs in energy conservation. Whether that happens will depend on the imagination of the politicians.

In the ultimate I haven't got any doubt that the Franklin was a significant factor in the Labor win — I think they probably would have got in anyway but with a much smaller majority, and the result may well have been in doubt. I think it was a big factor and it's been perceived as a big factor by the politicians. So hopefully the lesson has been learnt — that the national government must accept national responsibility for national areas. That transcends the saving of the Franklin.

What has happened, and it's a little ironic, is that as a result of the ultra-conservatism in two cases of two conservative Premiers — Bjelke-Petersen in the Koowarta case and Gray in the Dams case — we now have decisions of the High Court which emphasize the wide-ranging powers that the national government has, not only in the external affairs power but in the corporations power. I think the way is open for the Federal Government to take a more active role in conservation than it has in the past. We now ought to be looking at how the corporations power can be used to achieve conservation goals.

The other obvious area is looking at the other international conventions to which Australia is a party — on endangered species and wetlands and so on. We've got to work up proposals for legislation which aren't so radical as to dismay the States' righters too much. So over the next two or three years there is a series of opportunities to open the way to a national body of law that deals with the major environmental questions in Australia.

But the vast majority of land-use decisions will remain under State control because they have no international or national ramifications.

The scope of the external affairs power was put into context by Professor Leslie Zines, who was one of the counsel for Tasmania; he ended up by saying that we shouldn't regard the Federation as having come to an end; all that has happened was just another step in an historic tendency in High Court decisions for the area of power for the Commonwealth to be expanded.

It's not much good winning at law, though, if you haven't got a sufficient groundswell of public opinion behind you, because it's so easy for governments to change the rules. If you win at law but the Government is persuaded that public opinion is in favour of that project then that project will be approved and go ahead. If they have to change the law they'll do it.

The Parramatta Park litigation indicates how easy it is for a government to do it, even after there's been a successful legal action.

If there's a good legal case that's one thing but don't sit back on your haunches and think that by winning at law you've won the battle. Unless you have won over public opinion, or at least a sufficiently big proportion of that to make the Government take notice, winning in the courts is not really winning at all.

The 1983 Federal Election
ROGER GREEN

In July 1982 the Australian Labor Party, at its national conference in Canberra, adopted a policy of strong opposition to hydro-electric development on the Lower Gordon and Franklin Rivers. With a Liberal-National Government that refused to stop such development, the Labor policy created a difference between parties that could become an election issue.

By 14 December 1982 the two parties' positions were clearly stated and opposite. The Liberal Cabinet had announced a policy of non-intervention in Tasmania the week before. Even though Malcolm Fraser had supported the World Heritage listing of the Western Tasmania Wilderness National Parks, in his absence his government gagged debate on the Democrats' World Heritage Bill. The Labor Party voted for the Bill.

On the same day that the Labor environment spokesman, Stewart West, introduced the Bill into the House of Representatives two other Labor frontbenchers, John Button and Neal Blewett, were in Strahan for the start of the blockade. There wasn't much doubt whose side the Labor Party were on. The Opposition Leader, Bill Hayden, visited a month later.

On 19 December 1982, ACF drew conservationists from around the country to Tullamarine airport where the group decided that the South West issue was of such importance that the normally non-partisan conservation movement should take a stand at the next election. Unless the Liberal Government moved immediately to stop the dam that stand would be against the Liberal Party.

Through January, in spite of a blockade on the Gordon River and Malcolm Fraser's offer to fund an alternative power scheme, work on the dam continued. On Thursday 3 February 1983 Bill Hayden resigned as Leader of the Opposition and Malcolm Fraser called an election.

The next Sunday the National South West Coalition met for a second time and decided to campaign for the

Labor Party in the House of Representatives and the Australian Democrats in the Senate.

From the first meeting of the National South West Coalition just before Christmas 1982 I set out to rally support for the decision in the conservation movement and to plan an election campaign.

Organization in Victoria was easy. Wilderness Society and ACF groups already operated in marginal seats around Melbourne and Bendigo and had good communications with head offices in Melbourne. There were plenty of full-time volunteers. Karen Alexander found volunteers to organize in Brisbane — a place with marginal seats and a high level of sympathy for the cause.

New South Wales was more difficult. The marginal seats were mostly in the country and had had little contact with the Franklin campaign. Also, the different strands of the South West conservation movement in Sydney would need to co-operate. Shortly after Christmas a co-ordinating committee for NSW was set up but unfortunately it did not include all those groups wishing to be involved.

While I was in Sydney I began asking experts in politics for advice. I spent most of the next few weeks trying to get practical suggestions from political scientists, political commentators, Labor Party strategists and long-time conservationists. The questions I asked were: what should we advise voters to do, where should we campaign and should we run candidates?

The academics offered very little of use, tending to be concerned with the moral problems posed by alignment with political parties. They struggled with the problem of how to maintain the conservation movement's neutrality while trying to affect the outcome of an election. Professor Don Aitkin of the Australian National University had some practical ideas but urged us not to use them. He thought it was an impertinence for us to threaten the

Government. We should allow economic issues to take their rightful priority. All the academics were worried about what we *should* do. But we already knew that we *had to* change the government. We just needed to know how to do it.

The best practical ideas came from the ALP, in particular the party's national secretary, Bob McMullan, and his predecessor, David Combe.

Bob McMullan and I had been discussing marginal seats for some time but at a mid-January meeting with him and Geoff Prior at the ALP Secretariat in Canberra a new idea illuminated our sketchy plans. Based on our experience in the Flinders by-election, which had cost ACF and TWS $10,000, conservationists were thinking of campaigning in about 15 seats. But we had to make the most effective use of our money and people. Because we had more of the latter than the former we had to devise a labour-intensive campaign, doorknocking, rather than a capital-intensive campaign, advertising. To make best use of our labour we had to identify not only the most marginal seats but also the most important areas within those marginal seats. We would not be able to doorknock whole seats containing up to 40,000 dwellings.

For some years political analysts have tried to produce a demographic profile of the Swinging Voter. Political parties could then tailor their campaigns to those relatively few people in the middle who decide the outcome of elections. The analysts have had little success. However, from opinion surveys on conservation questions we had found socio-economic qualities possessed by the Conservation Sympathizer. If we could reach most of the Conservation Sympathizers in an electorate those unidentified Swinging Voters amongst them could decide the seat. Geoff Pryor suggested the use of census data to locate Conservation Sympathizers. From that moment I knew what to do.

A week later I was in the study of the pollster Irving Saulwick, who lives in the Melbourne bayside suburb of Beaumaris, leafing through his computer printouts. Saulwick is a gentle, humane intellectual whose surveys contain a wealth of sociological data. His house is as grand, rambling and leafy as the man.

Saulwick's surveys of opinion on South West Tasmania and similar conservation issues revealed four statistically significant traits of those who want our natural heritage preserved. The Conservation Sympathizer is young, most likely under forty, a student or tertiary-educated and professes no religion. I found no correlation between support for conservation causes and income levels or types of occupation.

To find where my stereotyped Conservation Sympathizer lived I first had to navigate the maze of the Cameron Offices at Belconnen in Canberra. I found the Australian Bureau of Statistics and, as sometimes happens in Canberra, the first officer I met was a keen supporter. His children were arrested on the Gordon River. I soon had a complete 1981 Census, maps and data on microfiche.

That evening, late in January 1983, I had dinner with some Parliament House journalists and Labor staffers who had given up the Franklin as lost. They could not see Labor winning an election whenever it was called. I tried to justify my optimism.

That weekend I started work on the microfiche. The national census figures are pieced together from fragments known as collection districts, small areas of about 200 houses. Each collection district is analyzed into many characteristics including age, religion, education level and student status. By studying collection district data we could find small areas with high concentrations of Conservation Sympathizers. These areas were divided into three levels of priority and electorate maps with three colours were made. Using these target-area maps the electorate organizers could direct doorknockers to the most promising blocks. Doorknocking is an arduous and often depressing activity. By eliminating large parts of each electorate volunteers could cover target areas and be encouraged by more positive responses from the other side of the flyscreen.

By early January about twenty marginal seats had been selected for closer attention. I was looking for a number of qualities: a small swing needed for the Government to lose the seat, a local branch of the Wilderness Society, ACF or another active South West conservation group, popular interest in conservation and short distances between population centres. Small city electorates that can be traversed by foot are much better places to campaign than country seats with many scattered towns.

Opinion polls showed our highest support was in Victoria and South Australia though only Kingston in South Australia was marginal. NSW and Queensland followed. Perth had many marginal seats and conservation sympathizers but as we had a shortage of local organizers and media interest we left it to Bob Hawke to win.

From the start we agreed that the only campaign in Tasmania should be for Norm Sanders as Australian Democrat candidate for the Senate. Other Tasmanian activists could be moved to sunny Queensland and country NSW though they were reluctant to leave the blockade. Many remained in Strahan and up the Gordon River until election day.

After much debate about the merits of running candidates in the election only Milo Dunphy decided to stand, in the safe Liberal seat of Bennelong in Sydney. He took many votes from John Howard, finally gaining 12.7% of the total. It was the highest vote of any House of Representatives candidate outside the major parties.

By late January our overall position was becoming clear. Both the Democrats and the ALP had strong anti-dam policies. But their aims were different: the ALP needed to win a majority of seats in the House of Representatives to become the government, the Democrats wanted enough Senators to hold the balance of power in the Senate. Each party wanted unequivocal support for the chamber of their greatest interest and was prepared to accept conservationists supporting the other party in the other chamber. We could please them both.

So with relatively little fuss the National South West Coalition meeting on Sunday 6 February decided to urge a vote for the ALP in the House of Representatives and the Democrats in the Senate. At the press conference held in the middle of the meeting at Tullamarine airport, thirteen priority seats were announced: five in NSW, five in Victoria, two around Brisbane and one in Adelaide. Based on the $10 000 cost of the Flinders by-election campaign a budget in the vicinity of $200 000 was approved, to be underwritten by ACF and the Tasmanian Wilderness Society.

Melbourne in February 1983 was oppressed by long, hot days. Dust storms blew in from the west, bushfires raged and killed in the east. Elemental themes and the images of Bob Hawke and Malcolm Fraser dominated the election campaign.

South West campaign workers battled with telephones in their stuffy headquarters in the city's environment centre. The designs for printed materials were late, marginal electorates wanted to do things their own way, fund-raising seemed to be far behind expenditure and Bob Brown's itinerary refused to obey the usual physical laws of space and time. I finished writing a set of guidelines for marginal electorate organizers and then set off for an electorate in Melbourne's eastern suburbs where a personality clash threatened to disrupt the campaign.

'Head office' intervention tipped the scales to one side; though two workers departed, the effectiveness of those remaining increased by a greater amount.

Tension between the two major partners in the South West Coalition, over expenditure and over the use of the Wilderness Society's name in the campaign, was kept to a simmer. There was also a struggle between the misers and the big spenders. However, in spite of spending nearly $50 000 on a full-page colour newspaper advertisement, the whole campaign came in under budget at $198 000. Almost all of the money was raised through an appeal to TWS and ACF members.

Another struggle was between the Melbourne office and the provinces. Outside the thirteen chosen electorates many groups wanted to participate in the election and they weren't interested in fund-raising. Suddenly local groups told us that seats requiring 12% swings to fall were really marginal. Spontaneous campaigns that even went to the length of financing and printing their own how-to-vote cards sprang up in Melbourne, Sydney, Armidale, Brisbane, North Queensland and Perth.

Gaining publicity was hard. Many days were spent dreaming up new items only to see the evening bulletins filled with Fraser and Hawke. Only in the last week of the campaign, after Tasmanian police evicted blockaders from the national park on the banks of the Gordon River, did the South West return to the headlines. That story was followed by a rally in Melbourne, and the Queensland Police having the good sense to ban Franklin River how-to-vote cards — we had been having trouble attracting media attention in Brisbane. The hundreds of arrests in the South West on G-Day, the day before the electronic media blackout, put the wilderness back on top of the television news.

During the blackout there was little to do. Except in Brisbane, all the how-to-vote cards had been distributed, the public meetings were over.

We had a couple of long breakfasts in the Hotel Windsor, Melbourne's recently-refurbished grand hotel. Mr Fraser was a guest at the hotel. On the Friday morning before election day eight greenies savoured Eggs Benedict and dabbed marmalade on toast. I was sipping tea when the Prime Minister's senior economic adviser entered.

I asked him what he thought of the state of the parties. He was feeling 'superconfident'. After weeks of opinion polls tipping a Labor victory there had been a shift. He had just seen a poll, to be published later that day, that showed the Liberals rapidly closing the gap. I sat down and toyed with my silver teapot.

Election day was mercifully cool. I handed out how-to-vote cards at Eltham Primary School. In the evening it was scrutineering at Templestowe. Of those who voted ALP 16% followed the Franklin card instead of the official ALP card. That showed significant interest in the conservation issue.

The first party was fairly nervous. People were drinking heavily. The second held more hope. A late swing in Western Australia ensured the election of a Labor Government. I didn't believe it until 1 a.m. when Malcolm Fraser resigned as Leader of the Liberals.

The third party was joyful. Hugs and kisses. Cheers echoed through the woods at Lower Plenty. Bob Brown was there. Everyone danced and sang, 'It's not just a river, it's one of a kind... the Franklin River is the place of things to come.'

Opinion polls taken within a week of the election by the major political parties and an independent organization all showed that an average of 2% of Australians had voted the way they did because of the Tasmanian dam. Areas targeted by the campaign showed much higher figures. Large numbers of Tasmanian pro-dammers voted Liberal. Tasmania was the only state to swing to the Liberals.

But more seats on the mainland were decided by the dam. The ALP policy and the campaign for the Franklin won the party about six seats that were decided by margins of less than 2%. While the Franklin issue did not decide the Government, the 1983 election campaign certainly demonstrated the political importance of conservation.

Wild Rivers Saved

*'We are one nation
and not just a collection of 6½ states.'*
BOB HAWKE

Bob Hawke was born in Bordertown, South Australia on 9 December 1929. He studied at the University of Western Australia, Oxford and the Australian National University before joining the ACTU. In 1959 he became the trade union advocate in the national wage case.

As President of the ACTU from 1970 to 1980 he earned a reputation as a forceful negotiator in industrial disputes. Bob Hawke was President of the ALP from 1973 to 1978 and in 1980 became the Member for Wills in the Australian Parliament.

In July 1982 he supported a motion at the Labor Party national conference which called for an end to hydro-electric construction on the Franklin and lower Gordon Rivers.

Bob Hawke became Leader of the Opposition in February 1983 and a month later defeated Malcolm Fraser to become Prime Minister of Australia. Within four months his Government passed World Heritage legislation, took it to the High Court and stopped the dam. Years of desperate campaigning had borne fruit.

When I spoke to him in his Parliament House Office in August 1983 Bob Hawke had just come from a long Cabinet meeting that had been discussing payments to Tasmania for the employment of HEC workers. The Prime Minister seemed tense and tired.

This decision has significance in a number of ways:
— it has a constitutional significance in that it has clarified an important area of power. In other words we haven't created a new head of power but the High Court has interpreted the Constitution in a very important way which has implications for the future. It doesn't mean that the Government can go off and conclude some international treaty for the sake of then having some power to act within Australia; it has got to be in pursuit of an international convention properly arrived at; but that's been clarified.
— secondly it has, and in my opinion this is the most important aspect of it, it has emphasized that we are *one* nation and not just a collection of 6½ states — if you can

talk about the Northern Territory as being half way towards statehood. The concept that we are one nation with national responsibilities and obligations, and rights, is very important.

— thirdly, in regard to the environmental issue, it has importantly established that economic considerations are not necessarily, in every circumstance, the only or the predominating considerations; that there are other factors which properly have to be taken into account.

I love the bush. We used to have a place down in Gippsland — I didn't own it — but it was a little farm in a remote valley down there when the kids were growing up. It had a little old house on it. It was part of a property of a doctor-friend of mine and he just made this available to us and we used to go down there a lot and it was just marvellous being around the bush with the kids playing. I had a great attachment to it.

The word 'wilderness' doesn't, of itself, mean anything. What's important is that there are areas of our physical inheritance, our natural inheritance, which have special features about them and which, if possible, should be preserved. This may be wilderness, it may be some other aspect of that natural inheritance.

In assessing values as a nation, as a people, we have a broad range of considerations that we take into account. We do have a responsibility to the future, in terms of what we hand on to them.

As a member of the Parliamentary Party during 1981 and '82 South West Tasmania became an issue that we had to address; we had to have a view about it at our national conference in '82. I thought about it very seriously and looked at all the considerations and I had no doubt that the view which the Party came to adopt, and which I supported vigorously, was the correct one.

We went into the election campaign with an

unequivocal commitment to this position and as soon as we were elected then I ensured that my relevant Ministers, and it was particularly the Attorney-General, move as quickly as possible to give effect to that commitment. We gave it a very, very high priority.

You see different estimates of the issue's electoral importance. It won us votes and it lost us votes. It lost us Tasmania: we didn't win a seat in the House of Representatives, but that wasn't a consideration in my mind.

Since the election the only difficulty really has been the attitude of the Premier of Tasmania who has tried to play politics. As far as officials are concerned — at my level and the state level and others, including for instance the Warden of Queenstown who came here when the Premier wouldn't come, and the Leader of the Opposition and a whole range of people including farm representatives, representatives of EZ — there was very good co-operation.

We're going about the job, in fact at this Cabinet meeting today we've confirmed arrangements in regard to projects which mean that we've now virtually tidied up all work for those who would otherwise have been employed for '83-'84. The only difficulty has been the politicizing of it by the Premier of Tasmania.

I made it clear to the people of Tasmania in the election campaign that there were two legitimate considerations — my line throughout was, No-one wants the dam as a dam, there's no-one who said, Look, we've got to have a dam because we want a dam' — there were two things: they were concerned about future power requirements and they were concerned about the employment of those who would otherwise have been employed.

I gave the commitment that we would meet those two requirements and that's what we're doing. It has involved some problems in terms of budgetary arrangements but I made that commitment and we kept it.

*'I reckon it would be worth
the whole existence of my trucking business.'*
KEVIN BAILEY

Kevin Bailey's yard is littered with wheeled vehicles — bicycles, lawnmowers, motorbikes, cars and a panel van. When I met him he was welding together the tailpiece of his Volvo N7 truck 'better than it was made'.

Kevin Bailey is a Strahan contractor who hires out his trucks, backhoes and loader for local construction jobs. He was one of the contractors used by the HEC on its Gordon-below-Franklin project.

He was born in Strahan on 24 January 1948. He went to high school in Queenstown before following his father into trucking. He has built up quite a prosperous business.

In the first half of 1983 most of Kevin Bailey's work was with the Hydro-Electric Commission: he had trucks and backhoes on the Crotty Road and at Warners Landing. The HEC was paying for three drivers and $250 000 worth of machinery. At the same time Kevin ws working in the HEC compound on the Strahan waterfront, often being called on to cut blockaders out of their chains.

After the damworks stopped on 1 July 1983 Kevin Bailey's men and machines were employed on Commonwealth-funded cleaning-up operations and alternative employment projects such as the road from Strahan to Zeehan. Kevin hopes to win contracts for work on new hydro-electric proposals such as the King scheme.

The work around Strahan's not real big money. I could survive myself doing local private work — trucking, drain-digging, excavations — I just wouldn't be able to keep new gear on. Probably 80% of my business is with the Hydro.

The Hydro offered me other jobs on the dam. I reckon it would be worth the whole existence of my trucking business. There's just not the money around anywhere else to expand. With the Hydro you can run new gear and buy new gear all the time. You can invest.

My father used to be the ganger on the Zeehan railway line. They closed that down in '59 or '60 and so he bought this old truck and went potholing for the Council. It sort of appealed to me and I just carried it on from there. When he died I was left on my own and I decided to build a business out of it and that's where we took off.

I was prepared to do anything, giving good service, working long hours. As it gets bigger it gets worse, your tax burden gets heavier. Your worries pile up as you get bigger. Often I think of going back to twelve years ago when you weren't getting so much money but there weren't so many worries.

I was doing local work, we never even moved out of Strahan. It was just work for the Strahan Council — they kept us employed. There was a bit of a building boom around — I was doing the excavations for the blocks.

Then I bought an old front-end loader and started work for the Forestry, all their roads. I gradually got enough money to buy a backhoe and that's when things started moving. I was the only backhoe on the West Coast eleven years ago. I started doing pipelaying for the EZ Company, work at Renison, work at Queenstown. Mainly the bigger type of excavations.

In the last four or five years the building's slackened off. Last year I was out of work for three months. I was paying my blokes money. About the middle of '82 I wasn't doing any work at all.

Then the Hydro came along and hired all my gear off me, except this truck, and I've never been more contented. There's money coming in every week and you can run a budget for your business.

Where they're building the Crotty Road I consider not very good countryside at all. It looks like the only thing it'd be good for is to put a road in there anyway and quarry it or do whatever's needed to be done. There was nothing happening down there until the Hydro started putting roads in. It is opening the countryside up and you are going to be able to drive to more scenic places.

At Warners Landing all you can see is a very small patch on the river, the rest of the work went on behind Warners.

From my point of view the dam was a necessity for Strahan. No doubt there's other people would disagree that are running boats and things like that — they reckoned it would hurt their tourist industry. I can't see it. I think it would make competition for their people and I think that's really what they would be going crook about.

If it hurt me I'd go crook. I can understand these boat-owners going crook but there is a boat-owner in Strahan who reckoned the dam would be good for him. I could only see it being good for Strahan. There are people in Strahan who wouldn't get anything out of the dam, who wouldn't get anything out of the Hydro, but they're for the dam. They're people interested in the well-being of Strahan.

The very first experience I had with the blockade was I was driving along the road to Strahan in the front-end loader and this thing — I call it a thing, he had his hair shaved all different shapes, it was dyed all different colours — he runs out in front of the front-end loader and I thought, 'Well, this is it.' I wasn't working for the Hydro at the time.

So I put the front-end loader in retard and lowered the bucket down on him until he got out of the road. And it shifted him. He gave up before the loader did. I never hurt him or anything, just made him scared, and he took off. He wasn't much of a good protestor, he wasn't.

Mostly I was in the Strahan compound. There was just as much action in the Strahan compound as anywhere. There was more action.

I thought it was very silly. There was a hell of a lot of greenies who were good people to talk to, but I lost faith in them. Like I'm talking to you now I'd be talking to a greenie and when you'd go to work in the morning he'd be chained to your front-end loader, or chained to your truck. And that was very annoying.

Sometimes you put your gear on the line because you've had to stop in a bad position because you had two or three people standing in front of you or in your bucket or on your wheels or something like that. A couple of times we'd be right on the brink of pushing a fill into the water down there and they'd get in behind you and you couldn't move. You were stuck there till the police come to shift them.

We were instructed by the Hydro engineers all the time not to get violent or push them out of the way. We had to be passive with them and try and understand them but it got very hard.

They had a day called G-Day. That was their big final push before the election and the Hydro fellas from Tullah and that all came down so they could counteract it. The greenies never did anything. They were going to chain themselves to everything but they didn't. The Hydro blokes went back that afternoon. We thought that was the last of the greenies. But the very next day down they were, all tied up.

That was the day I really got crabby with them, called them every bloody thing I could think of. I used to do the welding for the Hydro and so I used to do the cutting of the chains with oxy gear. That particular day I didn't feel very inclined to try to stop the sparks getting on them. I let as many sparks go down their legs as I could. Just a mild bit of an injury, a bit of a sting, the same sort of thing as I get when I'm working myself. At the same time I called them all the bastards I could think of.

We had a Coles crane with a 60 foot boom on it. There was this fella, it must have been his day to get locked up. Him and this girl climbed up to the bloody top of it. It was a very precarious position, they could have fell down out of it. The girl was terrified when she got up there. It was 60 feet straight up on the end of a boom. I had to lower the crane down very gradually and cut them down.

They used to take a big risk in the things they'd do and we were instructed to help them out of the situation they'd got themselves into. Some of their friends would become abusive towards us because they thought it was doing the wrong thing, getting them out of it. But we were only acting on their safety all the time.

There was one day I was shifting rock with the front-end loader, building a breakwater, and two or three silly buggers went and climbed on a couple of big rocks that I had to shift. One of them was right on the balance, if it had fallen down it would have broken their legs. So I had to sit with the loader, holding the rock, till the police come and shift them.

The funniest thing I ever seen was this day we went down and there was two or three chained to each gate. So we cut them off. Then this crane driver, an old fella who likes a few beers of a night-time and he usually comes to work pretty seedy, didn't actually stagger over to his crane but he just wandered over, he's a pretty slow old bugger, he wandered over to the crane and opened the door and there's a greenie in there who said, 'Hello,' and the old bloke nearly had a heart attack. We had to cut him out, he'd chained hisself in.

They used to pinch the Hydro chain and chain up with us. A new lock every time too.

This old duck, she'd have to be 60, a grey-haired old piece, she was in the Coles crane there one day. I had cut a few off the boom, they were all chained to the gates, a couple chained to the loader, a couple chained to the barge and when it come this turn to cut this old duck off, I thought she was chained to the crane. But she'd tied herself with string. When I got up there she said, 'You don't have to worry about the welder on me, just a sharp pocket knife.' She'd tied herself with string!

One day we went down there and here's this bloke climbed all the way up the centre of the boom of this crane. He's sitting up there playing this old melodium. Giving us a good tune too.

We became good friends with a lot of them. On election day there was a couple of nice young ladies down there handing out how-to-vote cards for Norm Sanders. I was handing out how-to-vote-Liberal cards. I'm a very strong Liberal. I was strong Liberal long before the dam issue, I've been Liberal ever since I've been working. These couple of girls were really friendly, just friendly nice people, doing what they think was right.

But then we'd get the idiots who'd come along. There was three or four leaders that, if we'd ever got the chance, we'd probably have bloody hammered them, because they seemed to get everyone worked up into a frenzy and two or three would go and do the thing and these blokes would sit back and get out of it every time. They'd stand back and then urge the next ones on again tomorrow.

There were the genuine conservationists — people who had just come there — and they'd protest just as much as the others but they wouldn't chain theirselves up and hinder your work. They'd stand around and say, 'Down with the Hydro' and all this — well, we didn't mind that.

I become very wild when they stopped me from working. One day I couldn't work for about four hours. The machine was tied up, I was getting paid.

On the Friday night afterwards I was down in the pub and this lady come up to me and she said, 'Mr Loader Driver, geez you was crabby the other day, wasn't you?'

I said, 'Yeah, I was, I really was.'

She said, 'Well what were you crabby about? Your machine wasn't working and you was getting paid for it.'

I said, 'Yeah, that's the whole thing. You people don't realize that to earn money you should be bloody working for it.' That keeps everything in balance then. There's too many people expecting money for nothing. I'll take money if I get it for nothing but I really do like working and getting satisfaction out of doing a job and then getting paid for it.

I've got no faith in Bob Hawke at all. With his policies I can't see him getting away from communism. I think that we're getting more towards communism that way than any other way and that's something to be feared of in Australia.

'What we wanted to do was build a dam.'
WARREN LOWRY

Warren Lowry is one of the workers affected by the halting of work on the Gordon-below-Franklin dam. He operated Kevin Bailey's backhoe at Warners Landing, digging drains, sewers and cable trenches for the camp there. When I spoke to him on the day of the High Court decision, 1 July 1983, he had just returned to Strahan after two weeks up the Gordon River.

How did he feel about the decision stopping the dam?

Bloody terrible, bloody terrible. At the moment I haven't got a bloody job. They've promised us other work but how long's it going to take to start? You don't know. They reckon some of the jobs you can just walk into straight away. But they have to survey it, it's going to take months to do that.

But we don't want another job, what we wanted to do was build a dam and that was it; don't want any other job. It was good working with the Hydro down there. Got on all right with all the blokes and the bosses, we didn't want no other job. We wanted to do what we was doing.

Warren Lowry worked at Warners Landing through the first half of 1983. The blockade of HEC works there was at its height from the arrival of the first bulldozer in early January till G-Day on 1 March.

The greenies and that, they were just terrible down there. You didn't know what was what. They'd be bloody getting in your road, climbing over your machines, things like this. The first month was the worst, till they more or less got rid of the greenies and told them to get out of it.

There were lots of things we couldn't do because the Hydro wouldn't allow us to do them. We wanted to dig drains and that and they just wouldn't let us, they said we had to wait for the decision before we could wreck any wilderness or anything like that.

What did he think of the country?

In my situation it wasn't so bad because the dozers would come in and level it all out and I'd just have to go through and dig drains. The dozer drivers — it was pretty rough for them when they first started.

There's nearly three kilometres of road almost completed down there. It's all going to waste now. They've spent months levelling off the camp site, done all this drainage and it's gone now. It's not worth nothing.

Shortly after the High Court decision Warren Lowry began work with the Hydro-Electric Commission on the upgrading of the tourist road from Zeehan to Strahan, a Commonwealth-funded alternative work project.

'The ripples of hope are already way out.'
BOB BROWN

This win has shown that a community of people who are concerned for the world's future can achieve a change in ingrained and, in the long run, destructive attitudes. We could just as easily show that you can't win, but I maintained throughout this campaign that if we couldn't win in South West Tasmania then what hope was there for the bigger issues confronting mankind. Let's not kid ourselves, we could have lost very easily in South West Tasmania.

I think the ramifications are far wider than the Franklin River itself and there's no knowing that those ramifications won't become more important than that wilderness. The ripples of hope are already way out through the Australian community and will go far beyond that. You can see the ripples of antipathy backing up within Tasmania because they've got nowhere else to go, and it is being heightened by the *Mercury* and by other people in the community who, in their insensitivity, have been blinded to the fact that they possibly could lose. We were prepared to lose again but I fear that many people on the West Coast weren't given the opportunity to be prepared because they'd been led into believing that there was no way they could lose.

That's the sort of attitude which has done the worst things in the world — this feeling of invincibility and macho feeling that might is right and nothing can stop you. That's what we've got to replace with a greater humility, a recognition that we're all fallible.

Where decisions become momentous ones we have to be able to find a moratorium so that we can step back and think about them, even if it takes centuries. There's this ubiquitous feeling that we have to plan things for now, it's outrageous to general community thinking that you should be thinking about people five centuries from now. Well that has got to become the norm and if it doesn't there will be no-one around in five centuries from now. A lot of very gentle and concerned people are going to be done very badly before that ethos comes to be. I'm not in the least bit unaware of the fact that somewhere along in the future I could be one of those. We've often joked here in Tasmania about what would have happened to us had we been an island republic a thousand kilometres further away from Australia. But we've only joked about it because we recognize that that's the tragedy of people in very many places around the world. We've got the best, most open, free, liberal society that the world has ever seen, we're part of that — not just in Australia but in other countries. And we shouldn't blind ourselves to the fact that that could be — you can argue that that's an aberration, that's by no means the norm for the future.

I may be involved in campaigning but to see it restricted, constricted and tied down to conventional politics is something that would alarm me greatly. I've thought about it, I've thought about getting into politics in Tasmania and really trying to do more to have this island a paradigm of good planning on the world stage but Tasmania is not the centre of the universe, nowhere else is either, but it's a dot in a very big world. I think the important thing is not people but ideas. Ideas change the way in which human communities work; ideas save the human community from itself. Then it needs people to put those ideas into action but the ideas have to be formulated and put forward first.

The most important thing is to push forward those ideas. One of the positive ideas in this Franklin campaign is the idea that things don't have to go wrong: the idea that an ideal can be fought by a community and fought successfully, and the idea that people can change things, not only for the better now but for the better for the long term.